Commodity Chains and World Cities

Commodity Chains and World Cities

Edited by

Ben Derudder and Frank Witlox

WILEY-BLACKWELL

A John Wiley & Sons, Ltd., Publication

Contents

List of Contributors

Ed Brown	Loughborough University
Neil M. Coe	University of Manchester
Peter De Langden	Eindhoven University of Technology, and Port of Rotterdam Authority
Ben Derudder	Ghent University
Peter Dicken	University of Manchester
Cesar Ducruet	French National Centre for Scientific Research (CNRS)
Niels Fold	University of Copenhagen
Viktor Goebel	Swiss Federal Statistical Office
Martin Hess	University of Manchester
Markus Hess	University of Luxembourg
Wouter Jacobs	Utrecht University
Stefan Lüthl	Munich University of Technology
Christof Parnreiter	University of Hamburg
Wim Pelupessy	Tilburg University
Saskia Sassen	Columbia University
Peter J. Taylor	Loughborough University
Alain Thierstein	Munich University of Technology
Ingeborg Vind	Statistics Denmark
Frank Witlox	Ghent University
Henry Wai-chung Yeung	National University of Singapore

1

World Cities and Global Commodity Chains:
an introduction

BEN DERUDDER AND FRANK WITLOX

Given the remarkable success of *Global Networks*, it seems fair to state that transnational spatial relations have become a key analytical lens through which the geographies of contemporary globalization are being studied. The purpose of this book is to assess the possible cross-fertilization between two of the most notable analytical frameworks, namely (i) the World City Network (WCN) framework, in which researchers have studied the emergence of a globalized urban system for the provision of a host of advanced corporate services (for example finance, insurance, accountancy, advertising, law); and (ii) the Global Commodity Chain (GCC) framework, in which researchers have scrutinized the interconnected functions, operations and transactions through which specific commodities are produced, distributed and consumed in a globalized economy. We should hereby immediately emphasize that our adoption of the WCN/GCC terminology does not imply an explicit favouring of the specific concepts advanced by Taylor (2004) and Gereffi and Korzeniewicz (1994) over other, related concepts. Rather, this choice is more reflective of the need for a useful shorthand when addressing the research literatures dealing with the rise of transnational central place systems (the WCN approach) and transnational production systems (the GCC approach) respectively.

Both literatures have emerged as critiques of conventional, state-centric social science interpretations of their subject matters, and they both propose what might be called 'global network alternatives': both WCN and GCC scholars stress that, to understand the dynamics of 'development' in a given place, research should focus on how places are being transformed by their insertion in networks of commodities, knowledge, capital, labour, power and how, at the same time, places and their institutional and social fabrics are transforming those networks as they locate in place-specific domains.

WCN research has emerged as a critique of mainstream social science interpretations of urban systems. The established way of researching urban

1

systems has long been through analyses of so-called 'national urban hierarchies'. Usually using data on population sizes or economic specializ-ation, cities from a particular state were assumed to constitute an auton-omous city-system as if the rest of the world did not exist. This approach obviously had some analytical purchase so long as a fair degree of economic and societal cohesion was maintained at the state level. However, it is equally clear that this framework has increasingly worked to the detriment of properly understanding major cities such as London and New York, which derive ever-larger portions of their centrality from their function in the global economy at large. Despite a number of earlier attempts to devise alternative frameworks, it was only when such cities came to be interpreted, first as international financial centres (Cohen 1981), then as world cities (Friedmann 1986), and further as global cities (Sassen 1991), that a literature emerged in which the study of cities, or some at least, gradually broke free of state-centric interpretations (for example, Rozenblat and Pumain 1993). Taylor's (2004) theoretical and empirical research in the context of the Globalization and World Cities (GaWC) research group and network has especially brought the relevance of a 'global network approach' to centre stage. Drawing on the work of Sassen (2001, 2002), Taylor maintains that one of the most powerful examples of the new geographies of contemporary globalization relates to the fact that major international financial and business centres across the world are interlinked in a single urban network. The intensity of transnational transactions among these cities – particularly through financial markets and transactions in advanced corporate services – has augmented sharply throughout the last two decades. Taylor's basic contention, therefore, is that major cities increasingly draw their functional centrality from their connections with other cities across the world. As a consequence, in recent years, cities have increasingly been studied as nodes in *Global Networks*.

GCC research, in turn, has emerged as part of a more encompassing critique of conventional conceptions of large-scale economic flows. In mainstream economics, the usual way of analysing large-scale com-modity flows has been through international trade theories. In general, these theories assert that, in an international economy, economic development emerges from whatever absolute, comparative or com-petitive advantages a country or region may have. It has, however, become increasingly obvious that the basic assumptions underpinning these classical trade theories are fatally flawed by their state-centric spatiality: ever-rising shares of intra-firm trade reveal that the geographies of trade are far more complex than only 'one step'-trade between producers in one country and consumers in another. Rather, production and trade patterns are increasingly guided by the strategic behaviour of firms, and (fixed) factor endowments of countries have therefore become less and less important in explaining commodity flows (Yeung 1994). In spite of a number of earlier attempts to devise alternative frameworks, it was only with the specification of the 'Global Commodity Chain' (GCC) paradigm by Gereffi and Korzeniewicz (1994) that relatively coherent alternatives for conventional trade theories have been worked out. In the last decade and a half or so, this GCC paradigm has been elaborated, respecified and further developed, whereby some authors have used different terminologies to stress the analytical specificity of their approach. In this context, the analytical frameworks focusing on 'Global Value Chains' (GVCs) (Gereffi et al. 2005) and 'Global Production Networks' (GPNs) (Coe et al. 2004; Henderson et al. 2002) have come to dominate this literature. However, notwithstanding a fair number of – sometimes profound – conceptual differences between these frameworks (see Bair 2005; Coe et al. 2008a; Hanssens et al. 2008), it seems fair to state that they converge in their emphasis on the relevance of value creation and its distribution and control within transnational and localized networks. Or, as Henderson et al. (2002: 442) suggest with respect to the study of globalized production in a GPN framework: 'Such processes are better conceptualized as being highly complex network structures in which there are intricate links – horizontal, diagonal, as well as vertical – forming multi-dimensional, multi-layered lattices of economic activity. For that reason, an explicitly relational, network-focused approach promises to offer a better understanding of production systems.' Rather than conceptualizing the global economy through a series of economic containers, these new analytical lenses allow social scientists to study the worldwide map of production, consumption, investment and trade from the perspective of global networks.

Given this metaphorical and formative usage of a 'global networks' perspective, it is no surprise that the original *Global Networks* journal has published a number of articles from both literatures.[1] However, although sharing a common meta-geographical outlook and a loose world-systems analysis progeny, both literatures have developed independently with little or no cross-referencing.[2] This book aims to take advantage of these parallels to investigate how both models may benefit from each other or even be integrated to provide a basic spatial skeleton for understanding the networked processes underpinning contemporary globalization.[3] To this end, we have brought together researchers from different backgrounds (human geography, economics, sociology) and different parts of the world to tease out some key aspects of such cross-fertilization.

It is at this point perhaps useful to point to three important caveats. First, the lack of intersections between both literatures is perhaps less clear-cut than we have suggested up to this point. For instance, part of the world cities literature explicitly deals with the urban geography of control within transnational and localized networks of firms. Thus the empirical research presented in Alderson and Beckfield (2004) and Taylor et al. (2009) can be read as an analysis of the localization of control in Global Commodity Chains through a world cities lens. A second qualification relates to the fact that the chapters in this book only cover a limited number of topics, sectors and regional settings. Much more – and perhaps very different – work remains to be done. Or, as Brown et al. (this book) point out: bringing two such wide-ranging literatures together is a very large task whatever their degree of synergy, and there are therefore inevitably aspects that are underplayed or perhaps even outright neglected. Third, the degree of synergy between both approaches is in itself a function of the actual or perceived coherence within both literatures. It is obvious that the consistency within GCC and WCN research only exists at a rather general level. The widely adopted GPN framework of Dicken et al. (2001), for instance, is the latest specification in the broad GCC literature that has evolved over the last two decades or so to explain how globalized industries are organized and governed (alongside the GCC and GVC frameworks, see Coe et al. 2008a). Similar observations can be made with respect to WCN research, where terms such as 'world cities', 'global cities' and 'global city-regions' are used alongside each other as different approaches for understanding globalized urbanization (see Derudder 2006; Scott 2001). The major implication for the present discussion is that different specifications of the GCC and WCN frameworks are not a trivial matter of semantics. However, for reasons of clarity, in the remainder of this introduction we shall continue to use the WCN/GCC terminology, even if authors use a different concept in their chapters. Readers should, however, bear in mind that any attempt to combine insights from both literatures will need to come to terms with this 'internal' multiplicity.

Steps towards cross-fertilization

Brown et al. (this book) explore the possible cross-fertilization between both literatures by returning to their common origins in world-systems analysis. They argue that some critics of Wallerstein's theoretical framework misinterpret the subtleties of the 'core' and 'periphery' concepts: they re-emphasize that these concepts should be conceived as bundles of complex mechanisms that create contrary outcomes rather than as their spatial outcomes *per se*. They take this observation as a starting point for exploring the possible linkages between both analytical frameworks in world-systems terms, and illustrate their approach through WCN process additions to understanding the coffee commodity chain and GCC additions to understanding Mexico City and Santiago de Chile's position in the WCN.

Although somewhat less explicit about the adoption of a world-systems framework, it is clear that Parnreiter (this book) continues his own research on WCN/GCC-linkages along the lines set out in Brown et al. (this book). His chapter examines functional connections between WCNs and GCCs by exploring the linkages between business services firms located in Mexico City and the globalization of the 'Mexican' economy. In his earlier work, Parnreiter (2003) already emphasized that a WCN-interpretation of Mexico City only made sense when functional linkages could be made with the country's increasing export production. In this chapter in this book, he provides some preliminary evidence of these functional connections by showing that there are indeed significant flows from business service firms in Mexico City to the companies responsible for the globalization of the 'Mexican' economy. The explanation for this spatial correlation is based on the need for access to 'localized' knowledge and the desire to maintain close contacts with clients.

Vind and Fold (this book) agree with our position that a combined GCC/WCN approach may improve our understanding of globalization processes, but they are far more sceptical about the added value of world-systems analysis in this context. They approvingly cite Jennifer Bair (2005: 158), who noted that recent research has moved 'away from the type of long-range historical and holistic analysis characteristic of the world-systems school', and has rather 'evolved as a network-based, organizational approach to studying the dynamics of global industries'. Vind and Fold therefore stress that – in line with recent GCC/GVC/GPN research – far more weight should be given to the role of firms as the organizing agents of capitalism. The more specific starting point of their own chapter is their contention that WCN research should pay more attention to the spectacular growth of many so-called

'Third World' cities such as Ho Chi Minh City. Like many booming cities in coastal China, this growth is primarily due to rising export-oriented industrialization and the concomitant immigration from rural hinterlands as these cities are integrated in GCCs. They illustrate this claim through a GCC analysis of the electronics industry located in Ho Chi Minh City and the agricultural sector in its rural hinterland, the Mekong Delta.

The explicit rebuttal of world-systems analysis in Vind and Fold's chapter leads to the question of other possible meta-narratives. However, in line with recent evolutions within the social sciences in general and human geography in particular, most other authors seem to shy away from adopting totalizing meta-narratives. The theoretical frameworks in most of the other chapters often consist of more eclectic narratives. The most obvious example here is Castells's (2000) wide-ranging argument that the world is being transformed from a 'space of places' into a 'space of flows'.[4] Both literatures can be seen as exemplary for Castells-like approaches of the geographies of contemporary globalization; it is therefore no surprise that most of the chapters in this book explicitly invoke Castells's work to structure their own research (for example Jacobs et al. this book; Lüthi et al. this book). However, despite Castells's prominent position in this literature, we sense that it is warranted to describe the many references to his work as 'eclectic' in that it seems to provide a number of useful metaphors more than anything else.

Hesse (in this book) explores the relevance of more recent theorizations of contemporary globalization by drawing on Sheppard's (2002) topical work on 'the times and spaces of globalization'. In this publication, Sheppard urges social scientists to consider the 'positionality' concept alongside more traditional approaches emphasizing the relevance of place, scale and networks. 'Positionality' is hereby advanced as a concept that captures the shifting, asymmetric and path-dependent ways in which the future of places depend on their interdependencies with others, so that the early understanding of spatial interaction is moving forward to a more relative notion of places in networks. Hesse uses this analytical lens to revisit the role of urban places in terms of their capability to attract, manage and redirect flows in such networks. This leads him to consider the role of seaports and port cities. He approvingly quotes Coe et al. (2008b: 276) who argue that, because of the vastly increased complexity and geographical extensiveness of GPNs, and the need to coordinate and integrate extraordinarily intricate operations as rapidly and efficiently as possible, the consideration of the logistics problem is absolutely central in this research domain.

Port cities and seaports are thus obvious settings for examining the intersections between advanced corporate services and commodity flows. Jacobs et al. (this book) also draw on this insight, and further sustain their choice for this particular geographical setting through the observation that ports are logistical nodes and sites of production in GCCs, while the port-city is potentially a centre for maritime and port-related advanced business producer services. They assess to what degree business services firms (as critical nodes in WCNs) co-locate near firms active in port-industrial complexes (as key logistical nodes in GCCs), as it can be assumed that physical proximity will foster the exchange of ideas and the building of trust (see also Parnreiter this book). To this end, they present a systematic comparison of the location of maritime producer services and port throughput figures, which is then used to identify different types of port cities.

Jacobs et al. suggest some appealing interrelations between WCNs and GCCs. However, because their study simply assesses the degree of co-location of logistics/production and maritime-related servicing, it remains somewhat difficult to identify the functional and spatial linkages between both. In this respect, the chapter falls short of the work of Rossi et al. (2007), who analyse the interrelations between the location of advanced corporate services firms and their clients in Brazil. The latter approach allows for an actual mapping of the functional and spatial linkages between production and its servicing, and this is taken up in great detail in the empirical analysis of Lüthi et al. (this book). Drawing on an extensive study of the linkages between service firms and their clients in the greater Munich area, Lüthi et al. put significant empirical flesh on the bones of conceptual research emphasizing the relation between WCNs and GCCs. They begin by looking at the ways in which multi-location firms from the so-called 'knowledge economy' develop their intra-firm networks internationally, after which they establish the (spatial location of the) partners with whom these firms have working relationships along individual GCCs. Their findings point to the existence of a multi-polar megacity-region (MCR), in which connectivity decreases as distance to Munich and the surrounding secondary nodes in the MCR increases.

Avenues for future research

Notwithstanding the many different approaches, topics and regional settings that can be discerned in the different articles, we believe they collectively point to the possible relevance of cross-fertilization between both literatures. One example of a potential benefit for WCN research relates to the possibility of a more de-centred approach to the study of globalized urbanization. The empirical focus in the chapters by Brown et al., Parnreiter, and Vind and Fold is on cities from the erstwhile 'Third World' (Mexico City, Santiago de Chile and Ho Chi Minh City). This is encouraging given the commonly voiced critique that WCN research has disproportionately concentrated on relatively few large metropolitan centres in the Western world.[5] Perhaps the most sharp critique along these lines has been formulated by Robinson (2002, 2005), who complains that restricting analyses of globalized urbanization to the presence of 'Western' business services firms implies that millions of people and hundreds of cities are dropped off the map in urban studies. Because of the focus on a narrow range of economic processes (namely 'advanced' servicing of globalized production), myriad other connections between cities are being ignored in this literature.[6] Through the consideration of a GCC framework with its more generic approach to flows of value and commodities, research on WCNs may identify other, more suitable ways of understanding cities from the 'Global South'.

An example of a potential benefit for GCC research relates to a more refined conceptual and spatial analysis of the relevance of crucial service inputs. Indeed, one of the main critiques of previous GCC research has been that it has lacked a comprehensive treatment of the role of financial capital and key service inputs. Coe et al. (2008b: 268), for instance, recently admitted that although this is 'an area worth reflecting on', the impact of financial capital and the spatialities of the global financial system have not yet been widely debated in GCC research (despite an early call by Rabach and Kim (1994) to explore the 'service sector nexus').[7] Analyses such as those by Luthi et al. (this book), who explore the financial and service inputs in individual GCCs, may therefore assist in helping to fill this hole in GCC research.

As pointed out in the introduction of this editorial, much more – and perhaps very different – work remains to be done. In that respect, the commentaries in this book by Coe et al. and by Sassen provide a number of perceptive suggestions on possible ways forward. However, we hope that the different chapters in this book will prove to be useful first steps towards cross-fertilization between the ideas advanced in both literatures separately. We look forward to reading critiques, embellishments and further ideas.

Notes

1. Previous GCC-papers in *Global Networks* include Dicken et al. (2001); Hassler (2003); Morgan (2001); Palpacuer and Parisotto (2003); Rothenberg-Aalami (2004); and Tokatli (2007). Papers contributing to the WCN literature include Beaverstock et al. (2002); Choi et al. (2006); Derudder and Taylor (2005); Faulconbridge and Muzio (2007); and Neal (2008).
2. Two notable exceptions are the research by Parnreiter et al. (2004) and Rossi et al. (2007). Parnreiter et al. examine what they aptly term the 'missing link' between Global Commodity Chains and global city-formation in Mexico City and Santiago de Chile. Rossi et al., in turn, analyse the interrelations between the location of advanced corporate services firms and their clients in Brazil.
3. The original idea for bringing together research dealing with the cross-fertilization between both perspectives emerged from a number of exchanges in the context of a possible EU-funded research consortium in the course of 2003. The idea was later specified in Parnreiter (2003) and Parnreiter et al. (2004), after which we took the initiative to organize two sessions followed by a discussion panel on 'World City Networks and Global Commodity Chains' at the annual meeting of the Association of American Geographers (AAG) in Boston in 2008.
4. Castells's work has been widely used in both literatures. WCN researchers, for instance, often refer to Castells's (1996: 415) observation that Saskia Sassen's work provides perhaps 'the most direct illustration' of the logic of hubs and nodes as anchor points in a 'Network Society' (for example Derudder and Witlox 2005, 2008); Taylor 2004. Meanwhile, Coe et al. (2004) and Henderson et al. (2002) also refer to Castells's writings when positing the GPN framework as a means to understand the 'territorial embeddedness' of myriad transnational flows.
5. This problem can, for instance, be observed in some of the empirical GaWC research that explicitly draws on Sassen's conceptual framework. A large number of GaWC's empirical analyses after the seminal Beaverstock et al. (1999) article have been based on the corporate geographies of 'leading' business service firms (for example Derudder et al. 2003; Taylor et al. 2002). One of the criteria for firms to be included in the analyses is that they should have a presence in what Derudder et al. (2003) dub the 'three prime globalization arenas' – northern America (the USA and Canada), Western Europe and Pacific Asia. This criterion has clearly resulted in a dataset with a very large presence of APS firms with Euro-American origins, so that some of the main conclusions in the GaWC studies regarding the perceived dominance of Western and Pacific Asian cities may well have been a self-fulfilling prophecy.
6. Perhaps more substantively, some researchers take issue with the fact that cities outside the West are assessed in terms of pre-given standards of (Western) world city-ness (for example Robinson 2002: 531–2). Massey (2007) has recently taken up this critique, and thereby urges us to consider additional implications of this neglect of an array of economic processes and a number of regions in the Sassen/GaWC research. She suggests that use of the term 'advanced' when studying the urban geography of these largely Western business services firms

9

implicitly grants these services (and the firms and the cities that provide them) a normative status. She therefore calls for approaches that 'expose the hegemonic geographical imaginations' and even 'take the further political step of proposing alternatives' (Massey 2007: 24).

7. To an extent, this is because GPN analysis has tended to treat services as separate networks within which knowledge is the product traded (see Clancy 1998).

References

Alderson, A. S. and J. Beckfield (2004) 'Power and position in the world city system', *American Journal of Sociology*, 109, 811–51.

Bair, J. (2005) 'Global capitalism and commodity chains: looking back, going forward', *Competition and Change*, 9 (2), 153–80.

Beaverstock, J. V., R. G. Smith and P. J. Taylor (1999) 'A roster of world cities', *Cities*, 16 (6), 445–58.

Beaverstock, J. V., M. A. Doel, P. J. Hubbard and P. J. Taylor (2002) 'Attending to the world: competition, cooperation and connectivity in the World City Network', *Global Networks*, 2 (2), 111–32.

Brown, E., B. Derudder, C. Parnreiter, W. Pelupessy, P. J. Taylor and F. Witlox (2010) 'World City Networks and Global Commodity Chains: towards a world systems integration, *Global Networks*, 10 (1), 12–34.

Castells, M. (1996) *The information age: economy, society, and culture Vol. I – The rise of the network society*, Oxford: Blackwell.

Castells, M. (2000) *The information age: economy, society, and culture Vol. I – The rise of the network society* (2nd edition), Oxford: Blackwell.

Choi, J. H., G. A. Barnett and B. S. Chon (2006) 'Comparing World City Networks: a network analysis of Internet backbone and air transport intercity linkages', *Global Networks*, 6 (1), 81–99.

Clancy, M. (1998) 'Commodity chains, services and development: theory and preliminary evidence from the tourism industry', *Review of International Political Economy*, 5 (1), 122–48.

Coe, N. M., M. Hess, H. W-c.Yeung, P. Dicken and J. Henderson (2004) 'Globalizing regional development: a Global Production Networks perspective', *Transactions of the Institute of British Geographers*, 29 (4), 468–84.

Coe, N. M., P. Dicken and M. Hess (2008a) 'Global Production Networks – debates and challenges', *Journal of Economic Geography*, 8 (3), 267–69.

Coe, N. M., P. Dicken and M. Hess (2008b) 'Global Production Networks: realizing the potential', *Journal of Economic Geography*, 8 (3), 271–95.

Coe, N. M., P. Dicken, M. Hess and H. W-c. Yeung (2010) 'Making connections, Global Production Networks and World City Networks', *Global Networks*, 10 (1), 138–149.

Cohen, R. (1981) 'The new international division of labour: multinational corporations and urban hierarchy', in M. Dear and A. J. Scott (eds) *Urbanization and urban planning in capitalist society*, London: Methuen, 287–318.

Derudder, B. (2006) 'On conceptual confusion in empirical analyses of a transnational urban network', *Urban Studies*, 43 (11), 2027–46.

Derudder, B. and P. J. Taylor (2005) 'The cliquishness of world cities', *Global Networks*, 5 (1), 71–91.

Derudder, B. and F. Witlox (2005) 'An appraisal of the use of airline data in assessing the World City Network: a research note on data', *Urban Studies*, 42 (13), 2371–88.

Derudder, B. and F. Witlox (2008) 'Mapping global city networks through airline flows: context, relevance, and problems', *Journal of Transport Geography*, 16 (5), 305–12.

Derudder, B., P. J. Taylor, F. Witlox and G. Catalano (2003) 'Hierarchical tendencies and regional patterns in the World City Network: a global urban analysis of 234 cities', *Regional Studies*, 37 (9), 875–86.

Dicken, P., P. F. Kelly, K. Olds and H. W-c.Yeung (2001) 'Chains and networks, territories and scales: towards a relational framework for analysing the global economy', *Global Networks*, 1 (2), 89–112.

Faulconbridge, J. R. and D. Muzio (2007) 'Reinserting the professional into the study of globalizing professional service firms: the case of law', *Global Networks*, 7 (3), 249–70.

Friedmann, J. (1986) 'The world city hypothesis', *Development and Change*, 17 (1), 69–84.

Gereffi, G. and M. Korzeniewicz (eds) (1994) *Commodity chains and global capitalism*, Westport, CT: Praeger Publishers.

Gereffi, G., J. Humphrey and T. J. Sturgeon (2005) 'The governance of Global Value Chains', *Review of International Political Economy*, 12 (1), 78–104.

Hanssens, H., B. Derudder and F. Witlox (2008) 'De wereldeconomie als netwerkeconomie: een analyse van de voornaamste onderzoeksparadigma's', *Kwartaalschrift Economie*, 5, 279–305.

Hassler, M. (2003) 'The global clothing production system: commodity chains and business networks', *Global Networks*, 3 (4), 513–31.

Henderson, J., P. Dicken, M. Hess, N. M. Coe and H. W-c.Yeung (2002) 'Global Production Networks and the analysis of economic development', *Review of International Political Economy*, 9, 436–64.

Hesse, M. (2010) 'Cities, material flows and the geography of spatial interaction: urban places in the system of chains', *Global Networks*, 10 (1), 75–91.

Jacobs, W. C. Ducruet and P. de Langen (2010) 'Integrating world cities into production networks: the case of port cities', *Global Networks*, 10 (1), 92–113.

Lüthi, S., A. Thierstein, and V. Goebel (2010) 'Intra-firm and extra-firm linkages in the knowledge economy: the case of the emerging mega-city region of Munich', *Global Networks*, 10 (1), 114–137.

Massey, D. (2007) *World city*, London: Polity Press.

Morgan, G. (2001) 'Transnational communities and business systems', *Global Networks*, 1 (2), 113–30.

Neal, Z. (2008) 'The duality of world cities and firms: comparing networks, hierarchies and inequalities in the global economy', *Global Networks*, 8 (1), 94–115.

Palpacuer, F. and A. Parisotto (2003) 'Global production and local jobs: can global enterprise networks be used as levers for local development?', *Global Networks*, 3 (2), 97–120.

Parnreiter, C. (2003) 'Global city formation in Latin America: socioeconomic and spatial transformations in Mexico City and Santiago de Chile', paper presented at the 99th Annual Meeting of the Association of American Geographers, 4–8 April, New Orleans, http://www.lboro.ac.uk/gawc/rb/rb103.html.

Parnreiter, C. (2010) 'Global cities in Global Commodity Chains: exploring the role of Mexico City in the geography of governance of the world economy', *Global Networks*, 10 (1), 35–53.

Parnreiter, C., K. Fischer and K. Imhof (2004) 'The missing link between Global Commodity Chains and global cities: the financial service sector in Mexico City and Santiago de Chile', http://lboro.ac.uk/gawc/rb/rb156.html.

Rabach, E. and E. M. Kim. (1994) 'Where is the chain in commodity chains? The service sector nexus', in G. Gereffi and M. Korzeniewicz (eds) *Commodity chains and global capitalism*, Westport, CT: Praeger Publishers, 123–42.

Robinson, J. (2002) 'Global and world cities: a view from off the map', *International Journal of Urban and Regional Research*, 26 (3), 531–54.

Robinson, J. (2005) 'Urban geography: world cities, or a world of cities', *Progress in Human Geography*, 29 (6), 757–65.

Rossi, E. C., J. V. Beaverstock and P. J. Taylor (2007) 'Transaction links through cities: "decision cities" and "service cities" in outsourcing by leading Brazilian firms', *Geoforum*, 38 (4), 628–42.

Rothenberg-Aalami, J. (2004) 'Coming full circle? Forging missing links along Nike's integrated production networks', *Global Networks*, 4 (4), 335–54.

Rozenblat, C. and D. Pumain (1993) 'The location of multinational firms in the European urban system', *Urban Studies*, 10, 1691–709.

Sassen, S. (1991) *The global city: New York, London, Tokyo*, Princeton: Princeton University Press.

Sassen, S. (2001) *The global city: New York, London, Tokyo* (2nd edition), Princeton: Princeton University Press.

Sassen, S. (ed) (2002) *Global networks: linked cities*, New York: Routledge.

Sassen (2010) 'Global inter-city networks and commodity chains: any intersections?', *Global Networks*, 10 (1), 150–63.

Scott, A. (ed) (2001) *Global city regions: trends, theory, policy*, Oxford: Oxford University Press.

Sheppard, E. (2002) 'The spaces and times of globalization: place, scale, networks, and positionality', *Economic Geography*, 78 (3), 307–30.

Taylor, P. J. (2004) *World City Network: a global urban analysis*, London: Routledge.

Taylor, P. J., G. Catalano and D. R. F. Walker (2002) 'Measurement of the World City Network', *Urban Studies*, 39 (13), 2367–76.

Taylor, P. J., P. Ni, B. Derudder, M. Hoyler, J. Huang, F. Lu, K. Pain, F. Witlox, X. Yang, D. Bassens and W. Shen (2009) 'The way we were: command-and-control centres in the global space-economy on the eve of the 2008 geo-economic transition', *Environment and Planning A*, 41 (1), 7–12.

Tokatli, N. (2007) 'Networks, firms and upgrading within the blue-jeans industry: evidence from Turkey', *Global Networks*, 7 (1), 51–68.

Vind, I. and N. Fold (2010) 'City networks and commodity chains: identifying global flows and local connections in Ho Chi Minh City', Global Networks 10 (1), 54–74.

Yeung, H. W-c. (1994) 'Critical reviews of geographical perspectives on business organizations and the organization of production: towards a network approach', *Progress in Human Geography*, 18 (4), 460–90.

2

World City Networks and Global Commodity Chains: towards a world-systems' integration

ED BROWN, BEN DERUDDER, CHRISTOF PARNREITER,
WIM PELUPESSY, PETER J. TAYLOR AND FRANK WITLOX

The rise of contemporary globalization has generated many new geographies, but spatial patterns and relations have been a neglected theme in the myriad writings on globalization. The purpose of this chapter is to address this situation by comparing and contrasting two literatures that focus upon different models of transnational spatial relations: in the *World City Network* (WCN) literature researchers model worldwide inter-city relations; in the *Global Commodity Chains* (GCC) literature researchers model production processes in the global economy. One of the key properties our selected literatures have in common is that they both depict fundamental spatial models of flows: a *chain* of production nodes connected by commodity flows and a *network* of city nodes connected by information flows. However, while these literatures share a common world-systems analysis progeny, they have developed independently with little or no cross-referencing. In this chapter we take advantage of their shared origin to show how the two models might be integrated and thereby provide a basic spatial skeleton for understanding the processes behind globalization. Because the two literatures already share many of the same conceptual and discursive starting points rather than competing ones, we avoid the dangers of conceptual eclecticism often involved in attempts to bring together different discourses on the same topic.

World-systems analysis is one of the most prominent trans-disciplinary clusters of social scholarship (Wallerstein 2004). As well as being explicitly transnational, this school of thought encompasses the critical spatiality of the modern world system as core–periphery structuring of world space through ceaseless capital accumulation; it focuses attention on the spatial dynamics of uneven development. The models with which we deal in this chapter derive from this fecund source of ideas in different ways. Global Commodity Chain analysis originates from a concern to show how value is transferred from periphery to core thus sustaining or deepening uneven development. World City Network arguments derive from a concern about how global capitalism is concretely commanded and enabled in contemporary globalization.

Bringing two literatures together is a very large task whatever their degree of synergy. Our argument is divided into two substantive parts. In part one we outline the progress made thus far in mapping trans-state processes and providing analytic models for building new global geographies. This is where we present basic outlines of Global Commodity Chain analysis and World City Network analysis. Given the aim of subsequent integration, each description focuses largely on the fundamental 'space of flows' of each model eschewing much further elaboration to be found in the literatures. For the World City Network analysis this means neglecting city networks generated by actors other than advanced producer service firms (for an overview, see Derudder 2006); for Global Commodity Chain analysis it means neglecting more complex structures (beyond simple chains) to be found in, for instance, Global Production Network (GPN) research (for an overview, see Coe et al. 2008). At this stage of our work it is much more important to identify and consider some of the more fundamental limitations and weaknesses of each basic model and forms of analysis. Our contention is that each model can contribute towards reducing the limitations of the other. In part two we return to the world-systems origins of both models as a route towards their integration. The core–periphery framework is described as providing the spatial structure upon which the World City Network and Global Commodity Chain mechanisms operate. In this context we take the first step towards integrating the two models through exploring what each has to offer the other. This is argued both conceptually through connecting their two spaces of flows, and empirically through reviewing evidence from two selected research areas (the coffee commodity chain and world city formation in Mexico City and Santiago de Chile). In a working conclusion we suggest the first steps towards a more complete integration of Global Commodity Chains with the World City Network.

The two literatures: models and analyses

Both the literatures we employ encompass basic critiques of conventional social science interpretations of their subject matters. We begin each description of the models with these critiques to show how both literatures transcend state-centric thinking and are therefore particularly suited to developing new insights into globalization. After summary descriptions of each model we consider their limitations and omissions.

World City Network analysis

In mainstream urban studies the traditional way of researching inter-city relations has been through analyses of 'national urban systems'. Typically using non-relational data from national censuses, population sizes of cities defined a 'national urban hierarchy'. Models such as 'the law of the primate city' and 'rank size rule' were devised to describe this 'hierarchy' as if the rest of the world did not exist. The study of cities was nationalized, so that city relations were territorialized, to the severe detriment of properly understanding major cities like London and New York. It was only when such cities became interpreted, through a series of influential writings, first as international financial centres (Cohen 1981), then as world cities (Friedmann 1986; Friedmann and Wolff 1982), and further as global cities (Sassen 1991), that a 'world city literature' arose in which the study of cities, or some at least, broke free of national containers. More recently, we have moved from conceptualiz-ations of world city formation to conceptualizations of World City Network formation: cities are studied system-wide in the modern world system as a World-City Network (Taylor 2004).

The World City Network has been specified as an interlocking network in which relations between cities are constituted by intra-firm flows in the advanced producer service sector of the world economy (Taylor 2001). One of the features of the contemporary world economy is that 'services' are becom-ing more and more important. Sassen (1991) pointed out that a key sector of these services, the advanced producer services (such as inter-jurisdictional law and global advertising) used by multinational corporations, were becoming more and more concentrated in leading cities. There were good 'cluster' reasons for such concentration, as the firms operating in these services require information-rich environs to keep ahead in their business. But this need for knowledge did not lead to the concentration of these firms in just one or just a few 'mega service centres'; rather, a second requirement led to these services being offered across the world in cities covering all major regions. This second need of producer service firms was the requirement to provide their service where and when their clients needed it; and since the corporations they serviced were becoming global, service firms had no choice but to follow suit and go global themselves. The alternative option of farming out their work to partner firms in other cities was never seen as feasible because of the importance of maintaining brand integrity in a field that deals in information and knowledge. Thus, major service firms created worldwide office networks across the major cities of the world.

One of Sassen's main arguments is that global cities obtain their overall centrality because they are 'highly concentrated command points in the organization of the world economy' (Sassen 2001: 3). Thus, a key purpose of worldwide office networks is to enable transnational business to be conducted. Projects involving several jurisdictions, languages, cultures and budgets will draw upon knowledge resources from a range of relevant offices. These intra-firm connections, both electronic and human, flow across the world silently linking the tower blocks that dominate so many cityscapes in all regions of the world. It is the aggregation of all these intra-firm flows – of information, knowledge, instruction, strategy, plans, and personnel – that constitute the contemporary World City Network. It is in this sense that advanced producer firms are the 'interlockers' of world cities. Hence, when the network is modelled, it is presented as consisting of three layers – the network level at the world-economy scale; the nodal level, which is composed of the cities where the work of network formation takes place; and the sub-nodal level, which is defined by the firms that are the agents of the whole process. In this interpretation the World City Network is a web of 'global service centres', integral parts of complex networks of capital circulation and accumulation. It is important to note that the deliberate sidestepping of national states in this particular specification of the World City Network does not imply the suggestion that they do not matter in World City Network formation (for in-depth discussions of the multifaceted links between world city formation and state territorial development under conditions of contemporary globalization, see Brenner 1998; Olds and Yeung 2004). Rather, it means that such specification should not be a priori shaped by states; the observation that transnational inter-city relations are heavily influenced by national states is viable, but it should be advanced as a result of the analysis rather than being an artefact of its initial specification.

There are two main limitations of the world city literature; one is commonly voiced while the other is becoming increasingly important. The first is the concentration on a relatively few large metropolitan centres to concomitant neglect of all other cities. The most trenchant critique along these lines is by Robinson (2002: 536), who complains that 'millions of people and hundreds of cities are dropped off the map of much research in urban studies'. This exclusion is from two 'maps': (i) the geographical map of world cities wherein most cities in the 'South' are missing; and (ii) the conceptual map of world cities that focuses on a narrow range of global economic processes so that myriad other connections between cities are missing. However, *all* cities experience contemporary global processes, and globalization can therefore not be construed as affecting just a few privileged cities. Subsequently, Robinson (2005: 760) has conceded that the world city literature now covers 'a much wider range of cities around the globe', thus lessening the exclusion from the map. This attempt to broaden our understanding of the World City Network has seen the postulation of such ideas as 'globalizing cities' (Marcuse and van Kempen 2000) or 'cities in globalization' (Taylor et al. 2006).

The second main limitation of the world city literature relates to its rather underdeveloped *urban*-theoretical underpinnings (see, however, Brenner 2004; Hesse this book). It can be noted that the dominant arguments in this literature developed from efforts to try and make sense of contemporary *economic* processes: the two seminal contributions are by Friedmann (1986) figuring out implications of the 'new international division of labour', and Sassen (1991) trying to understand 'the composition of globalization'. Neither Friedmann nor Sassen begins with, or develops, a theory of cities *per se*. What cities are, and how they relate to one another, are questions that are left unexamined except as a vague hierarchical premise. It is the latter that leads to the privileging of the few. Taylor has argued that this situation can be rectified through a confrontation of the idea of a World City Network with the ideas of Jane Jacobs (1969, 1984, 2000) who treats cities as key economic entities. For Jacobs, vibrant cities expand economic life in ways that diversify economic processes within the city (she calls them 'the little movements') that in turn lead to complex relations with other cities (she calls these the 'big wheels' of commerce). Such a new conceptual context also recognizes Robinson's (2005: 757) emphasis on the inherent complexity of cities. Following this line of argument, the use of advanced producer services to define the World City Network is not that they encompass most or even a sizeable proportion of the myriad complex flows between cities, rather it is that, as cutting-edge industries, they are critical indicators of vibrancy in Jacobs's sense (Taylor 2006). Today, where there are concentrations of advanced producer services, there is manifest expansion of economic life.

Underlying both limitations and critiques of the world cities literature is the idea that these studies have largely failed to transcend their prime scale of interest, the global. World city studies need to address leading cities in the global economy to be sure, but there is no need to be ghettoized into one-scale analysis. Quite simply, the World City Network is built upon ramifications of operations across different scales through macro-regional and national to local

(Parnreiter 2003). Although recent attempts to analyse the city network in greater geographical detail (Brown et al. 2002; Derudder et al. 2003; Parnreiter 2002; Rossi and Taylor 2005) have extended our understanding beyond a limited number of leading cities, they fail to explain the connection to other scales. That is, these analyses are the end result of ever larger data sets that depart from the logic of considering only the nodes at the global scale, but they are weak at revealing how urban networks at national and regional scales are connected to the wider World City Network (but see Hall and Pain 2006). Again, these issues can be addressed by returning to Jacobs (1969) where she describes cities as process; Castells (1996) makes exactly the same point and this has been recently elaborated upon by Taylor et al. (2010; see also Taylor 2006) in their identification of the interlocking model as describing the process of city-ness. In this argument, city-ness is contrasted with the process of 'town-ness'; the latter refers to relations between an urban place and its hinterland – it is essentially local – whereas city-ness includes wider relations and city networks that are non local. Today's World City Network is global.[1] This network-making process can and does occur at different scales and separates contemporary studies of the World City Network from earlier primitive 'rosters of world cities' that essentialized the concept. Such work is correctly criticized by Shatkin (2007) but without paying attention to more recent literature. Cities constitute myriad processes in their city-ness; in the twenty-first century large numbers of cities incorporate world city-ness processes (advanced producer service provision as described earlier), some more than others. Nowhere, of course, is world city-ness the only process occurring as non-relational essentialist ideas may imply.

Global Commodity Chains

In mainstream economics the usual way of analysing large-scale commodity flows has been through international trade theories. In general, these theories assert that, in an international economy, economic development emerges from whatever absolute, comparative or competitive advantages a country may have. Many of the theories are based on the neo-classical Heckscher-Ohlin theorem with corresponding restrictive assumptions. The important market clearance condition may be loosened in the chain approach (Busch 2007: 443). Alternative and 'new' trade models tried to reduce some of the limitations by including demand considerations, imperfect competition, scale economics, technologies, dynamic factors and intra-industrial trade (Appleyard and Field 1997: 229–62).[2] However, even without recourse to a refined analysis, it can be noted that the basic assumptions underpinning these (neo-)classical trade theories are fatally flawed by their state-centric spatiality. The underlying supposition that national states are the spatial actors controlling the global economy is indefensible, while the spatiality of trade is of course far more complex than only 'one step' trade between producers in one country and consumers in another (Díaz 2003: 47–63). For instance, both intra-firm and intra-industry trade constitute an important – and increasing – share of world trade. This makes differentiation an important factor, not only for end products, but also for raw and intermediate materials flows. Furthermore, in the contemporary global economy, production and trade patterns are mostly guided by the strategic behaviour of firms and other economic actors, while (fixed) factor endowments of countries have become less important in explaining commodity flows (Bair 2009). Both industrial organization trends of outsourcing based on new technologies and economic policies of liberalization have made national states clearly insufficient as units of analysis. The overarching analytical disjuncture is that, in spite of the empirical evidence for the importance of trans-state economic flows (as presented in Dicken 2003), conventional theories of economic development have generally been organized around an international rather than a transnational framework. It was only when production and trade became interpreted, via the world-systems writings of Hopkins and Wallerstein in the 1970s (Wallerstein 2009), as a series of cross-border firm-based transactions, that a transnational literature on trade emerged.

Wallerstein and his colleagues hereby introduced the concept of 'commodity chain' as 'a network of labour and production processes whose end result is a finished commodity' (Hopkins and Wallerstein 1986: 159). The emphasis was on the material inputs *en route* to final consumption, the realization of capital. However, it was only with the advent of the work by Gereffi and Korzeniewicz (1994) that we can speak of a relatively coherent paradigm of 'Global Commodity Chains' focusing on value creation, its distribution and control within transnational networks, which extend in a chain of nodes from raw material exploitation, primary processing, through different stages of trade, services and manufacturing processes to final consumption and waste disposal. Taken as a whole, a Global Commodity Chain may link up different organizational models of production, trade and service providing processes, and can even include the generation of externalities and inter-market spillovers (Gereffi and Kaplinsky 2001; Pelupessy 2001). The Global Commodity Chain approach is basically an analytical political economy tool, where attention is focused on the systems of value creation employed by firms and other agents. The connections between these units are conceived of as a chain linking sequences of imperfect markets, reflecting the market power asymmetries that lead to unequal value distributions. The dynamics of any specific chain are determined by the input–output structure of the nodes or chain segments, their geographical location, institutional and socio-political framework and their governance or control structure that gives the commodity chain its hierarchical and unequal character, since '[a] chain without governance would just be a string of market relations' (Humphrey and Schmitz 2001: 20). The importance of the social embeddedness of a chain and eventual state intervention in its markets are hereby considered in the analysis of the socio-political dimension (Pelupessy 2001; Rammohan and Sundaresan 2003).

There are three main ways in which the Global Commodity Chain approach provides an effective analytical tool for understanding the governance structure of specific chains and their significance. First, there is the asymmetric capacity of participants in the chain to appropriate rents and the barriers to entry of the different nodes. These have a dynamic character, and may be eroded by potential competition (Kaplinsky 2005). Second, there is the behaviour of lead firms involved in the governance structure. This may refer to direct coordination of activities on a global scale, the identification and appropriation of dynamic rents, the assignment of specific roles to chain agents, as well as indirect rule setting for the chain. This may open the way for actors from developing countries to upgrade their position in specific Global Commodity Chains (Bair 2009: 29–30). Third, there are the different types of chains defined by the upstream or downstream location of lead firms(s), the kind of dominant or core production factor that they control and others, which are classified as either producer- or demand-driven commodity chains (Gereffi and Korzeniewicz 1994). The importance of the latter category has increased substantially in time and given rise to the concept of demand-responsive economies in for instance East Asia (Hamilton and Gereffi 2009). A recent special issue of *Economy and Society* (2008) elaborated on the relevance of global chain governance for conceiving the globalization of production and trade. In this context, four aspects are relevant: the historical context, geographic and sectorial unevenenness, specialization, differentiation and changing patterns of ownerships (Gibbon et al. 2008).

Rather than conceptualizing the global economy through a series of exclusively market-oriented containers, the Global Commodity Chain approach allows us to focus on system-wide networks of labour and production processes. As a consequence, this approach is better geared to reveal the spatial ordering of social relations that are being continually reproduced through every day practices of production, distribution and consumption in a globalized economy. Nevertheless, because the focus of the approach is upon the spaces of flows involved in the production of particular commodities, commodity chain research has been less successful in specifying how chains contribute towards the complex dynamics of the broader economic system in which they are located (Bair 2003).

Some would go further in this critique. Coe et al. (2004) and Smith et al. (2002) argue that, despite the global focus of the commodity chain approach, it still remains preoccupied with the nation-state as geographical scale of analysis. They back this up through reference to Gereffi's paper on the prospects for 'industrial upgrading', which he defines as 'improving the position of firms or nations in international trade networks' (Gereffi 1999: 39). The result, Coe et al. (2004) and Smith et al. (2002) argue, is that Global Commodity Chain analysis 'has surprisingly little to say about regional and subnational processes, because of the focus on the international dimensions of commodity chains and global divisions of labour' (Smith et al. 2002: 49). However, recent Latin American empirical studies gave more attention to local and subnational impacts of global chains (Díaz 2003: 172–93; a conceptual framework on integrating vertical and horizontal analysis of value chains is given by Bolwig et al. 2008).

Global Commodity Chain research also lacks a comprehensive treatment of the spatiality of commodity chains (Leslie and Reimer 1999). Despite the theoretical insight that a Global Commodity Chain connects inputs from different parts of the world, pulls them together in specific sites and provides output to different locations, the study of the actual geographies of these commodity chains has remained relatively underdeveloped. Although a number of writings have focused on the role of Global Commodity Chains in regional development and the potentials of localities (for example Schmitz 2000, and some contributions in the volume edited by Hughes and Reimer 2004), an overarching spatial conceptualization remains an unfulfilled task. That is, there is a critical need to trace commodity chains spatially, as place-bound linkages between different localities.

Another more specific limitation in Global Commodity Chain research is that the empirical scope of analysis has been somewhat limited, with the majority of studies focusing on a number of primary commodities and industrial sectors. Services, in particular, despite an early call for exploring the 'service sector nexus' (Rabach and Kim 1994), have not been analysed particularly effectively in commodity chain research, either in industries where the service constitutes a commodity in its own right or where it is used to facilitate the production of other more tangible commodities (for an interesting recent effort to overcome these deficiencies, see Li Yang and Yu 2007).[3] However, it is perhaps above all the lack of attention that has been paid to understanding the crucial role of producer services in setting up and sustaining global networks of production that has been the most crucial omission in this literature (Daniels and Bryson 2002).

World-systems integration

The main contention of this chapter is that the route to integrating World City Network with Global Commodity Chains is through emphasizing their common world-systems origins. But before we proceed it must be noted that their relations to the development of world-systems analysis are quite different. For instance, whereas in early *Political Economy of the World-System Series* volumes, number 16 on commodity chains could reproduce pioneer papers by Wallerstein and Hopkins, the founders of the world-systems approach (Gereffi and Korzeniewicz 1994), these authors are absent from number 14 on 'Cities in the World-System' (Karaba 1991). In fact there has been a debate about the neglect of cities in world-systems analysis (Smith 2003). Wallerstein's (1984) only paper on 'cities' is actually about urbanization, a process he subsequently renamed 'de-ruralification'. Thus, despite early important studies within this school of thought (for example Chase-Dunn 1983; King 1990; Timberlake 1985), cities have not been central to world-systems research in general and Wallerstein's writings in particular in the way that commodity chains have. Perhaps the most city-centred theoretical contribution to the research that presents itself as 'world-systems analysis' is the work of Arrighi (1994, 2007). In particular, Arrighi's 1994 work, *The long twentieth century*, in which he reinterprets the history of capitalism since the thirteenth century as a series of alternations between 'material expansions' and 'financial expansions', is relevant in this context. Although in many ways intellectually close to Immanuel Wallerstein, in this work Arrighi tends to focus less on spatial divisions of labour and more on anchoring transnational material/financial networks across space. Although his main objective is not to understand cities *per se*, his focus on the territorial interlocking of the different flows leads him to consider the relevance of fourteenth-century Italian city-states to the emergence of global capitalism and, after the consolidation of the interstate system in cities such as Antwerp, Seville and Lyons, to their role as central market places for the trans-statal activities of foreign business organizations (Arrighi 1994: 128).

This means that although core–periphery distinctions are central to Global Commodity Chain analysis, allusions to links between the World City Network and core–periphery are limited to their apparent (if not commonsensical) coincidence. The real linkages remain obscure and are passed over in silence. For instance, in the seminal paper that was one of the world cities literature's original texts, Friedmann (1986) explicitly invokes world-systems analysis in his hierarchical classification of cities through including a division between cities in 'core countries' and cities in 'semi-peripheral countries'. But the world-systems analysis Friedmann calls upon remains at this basic conceptual level; there is nothing on how cities are implicated in the creation of core–periphery structures through commodity chains. Cities are described as 'control and command centres' through their housing of multinational corporate headquarters, but how this translates into the operation of, and control over, commodity chains is not broached. Saey (1996: 122) is the most severe critic in this respect arguing that the apparent spatial correlation between world-city formation and core processes is in and by itself insufficient to speak of a systematic relation between both structures. As a consequence, it can be noted that the title of Knox and Taylor's *World cities in a world-system* (1995) reflects an ambition rather than a reality.

However, as pointed out in the previous section, Taylor (2004, 2006) has recently brought back world-systems thinking into the study of world cities by using Jane Jacobs's categories of economically dynamic and stagnant cities, albeit again without reference to commodity chains themselves. It is Parnreiter (2003; Parnreiter et al. 2007) who has addressed the problematic absence of conceptual linkages between both approaches in an analysis of world city formation in Mexico City and Santiago de Chile, and it is this work that is discussed later in this section.

Core–periphery structure

In contrast to our argument here, Dicken et al. (2001: 99–100) have explicitly complained about the 'world-systems ancestry' of commodity chain analysis with its core–periphery framework, and Leslie and Reimer (1999: 404) have objected to the 'highly dualistic language' that leads to a 'surface level' geography. Many core–periphery models that abound in the social sciences can be justly criticized for their simplistic dualism but this is not the case with world-systems analysis. Hence, the criticisms above are based on a misunderstanding of the subtleties of the core and periphery concepts in world-systems analysis. Rather than 'surface' outcomes, core–periphery in world-systems analysis is a

25

deep structure from which both Global Commodity Chain formation and World City Network formation derive and whose mechanisms shape both types of spaces of flows. The key point about core and periphery in world-systems analysis is that they are not unchanging geographical categories; rather they are the spatial structures underpinning a very dynamic world economy.[4]

At the simplest level, core and periphery can be seen as bundles of systemic mechanisms that create contrary outcomes. Core processes are associated with historically high wage, high-tech, high profit inputs and outcomes (the work of lead firms in managing commodity chains is an example of a core mechanism); peripheral processes are associated with the opposite. Geographically, these processes have tended to concentrate and segregate (reflecting the evolution of market power, entry barriers and forms of chain governance). This produces places where core processes dominate and where peripheral processes dominate. For shorthand purposes these may be designated as 'core' and 'periphery' but they must never be seen as purely one or the other: so-called 'core countries' encompass numerous, if minority, peripheral processes; and the opposite is so for 'peripheral countries'.[5] Thus, Wallerstein's (1979, 2004) conceptualization, far from producing a simple 'dual world', suggests a most complex geography of interweaving contrary processes based upon a quite sophisticated social model. Importantly, in some places the contrary processes are approximately balanced – the concentration/ segregation has not transpired – and with no dominant processes, the outcome is referred to as semi-periphery.

The important point here is that the core–periphery model is central to both Global Commodity Chain and World City Network analysis. As regards Global Commodity Chain analysis, a major reason for using the model is to trace chains across the core–periphery boundary to expose the inequities of the geographies of how value is added and profit taken within the chain. In the case of World City Network analysis, delineating core/semi-periphery/ periphery by state jurisdictions has been replaced by city-based delimitations. For instance, the core is defined as locales in which core processes dominate: the cities and city regions of the three 'globalization arenas' – northern America, Pacific Asia and Western Europe – and peripheralization can be equated with Jacobs's (1984) description of the pernicious effects of dynamic cities on vulnerable locales beyond their city region in an extension of Frank's (1969) dependency thesis. Obviously, this revision of the core–periphery model takes the interweaving of the two processes to a more complicated geography than the usual definitions employing states as the constituents of the spatial categories (for example Arrighi and Drangel 1986; Terlouw 1992). This interpretation replaces the weak use of world-systems terminology in Friedmann (1986) where 'core ' cities are designated because they are located in 'core countries'.

What are the implications of this for integrating global commodity flows with the World City Network? First, basically *all* global commodity flows in the world economy include core-formation processes, which is why the chain cannot be initiated and sustained without world cities, wherever they may be located. These processes are needed to exercise control over commodity chains. Commodity flow branches bring value in from cities at all nodes and this leads to further consequent flows of profits to cities. This idea can be traced back to Sassen's original argument that world cities (or, in her terms, 'global cities') are centres for *both* the management and the command of the world economy. Although Sassen does not use the Global Commodity Chain terminology, her notion that a city's capacity to export producer services points to the capabilities for servicing and controlling global operations of firms exactly suggests what is elaborated here: world cities form critical nodes in numberless commodity chains because it is from these cities that core inputs required by all production chains are provided. It is in this sense that Sassen provides – although only analysing three major cities in considerable depth – an account that is valuable for understanding the structure of the world economy at large. Second, *all* cities are integrated into commodity chains, and that is how they are connected to the World City Network, even if their own input into the chain is only of a peripheral character. Thus, it is only from being within such spaces of flows that cities can be sustained within the world economy. Global Commodity Chains and the World City Network are therefore integral to the spatiality that is the core–periphery structure of the capitalist world economy.

World City Network process in Global Commodity Chains

A world city can be seen as a critical node within commodity chains, precisely for its insertion of advanced services into the production process. Thus, every world city is a service node in and for a myriad of chains, thereby obtaining its overall centrality. Our argument is that it is service intermediaries, the so-called producer services, located in world cities that maintain the connections between the networks of world cities and commodity chains. The innovation here is the assertion that service intermediaries, which provide the connectivity within urban networks, are also of particular significance for the efficient functioning of Global Commodity Chains because they offer key inputs (see also Jacobs et al. this book; Lüthi et al. this book). From a bank's initial lending of capital to initiate production, to the use of an advertising agency's services to facilitate final consumption, the provision of producer services through cities is essential in linking dispersed production and consumption sites and, therefore, to the successful operation of commodity chains. We illustrate this for the coffee Global Commodity Chain.

The coffee commodity chain constitutes a traditional primary commodity with long established systems of supply and demand across the globe, and is also currently an arena of rapid change including major price movements, significant readjustments in the distribution of income among the various participants within the chain (as the industry has been still further globalized) and major transformations in both how the final product is marketed and where (Daviron and Ponte 2005; Talbot 2004). A number of studies have attempted to apply a commodity chain (or value chain) analysis to the sector (Daviron and Ponte 2005; Fitter and Kaplinsky 2001; Pelupessy 1999; Talbot 2004). Their findings illustrate the economic polarization in the sector. On the one hand, despite the massive role that supermarkets play within the retail of coffee, the roasting companies have managed to maintain strong control of the coffee commodity chain. This has been achieved particularly through massive investment in advertising, bonus systems to maintain brand loyalty, blending and other non-price competition instruments (Pelupessy and Díaz 2008). On the other hand, austerity reforms via structural adjustment have robbed small growers of access to credit and state-sponsored marketing and extension services. As such, now 'producers sell only atomistically into commodity markets. These atomistic producers lack the capacity to combine forces' (Fitter and Kaplinsky 2001: 72). It is this more than anything that lies behind the regular crises facing coffee-producing areas.

Nevertheless, for all the strengths of commodity chain analysis, there is little or no recognition of the critical role of finance in the various stages of the production cycle (how it is obtained, managed and safeguarded at different points along the chain) and the changing relationship between the major players in the sector and the financial markets in the liberalized world of the past couple of decades (particularly in the expanded complexity and reach of trading in futures). There is also no explicit place for advertising agencies except as inputs to either roasting or trading activities. To an extent, this is because of the way in which commodity chain analysis has tended to treat services as separate chains within which knowledge is the commodity traded (Clancy 1998; Rabach and Kim 1994). However, to do so in the case of producer services has the effect of isolating the analysis of individual commodity chains such as coffee from the necessary service providers who enable the development and reproduction of the chain (see Vind and Fold, this book). Furthermore, it is worth reiterating that these are *producer* services and, as such, their knowledge commodity is not an end product in itself. Producer service knowledge commodities feed into other commodity chains that do lead to a final realization of capital (the concentration of financial rents by producer service providers and their relationship with other lead firms in the chain is a topic worthy of further detailed discussion).

The four major roasting companies are major global corporations and their myriad engagements within globalization are exceedingly complex. This global complexity is managed through headquarter and other governance levels as part of the command and control functions of world cities. These are the 'decision' cities through which advanced producer services are contracted (Rossi et al. 2007). These services are carried out in 'service' cities where the professional, creative and financial work takes place. It is this work that, to a large extent, makes possible the operation of the coffee commodity chains. A company like Nestlé will support its coffee commodity chains using banking/financial corporations, both local and global, to fund expansions; both insurance and law firms will be engaged for all projects that entail any risk; accountants and management consultants will be used to audit accounts and enhance profit margins to grow shareholder dividend; advertising agencies are crucial to marketing both nationally and globally. Thus, every stage in the commodity chain will involve professional, creative or financial inputs from cities; often chains will run through local cities (near production nodes), at other times through major cities distant from production nodes (for example the use of major advertising agencies in New York or major insurance corporations in London). Clearly, to function in an increasingly complex and globalizing world economy, commodity chains have to disseminate through city networks.[6] Figure 1 summarizes this suggested cross-fertilization by showing how cities play a crucial role in commodity chains through their dual function of servicing producers and final consumption.

Global Commodity Chain process in World City Network formation

Through modelling commodity chains we can draw attention to inter-city relations beyond the leading world cities, since these commodity chains reveal how many smaller settlements are connected to the World City Network through the various flows of capital, labour, goods and services. Global Commodity Chains explicitly include the stages of primary production, which

29

Figure 1: Model integration – one commodity chain and two world cities

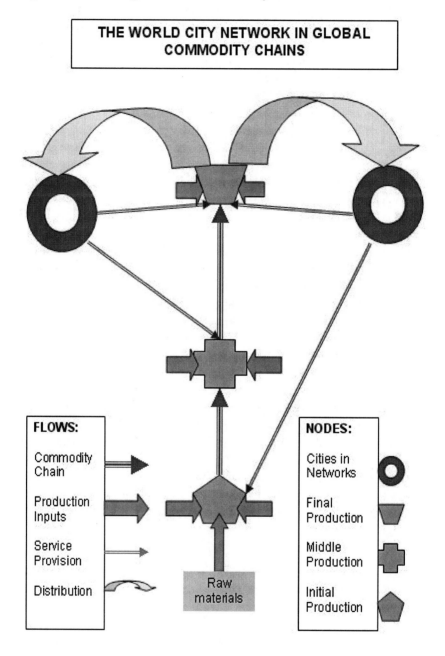

are located in rural areas and related to city-based transformation and trade processes (Jacobs 1969). Such an examination may thus help to develop a more spatially refined analysis of the World City Network, depicting also the specific roles of those cities seemingly at the margins of the World City Network. To do this, the data on the location strategies of individual companies may be extended with information on the geography of their clients (thus grasping backward and forward linkages). To this end, we need data on the geographic location of the clients of advanced producer firms (see Rossi et al. 2007). In particular, we need analysis of service provision through cities as a process that directly contributes to commodity chains; Parnreiter et al. (2007) have carried out just such a study of a specific financial process in Mexico City and Santiago (for a more detailed analysis of the Mexico City case, see Parnreiter, this book).

This research starts from the identification of the 'missing link' between two findings: Mexico and Chile are increasingly integrated in a variety of Global Commodity Chains, and globally organized advanced producer services are highly centralized in Mexico City and Santiago. It remained an assumption, however, that advanced producer services in both cities are essential in articulating production in the two countries with the world market. If world city-ness is to be understood as a *process* (that is providing advanced services for making global production feasible), then the multifaceted *links* between firms whose economic activities are geared towards the world market and service providers in a specific city have to be revealed.

Parnreiter et al. (2007) set out to explore one of those links through a study of the involvement of (local and global) financial institutions in issuing the bonds and shares of leading corporations in Mexico and Chile, starting from the assumption that the provision of this kind of financial service represents an important input for the functioning of a commodity chain. The study shows that between 1982 and 2004 most of the bond and share issues of the 50 top ranked Mexican and Chilean enterprises were handled by global financial institutions such as Citibank/Citigroup, JP Morgan/Chase Manhattan, Bank of New York, Banco Santander or ING Bank. More importantly, however, it was shown that the big corporations in Mexico and Chile prefer those global financial institutions that maintain offices in Mexico City and/or Santiago de Chile. Demand for financial service intermediaries is, therefore, concentrated in firms operating *both* at a global and a local scale. As a result, the locational strategies of banks and other financial institutions can best be summarized through the 'glocalization' concept (Swyngedouw 1997) or, in the words of UBS: 'We operate in two locations: Everywhere, and right next to you.' Two New York banks with local offices are particularly important: Citibank/

Citigroup services four of the Top 10 firms in Mexico and two of the Top 10 in Chile, while JP Morgan/Chase Manhattan provides financial services to three of the Top 10 firms in Mexico and to four of the Top 10 in Chile.

Parnreiter et al. (2007) attribute this preference for 'glocal' financial institutions to several factors. First, leading companies in Mexico and Chile seek out banks with sufficient global experience to place bond and share issues at major financial markets (in this case New York, Luxembourg, Frankfurt). Second, it is reasonable to assume that the Mexican branch of a transnational company chooses a bank already involved in the stock market transactions of the headquarters in, say, the United States. Third, the importance of a local office lies in so-called 'soft' factors, such as the initiation of business deals, an in-depth analysis of the company that sets out to issue bonds or shares, preparation of the 'pitch material' (such as information on financial position, investment strategies, profile of customers, or production description).

It is in this way that commodity chains instituted by leading corporations in Mexico and Chile are contributing towards Mexico City and Santiago's positioning in the World City Network. For instance, Citibank/Citigroup generate high value work in both cities through providing key inputs for several Global Commodity Chains. It does this by enabling investment for the Mexican oil company PEMEX or the Chilean copper company Codelco through bonds and shares at stock markets; by selling financial services to major retailers (for example Wal-mart Mexico, Controlada Comercial Mexicana); and by creating new commodity chains. Citibank/Citigroup acts therefore as an interlocker in the World City Network in their facilitation of myriad commodity chains. By playing a crucial role in both networks, 'glocalized' financial institutions provide the indispensable connection between the World City Network and Global Commodity Chains: *all* Global Commodity Chains 'run' through world cities, and *all* cities are integrated into commodity chains. Figure 2 summarizes this suggested cross-fertilization by showing how the operation of commodity chains is facilitated by myriad service provisions from cities.

An office in one city might, for instance, service a production node in its hinterland (for example a city financing the beginning of one chain and providing the advertising for the other chain), while on other occasions expertise from more than one office is used to service a producer (for example, the advertising for the right-hand chain is more complex and brings in expertise from offices in both cities); similarly, the latter chain requires a multi-office legal services (inter-jurisdictional) whereas the left-hand chain uses a law firm from its local city for a uni-jurisdictional legal requirement.

Figure 2: Model integration – one World City Network dyad and two commodity chains

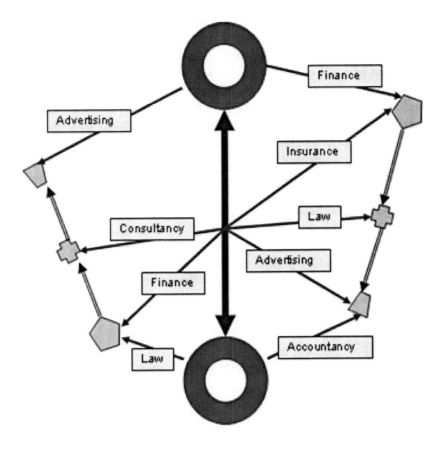

 Inter-city link formed by joint servicing projects

There are, however, important differences between the spatialities of commodity chains and the World City Network as well as between specific commodity chains (for example, primary production, manufacturing and services). On the whole, these differences stem from the degree of core-ness of the processes that constitute the flows sustaining the respective chain or network. While the World-City Network is by definition formed exclusively through the flows of high valued and highly monopolized activities, commodity chains are maintained by a multitude of flows. Although some of them are associated with core processes, many others are based on low-wage activities of producers, which are easy to substitute.

There are three interrelated spatialities to this difference. First, the prevalence of world cities differs markedly across the networks in question. Though commodity chains (like the coffee chain analysed above) necessarily run through world cities, these represent only a minor fraction of all nodes in the chain, while the prevailing localities in commodity chains are those cities and villages that tend to be 'off the world cities map' (Robinson 2002: 536). Second, there is a difference in the frequency and density of the connectivity to the 'global'. While world cities are linked to each other through multiple, extensive and constant flows, many localities are connected only through the flow of one or two items. The result is a (very) different degree of centrality within global networks. Third, the World City Network is geographically much more horizontally structured than commodity chains. Though the flows connecting Mexico City to other world cities are surely not even, there is no clear-cut hierarchy between the financial institution in New York and its regional office in Mexico City (Parnreiter et al. 2007). Conversely, all research on governance in commodity chains reveals that these are hierarchical and unequal in character.

Conclusion: what might an integrated research agenda look like?

Our ultimate goal is to produce a synthesis of World-City Network analysis and Global Commodity Chain analysis and this chapter is intended as a first step towards that objective. We have argued that both analytic frameworks have things to learn from each other and this can be a springboard to possible, eventual integration.

The first task is to create dense empirical evidence on how producer service firms in world cities interact with firms in commodity chains. The challenge consists in really *documenting* these flows of information and capital in at least two ways. Forward linkages of producer service firms and the (service) backward linkages of firms in commodity chains must be mapped to grasp: (a) the geographical reach of operations that emanate in world cities but that in many cases will go beyond the World-City Network; and (b) the spatial stretching of Global Commodity Chains towards specific world cities inputting producer services. In addition, the characteristics of the flows between producer service firms in world cities and firms in commodity chains have to be assessed with regard to the core-ness of the processes involved (for example, as value creation, or the possibility or grade of monopolization).

Second, to overcome the limitations of each model this new knowledge has to be fed back into the conceptualization of the two types of spaces of flows. As regards World-City Network formation, to identify the manifold linkages between world and non-world cities across different scales will help to understand how global cities relate to globalizing cities. Another expected result is a refined analysis of World-City Network formation itself. Mapping the geographical scales of service provision in a specific city, and detailing information on the core-ness (or not) of these inputs will lead to a comprehensive understanding of how big this city's wheels are (to use Jacobs's words) in making global production feasible. As for Global Commodity Chains, the full integration of services into their analysis and the related goal of treating the spatiality of the chain comprehensively are not ends in themselves. Rather, both efforts might lead to a more detailed understanding of where (or from where) control over production is exercised and how and where value is created and appropriated.

The cross-fertilization of the two models suggested represents the first step to their integration. If the integration proposed proceeds and eventually succeeds, world cities and Global Commodity Chains will no longer be treated separately. The creation and (unequal) distribution of value along commodity chains is organized in and governed from world cities, while – vice versa – the capacity to create the means of control of value creation and distribution and the power to deploy them is the underlying force in world city formation. This reciprocal relationship is because core formation processes are necessary for and hence inherent to both the organization of commodity chains and the formation of world cities.

Acknowledgements

We would like to thank the editor and two anonymous referees for their extensive and insightful comments, which have certainly helped to sharpen the line of argument in this chapter. This chapter draws on an earlier and broader elaboration of the argument, which can be downloaded as a GaWC Research Bulletin from http://www.lboro.ac.uk/gawc/.

Notes

1. Of course, external urban relations are a little more complicated than this: 'local' is itself variable as when hinterlands are arranged into central place hierarchies. The key point is whether the urban process is inward-looking – centred on place (town-ness) – or outward-looking – centred on flows (city-ness). For further discussion see Taylor et al. (2008).
2. For comparisons of the basic underlying assumptions of these models see Díaz (2003: 51, 56, 59).
3. Chain studies on tourism are also available (Clancy 1998; IFC 2006; Yilmaz and Bititci 2006).
4. In our reading, this critique of a 'surface level' geography in which 'core' is being equated with 'core states' misconceives Wallerstein's basic ideas. Admittedly, Wallerstein never elaborated what 'core' meant in geographical terms. However, in his writings, he uses the neutral term 'zones' when referring to core/periphery geographies, which may or may not be states. For instance, in the first volume of *The modern world-system*, Wallerstein (1974) points to the fact that northern France is 'in' the core while Mediterranean France is 'in' the semi-periphery. Many later writers use 'core' and 'core state' as synonyms for empirical rather than conceptual reasons (for example Arrighi and Drangel 1986; Terlouw 1992).
5. Even the most 'core' of all 'core zones' (namely the consecutive hegemons of the world system) encompass peripheral processes. For instance, at the height of its hegemony, the UK included a very typical peripheral process in a major way (the Irish famine); similarly at the height of US hegemony the 'South', a major division of the state, remained resolutely 'uncore-like' in both its economics and politics.
6. In addition to this extant complexity, the markets are themselves highly dynamic, creating new threats and opportunities to which the roasting companies have to respond with the help of their global service providers. Moreover, it is in the commercial milieu of the cities of the World-City Network where the consumption styles of urban consumers are created and recreated. The shifts in consumers' preferences towards non-material or symbolic attributes of goods are introduced and developed in urban areas, and frequently these are related to growing income levels. This suggests that there are more points of contact between commodity chain and World-City Network approaches: by recognizing the increasing consumer orientation of especially buyer-driven global chains, cities play an essential role in shaping consumer preferences, fashions and habits, which ascertain the flows of information along the chains; this again brings into the analysis consideration of the role of advertising and other producer services in creating and adapting new markets for coffee. Considerable internal changes to the governance of the coffee chain have been occasioned by new entrants into the retail market such as Starbucks and their competitors. These new firms have themselves made considerable use of professional and creative services. It is in major cities that these cutting edge marketing initiatives transforming traditional commodity chains are being developed and diffused. Thus, the neat circular argument for services beginning in cities at all stages of the chain and capital in the chain being realized through new retailing innovations in cities.

References

Appleyard, D. and A. Field (1997) *International economics*, New York: Richard D. Irwin Inc.

Arrighi, G. (1994) *The long twentieth century: money, power and the origins of our times*, New York: Verso.

Arrighi, G. (2007) *Adam Smith in Beijing: lineages of the twenty-first century*, New York: Verso.

Arrighi, G. and J. Drangel (1986) 'The stratification of the world-economy: an exploration of the semiperipheral zone', *Review*, 10 (1), 9–74.

Bair, J. (2003) 'From commodity chains to value chains and back again?', paper presented at 'Rethinking Marxism', University of Massachusetts at Amherst, available online at http://www.csiss.org/events/meetings/time-mapping/files/bair_paper.pdf, last accessed 22 October 2009.

Bair, J. (2009) 'Global Commodity Chains: genealogy and review', in J. Bair (ed.) *Frontiers of commodity chain research*, Stanford: Stanford University Press, 1–34.

Bolwig, S., L. Riisgaard, S. Ponte, A. du Toit and N. Halberg (2008) 'Integrating poverty and environmental concerns in to value chain analysis: a conceptual framework', *DIIS Working Paper*, 2008/16.

Brenner, N. (1998) 'Global cities, glocal states: global city formation and state territorial restructuring in contemporary Europe', *Review of International Political Economy*, 5 (1), 1–37.

Brenner, N. (2004) *New state spaces: urban governance and the rescaling of statehood*, Oxford: Oxford University Press.

Brown, E., G. Catalano and P. J. Taylor (2002) 'Beyond world cities: Central America in a space of flows', *Area*, 34, 139–48.

Busch, L. (2007) 'Performing the economy, performing science: from neoclassical to supply chain models in the agrifood sector', *Economy and Society*, 36, 437–66.

Castells, M. (1996) *The rise of the network society*, Oxford: Blackwell.

Chase-Dunn, C. (1983) 'Urbanization in the world-system: new directions for research', *Comparative Urban Research*, 9, 41–6.

Clancy, M. (1998) 'Commodity chains, services and development: theory and preliminary evidence from the tourism industry', *Review of International Political Economy*, 5, 122–48.

Coe, N., M. Hess, H. W-c. Yeung, P. Dicken and J. Henderson (2004) 'Globalizing regional development: a Global Production Networks perspective', *Transactions of the Institute of British Geographers*, 29 (4), 468–84.

Coe, N., P. Dicken and M. Hess (2008) 'Global Production Networks: realizing the potential', *Journal of Economic Geography*, 8 (3), 271–95.

Cohen, R. (1981) 'The new international division of labour, multinational corporations, and urban hierarchy', in M. Dear and A. Scott (eds) *Urbanization and urban planning in capitalist society*, Methuen: London, 287–315.

Daniels, P. and J. Bryson (2002) 'Manufacturing services and servicing manufacturing: changing forms of production in advanced capitalist economies', *Urban Studies*, 39 (5–6), 977–91.

Daviron B. and S. Ponte (2005) *The coffee paradox, global markets, commodity trade and the elusive promise of development*, London: Zed Books.

Derudder, B. (2006) 'On conceptual confusion in empirical analyses of a transnational urban network', *Urban Studies*, 43 (11), 2027–46.

Derudder, B., P. J. Taylor, F. Witlox and G. Catalano (2003) 'Hierarchical tendencies and regional patterns in the World City Network: a global urban analysis of 234 cities', *Regional Studies*, 37 (9), 875–86.

Díaz, R. (2003) 'A developing country perspective on policies for sustainable agribusiness chains: the case of Costa Rica', NICCOS, 43.

Dicken, P. (2003) *Global shift: reshaping the global economic map in the 21st century* (4th edition), London: Sage Publications.

Dicken, P., P. Kelly, K. Olds and H. W-c. Yeung (2001) 'Chains and networks, territories and scales: towards a relational framework for analysing the global economy', *Global Networks*, 1, 99–123.

Fitter, R. and R. Kaplinsky (2001) 'Who gains from product rents as the coffee market becomes more differentiated? A value chain analysis', *IDS Bulletin*, 32, 69–82.

Frank, A. (1969) *Latin America: underdevelopment or revolution?*, New York: Monthly Review Press.

Friedmann, J. (1986) 'The world city hypothesis', *Development and Change*, 17, 69–83.

Friedmann, J. and G. Wolff (1992) 'World city-formation: an agenda for research and action', *International Journal of Urban and Regional Research*, 6, 309–44.

Gereffi, G. (1999) 'International trade and industrial upgrading in the apparel commodity chain', *Journal of International Economics*, 48, 37–70.

Gereffi, G. and M. Korzeniewicz (eds) (1994) *Commodity chains and global capitalism*, Westport: Praeger.

Gereffi, G. and R. Kaplinsky (eds) (2001) 'The value of value chains: spreading the gains from globalization', *IDS Bulletin*, 32 (3).

Gibbon, P., J. Bair and S. Ponte (2008) 'Governing Global Value Chains: an introduction', *Economy and Society*, 37, 315–38.

Hall, P. and K. Pain (eds) (2006) *The polycentric metropolis: learning from mega-city regions in Europe*, London: Earthscan.

Hamilton, G. and G. Gereffi (2009) 'Global Commodity Chains, market makers and the rise of demand-responsive economies', in J. Bair (ed.) *Frontiers of commodity chain research*, Stanford: Stanford University Press, 136–62.

Hesse, M. (2010) 'Cities, material flows and the geography of spatial interaction: urban places in the system of chains', *Global Networks*, 10 (1), 75–91.

Hopkins, T. and I. Wallerstein (1986) 'Commodity chains in the world-economy prior to 1800', *Review*, 10 (1), 157–70.

Humphrey, J. and H. Schmitz (2001) 'Governance in Global Value Chains', *IDS Bulletin*, 32 (3), 19–23.

Hughes, A. and S. Reimer (eds) (2004) *Geographies of commodity chains*, London: Routledge.

IFC (International Finance Corporation) (2006) 'The tourism sector in Mozambique: a value chain analysis', (vols 1 and 2), IFC: Washington, DC.

Jacobs, J. (1969) *The economy of cities*, New York: Vintage.

Jacobs, J. (1984) *Cities and the wealth of nations*, New York: Random House.

Jacobs, J. (2000) *The nature of economics*, New York: Vintage.

Jacobs, W., C. Ducruet and P. de Langen (2010) 'Integrating world cities into production networks: the case of port cities', *Global Networks*, 10 (1), 92–113.

Kaplinsky, R. (2005) *Globalization, poverty and inequality: between a rock and a hard place*, Cambridge: Polity Press.

Karaba, R. (1991) *Cities in the world-system*, Westport: Greenwood Press.

King, A. (1990) *Global cities*, London: Routledge.

Knox, P. and P. J. Taylor (eds) (1995) *World cities in a world-system*, Cambridge: Cambridge University Press.

Leslie, D. and S. Reimer (1999) 'Spatializing commodity chains', *Progress in Human Geography*, 23 (3), 401–20.

Li Yang, C. and M. Yu (2007) 'The impact of producer services on manufacturing value chain', *International Journal of Services Operations and Informatics*, 2 (4), 421–38.

Lüthi, S., A. Thierstein, and V. Goebel (2010) 'Intra-firm and extra-firm linkages in the knowledge economy: the case of the emerging mega-city region of Munich', *Global Networks*, 10 (1), 114–37.

Marcuse, P. and R. van Kempen (eds) (2000) *Globalizing cities*, Blackwell: Oxford.

Olds, K. and H. W-c. Yeung (2004) 'Pathways to global city formation: a view from the developmental city-state of Singapore,' *Review of International Political Economy*, 11 (3), 489–521.

Parnreiter, C. (2002) 'Mexico: the making of a global city?', in S. Sassen (ed.) *Global networks, linked cities*, London: Routledge, 145–82.

Parnreiter, C. (2003) 'Global city formation in Latin America: socioeconomic and spatial transformations in Mexico City and Santiago de Chile', paper presented at the 99th Annual Meeting of the Association of American Geographers, New Orleans, 4–8 March also *GaWC Research Bulletin*, no. 103, available online at http://www.lboro.ac.uk/gawc/rb/rb103.html, last accessed 22 October 2009.

Parnreiter, C. (2010) 'Global cities in Global Commodity Chains: exploring the role of Mexico City in the geography of governance of the world economy', *Global Networks*, 10 (1), 35–53.

Parnreiter, C., K. Fischer and K. Imhof (2007) 'El enlace faltante entre cadenas globales de producción y ciudades globales: el servicio financiero en Ciudad de México y Santiago de Chile', *Eure*, 33, 100, 135–48.

Pelupessy, W. (1999) 'Coffee in Côte d'Ivoire and Costa Rica: national and global aspects of competitiveness', in H. van der Laan, T. Dijkstra and A. van Tilburg (eds) *Agricultural marketing in tropical Africa*, Aldershot: Ashgate, 109–30.

Pelupessy, W. (2001) 'Industrialization in Global Commodity Chains emanating from Latin America', *UNISA Latin American Report* 17 (2), 4–14.

Pelupessy, W. and R. Diaz (2008) 'Upgrading of lowland coffee in Central America', *Agribusiness: An International Journal*, 24 (1), 119–40.

Rabach, E. and E. Kim (1994) 'Where is the chain in commodity chains? The service sector nexus', in G. Gereffi and M. Korzeniewicz (eds) *Commodity chains and global capitalism*, Westport: Praeger, 123–43.

Rammohan, K. and R. Sundaresan (2003) 'Socially embedding the commodity chain: an exercise in relation to coir yarn spinning in southern India', *World Development*, 31 (5), 903–23.

Robinson, J. (2002) 'Global and world cities: a view from off the map', *International Journal of Urban and Regional Research*, 26 (3), 531–54.

Robinson, J. (2005) 'Urban geography: world cities, or a world of cities', *Progress in Human Geography*, 29, 757–65.

Rossi, E. and P. J. Taylor (2005) 'Banking networks across Brazilian cities: interlocking cities within and beyond Brazil', *Cities*, 22 (5), 381–93.

Rossi, E., J. Beaverstock and P. J. Taylor (2007) 'Transaction links through cities: "decision cities" and "service cities" in outsourcing by leading Brazilian firms', *Geoforum*, 38 (4), 628–42.

Saey, P. (1996) 'Het wereldstedennetwerk: de nieuwe Hanze?', *Vlaams Marxistisch Tijdschrift*, 30 (1), 120–3.

Sassen, S. (1991) *The global city*, Princeton: Princeton University Press.

Sassen, S. (2001) *The global city*, 2nd edition, Princeton: Princeton University Press.

Schmitz, H. (2000) 'Global competition and local cooperation: success and failure in the Sinos Valley, Brazil', *World Development*, 27, 1627–50.

Shatkin, G. (2007) 'Global cities of the South: emerging perspectives on growth and inequality', *Cities*, 24 (1), 1–15.

Smith, A., A. Rainnie, M. Dunford, J. Hardy, R. Hudson and D. Sadler (2002) 'Networks of value, commodities and regions: reworking divisions of labour in macro-regional economies', *Progress in Human Geography*, 26, 41–63.

Smith, D. (2003) 'Rediscovering cities and urbanization in the 21st century world-system', in W. Dunaway (ed.) *Emerging issues in the 21st century world-system*, vol. 2, Westport: Praeger, 111–29.

Swyngedouw, E. (1997) 'Neither global or local: "glocalization" and the politics of scale', in K. Cox (ed.) *Spaces of globalization*, New York: Guilford Press, 137–66.

Talbot, J. (2004) *Grounds for agreement: the political economy of the coffee commodity chain*, New York: Rowman & Littlefield Publishers.

Taylor, P. J. (2001) 'Specification of the World City Network', *Geographical Analysis*, 33, 181–94.

Taylor, P. J. (2004) *World City Network: a global urban analysis*, London: Routledge.

Taylor, P. J. (2006) 'Cities within spaces of flows: theses for a materialist understanding of the external relations of cities', in P. Taylor, B. Derudder, P. Saey and F. Witlox (eds) *Cities in globalization*, London: Routledge, 287–97.

Taylor, P. J., B. Derudder, P. Saey and F. Witlox (eds) (2006) *Cities in globalization*, London: Routledge.

Taylor, P. J., M. Hoyler and R. Verbruggen (2010) 'External urban relational processes: introducing central flow theory to complement central place theory', *Urban Studies*, 46, in press.

Terlouw, C. (1992) *The regional geography of the world-system: external arena, periphery, semiperiphery, core*, Utrecht: Faculteit Ruimtelijke Wetenschappen Universiteit Utrecht.

Timberlake, M. (ed.) (1985) *Urbanization in the world-economy*, New York: Academic Press.

Vind, I. and N. Fold (2010) 'City networks and commodity chains: identifying global flows and local connections in Ho Chi Minh City', *Global Networks*, 10 (1), 54–74.

Wallerstein, I. (1974) *The modern world-system I: capitalist agriculture and the origins of the European world-economy in the sixteenth century*, New York, Academic Press.

Wallerstein, I. (1979) *The capitalist world-economy*, Cambridge: Cambridge University Press.

Wallerstein, I. (1984) 'Cities in socialist theory and capitalist praxis', *International Journal of Urban and Regional Research*, 8, 64–72.

Wallerstein, I. (2004) *World-systems analysis*, Durham, NC: Duke University Press.

Wallerstein, I. (2009) 'Protection networks and commodity chains in the capitalist world-economy', in J. Bair (ed.) *Frontiers of commodity chain research*, Stanford: Stanford University Press, 83–90.

Yilmaz, Y. and U. Bititci (2006) 'Performance measurement in tourism: a value chain model', *International Journal of Contemporary Hospitality Management*, 18, 341–9.

3

Global cities in Global Commodity Chains: exploring the role of Mexico City in the geography of global economic governance

CHRISTOF PARNREITER

Global city research is guided by two basic arguments. The first is that global cities articulate local, regional and national economies into the world economy by providing producer services (such as finance, accountancy, consultancy, legal or real estate services) to companies that operate on different geographical scales. Second, it is maintained that global cities have emerged 'as highly concentrated command points in the organization of the world economy' (Sassen 1991: 3) because producer services are seen not only as techniques necessary for the smooth function of production networks, but also as means that constitute the capability for global control.

Though both claims are widely accepted, there is very little empirical evidence to document the management *and* the command functions of global cities. Complaints about the lack of adequate data for global city research are common, but much has been achieved since Short et al. (1996) wrote their critical account. Most progress was made in the empirical analyses of linkages between major cities hosting the most important (producer service) firms (see, for example, Derudder 2006; Taylor 2004; Taylor et al. 2009). Little research, however, has been devoted to showing how producer service firms in global cities help to link economies on different geographical scales. Even less effort was made to explore to what extent the presence of sizeable clusters of globalized producer service firms may lead to the qualification of a city as a command-and-control centre in the global economy. Hence, little is known about the actual practice of exercising management and command functions, which, needless to say, undermines the strength of the global city argument.

Despite this lack of evidence, the central argument in this chapter is that global cities are – and have to be understood as – critical nodes in Global Commodity Chains.[1] Because they are the places where producer services, in other words the means to deal with and to control complex cross-border

43

networks of production and distribution, are provided, each global city constitutes a significant juncture in numberless production networks, while each commodity chain contains several world cities (Parnreiter 2003). This claim is derived from Hopkins and Wallerstein's (1977: 114) spatial conceptualization of core areas, which are defined as areas with 'many relational sequences leading from or to them'. Though Hopkins and Wallerstein developed their concept of commodity chains only in the 1980s, and though Wallerstein never thought of cities as the cores of the world economy, the usefulness of this line of reasoning for the purpose of integrating the research literatures on world cities and on Global Commodity Chains is obvious (see also Brown et al. in this book). My assertion that global cities are key nodes in cross-border production networks has further roots in Sassen's account that producer services, which are highly concentrated in global cities, constitute the instruments for the management and the control of the dispersed world economy. Finally, my contention also emanates from Rabach and Kim's (1994: 123) notion that 'without the integrating and coordinating function fulfilled by services, GCC would not be viable'. These arguments clearly suggest that producer services constitute core activities in commodity chains, *and* that global cities are critical links in commodity chains.

The purpose of this chapter is to sustain this claim by providing qualified evidence for both assumed functions of global cities, namely the management and the command of Global Production Networks. This will be done through the analysis of forward linkages of producer service firms in Mexico City. I focus my empirical analysis first on service flows from firms in Mexico City to major companies engaged in global production in Mexico. I shall argue that Mexico City is necessarily a place in which to insert producer services into commodity chains originating in or running through Mexico.

Second, through the empirical analysis I seek to highlight whether and to what extent producer service firms in Mexico City exercise control over the production chains for which they supply services. Based on Sassen's (1991) conception of global cities as points of command and on Gereffi's (1994: 97) notion that governance of commodity chains means the authority to influence the creation and allocation of value within a chain, the objective is to explore whether the producer service sector in Mexico City plays a role in the shaping of value creation and distribution within the segments of Global Production Networks in Mexico, or whether global city formation in Mexico City is confined to contributions that merely enable the running of Global Commodity Chains. Thus, the question posed is: what is the position of Mexico City in the geography of governance in the world economy? My conclusion will be nuanced – the city's role varies by sector and firm-specific factors, and it also depends on the kind of producer services being analysed.

Through this exploration of whether governance functions are exercised in Mexico City, I hope also to contribute towards a more comprehensive grasp of the role of major cities in poorer countries in processes of uneven globalization. My contention is that such an understanding is necessary for a conception of the (changing) geography of governance, because both apocalyptic accounts (Davis 2006) and complaints that global city research is inadequate for understanding cities in poorer countries (for example, Robinson 2006) obscure the role of cities like Mexico City in the world economy.

The remainder of this chapter is organized as follows. After a brief discussion on the deeper integration of economic activities in Mexico into Global Commodity Chains and of global city formation in the country's capital, in the following three sections I shall examine the management and the control assumption of global city research, and discuss the specific place of Mexico City in the geography of governance. To document and analyse connections between Mexico City's producer service sector and companies in commodity chains running through Mexico I use different data sources. I draw on national accounts data, which are broken down by different types of producer services and analysed for different geographical scales, as well as on written information provided by global producer service firms in Mexico City, which offers detailed insights into the structures of the clients of the respective firms. This information is supplemented by insights gained from 13 semi-structured expert interviews with professionals in accountancy, finance, law and real estate firms, and with Alejandro Tagle Robles, deputy director of the National Register of Foreign Investment at the Ministry of Economics. Interviews lasted between 30 and 70 minutes and were conducted in Mexico City, mainly in October 2008 (two in October 2007). Most interviews were held in Spanish (two in German), and were recorded, transcribed and translated by the author. Interviews focused on the structure of clients, on different features of the services provided, on the position of the Mexican office *vis-à-vis* other offices of the respective service firm, and on the potential influence the service firm has on corporate decision-making. The results of the study are summarized in the final section.

Deeper integration into Global Commodity Chains and global city formation

Mexico City is a proper case because the country's economy has gone through a rapid course of globalization, and because there is sound evidence of ongoing global city formation. In the following section, I briefly discuss both aspects to provide the basis for the following examination of Mexico City's role in commodity chains.

Following the end of import substituting industrialization (ISI) in the early 1980s, Mexico became the third largest recipient of FDI among developing economies. Annual inflows grew by 1300 per cent (1980/85–2001/06), amounting to $US 19 billion in 2006. As a result, the share of Mexico's FDI stock in its GDP rose to 27 per cent (UNCTAD 2007). Manufacturing is the most important destination for FDI (46 per cent in 1999–2008), followed by financial and real estate services (together 26 per cent) (Secretaría de Economía 2008). Cross-border trade has also grown significantly. Exports have grown ninefold (up to $US 272 billion in 2007), and imports have increased twelvefold (1980/85–2002/07). As a result, the trade ratio rose to 65 per cent in 2006, up from 24 per cent in the early 1980s (UNCTAD 2008; World Bank 2008).

An even more significant feature of the globalization of the Mexican economy is that the composition of exports was altered fundamentally, with manufacturing amounting to 80 per cent of exports (2006–08), while the share of oil has decreased to 17 per cent. This indicates a changing integration of firms and cities in Mexico into Global Commodity Chains, transforming them into production platforms designed chiefly to serve the US market. Another salient feature is that the trade balance has been negative almost every year since Mexico joined the GATT/WTO in 1986. Even in manufacturing the trade balance is strongly negative, with the electronic and automotive industries the strongest importers (INEGI 2008a; UNCTAD 2008).

While Mexico's economy was being reoriented towards the world market, Mexico City – in the era of ISI the economic epicentre of the domestic market – underwent a deep transformation. The share of manufacturing in the city's gross regional product dropped from 24 to 19 per cent (1980–2003), while the participation of Mexico City in national industrial production was falling from 47 to 17 per cent.[2] This decline led to an overall reduction of Mexico City's participation in the national GDP, which in 2003 amounted to 31 per cent. Another major trend is the strong growth of producer services. Financial services increased their share in the city's GRP from 9 to 25 per cent (1980– 2003), while real estate, legal and headquarter services also grew above average.[3] In 2003 Mexico City's producer services accounted for more than a third of urban production, while the city's share in the national production of these services had risen to 76 per cent. By comparison, Monterrey, despite its economic upsurge in recent years, accounted for only 6 per cent. With 88 per cent of Mexico's added value stemming from Mexico City, financial services are the most concentrated services, followed by headquarter services (81 per cent) (Sobrino 2000; INEGI 2004). This rise of producer services indicates that Mexico City is changing from a predominantly national production centre, catering to and integrating the domestic market, to a hinge between economic activities carried out in Mexico and the world market (Parnreiter 2002, 2007). Support for this argument comes from studies that show that Mexico City's producer service sector is firmly inserted into the World City Network (Taylor 2004). Classified as an 'Alpha World City' in 2008, Mexico City had network connectivity comparable to Amsterdam or Frankfurt (Taylor et al. 2009).

Concomitant with the concentration of producer services, the headquarters of the main companies operating in Mexico have become more centralized. In 1993, the year before NAFTA was enacted, 255 of the Top 500 companies in Mexico were headquartered in Mexico City. Thirteen years later, the number had risen to 352. It is remarkable that today the centralization of head offices is even higher than in the times of ISI. It is also striking that the bigger a corporation is and the more global links it has (in terms of foreign ownership and exports), the stronger the concentration of headquarters in Mexico City. While 63 per cent of the Mexican owned Top 500 corporations are headquartered in Mexico City (2006), among foreign owned firms the share is 79 per cent (Expansión various years).

Thickening empirical evidence

After having shown that decision-making and high-level management became more concentrated in Mexico City since the end of ISI, the objective of this section is to scrutinize the notion that global cities articulate local, regional and national economies into Global Commodity Chains through the insertion of producer services. If this assertion is true, then neither the concentration of headquarters nor the growth of the producer service sector *per se* makes a global city. Rather, the key point for an empirical analysis of global city formation is that the demand for these services by companies within Global Commodity Chains must be confirmed. My contention is, therefore, that the World City Network has to have extensions at various geographical scales, including the national, and that is why the World City Network is built upon ramifications that link global cities to the countless non-global, but yet globalized cities, where production for global markets is carried out (Parnreiter 2003).

Sassen (2007: 201) suggests that the capacity of a city to export producer services points towards capabilities for servicing and controlling global operations of firms. Though she apparently alludes to cross-border exports, for the purpose of this chapter it is proper to apply a more generalized notion of exports. Do firms in Mexico City supply producer services that are used by firms throughout Mexico to enable the running of global production? In discussing this question, I seek to transform attribute data presented in the previous section (for example, number of headquarters or value added in producer services) into relational data that indicate flows between cities. Therefore, in the following I shall provide quantitative and qualitative information on forward linkages of the producer service sector, that is on interregional flows of services, with the aim of strengthening evidence for the argument that world cities are critical nodes within commodity chains, precisely for their insertion of producer services into the production process.

According to an input-output analysis of the Mexican economy (2003), 60 per cent of the producer services went to three economic sectors: 23 per cent were utilized by the wholesale and retail trade, 19 per cent by manufacturing and 18 per cent by the producer service sector itself (INEGI 2008b). Data on FDI inflows reveal that these sectors are firmly integrated into Global Production Networks: manufacturing attracts 49 per cent of all FDI (1994–2007), financial services 23 per cent, and wholesaling and retailing 9 per cent (INEGI 2008a). As a consequence, ownership in these sectors is strongly internationalized.

Because the input-output analysis cannot be broken down on a regional level, we do not know how much of the producer services used by the three sectors actually come from Mexico City. Nevertheless, the strong geographical concentration of value adding activities in producer services shows, along with information provided in Table 1, that there are substantial flows of producer services from Mexico City to other parts of the country. Taking the two major export industries as examples, Table 1 shows that cities where much of export manufacturing is carried out are not at all equipped to *manage* this production within global networks. The 11 *municipios* (districts), from which half the added value in the automotive industry and two-thirds of the added value in the computer and electronic industries come, have together only 2 per cent of all added value in producer services, and they house hardly *any* headquarter services. This suggests that the need to service export production is, at least partly, satisfied by producer services coming from Mexico City.

Table 1: Share in value adding activities in automotive industries, computer and electronic industries, and in producer services, selected *municipios*, 2003, %

District (Federal State)	Share of value added in automotive industry	Share of value added in producer services	District (Federal State)	Share of value added in computer and electronic industries	Share of value added in producer services
Cuautlancingo (Puebla)	15.8	0.1	Juárez (Chihuahua)	26.2	0.6
Silao (Guanajuato)	11.5	0.0	Tijuana (Baja California)	14.8	0.5
Juárez (Chihuahua)	7.5	0.6	Mexicali (Baja California)	7.1	0.3
Ramos Arizpe (Coahuila)	5.8	0.0	Aguascalientes (Aguascalientes)	6.3	0.2
Toluca (Edo. de México)	5.3	0.2	El Salto (Jalisco)	5.7	0.0
Nuevo Casas Grandes (Chihuahua)	4.0	0.0	Reynosa (Tamaulipas)	5.6	0.3

Source: Own calculations, based on INEGI 2004.

That said, it is also necessary to point out that the importance of producer services as inputs varies considerably across economic sectors. In wholesale and retail trade they make up 45 per cent of all inputs, while in manufacturing the relatively small contribution that producer services make to the added value is striking. Whereas in several OECD countries producer services account for 15–20 per cent of all inputs to manufacturing (Daniels 2007: 112), in Mexico they comprise only 5 per cent. The fact that the demand for producer services provided (mainly) by Mexico City based service firms varies significantly among economic sectors and sub-sectors, suggests that Mexico City's role as a global city is very different in, for example, the automotive chain and the many chains that end in the 1104 supermarkets owned by Wal-Mart Mexico.

As regards manufacturing, the minor importance of producer services provided in Mexico City can be attributed to the poor embeddedness of export manufacturing in the economy. Export industries are characterized by a 'specialization in segments of commodity chains reliant on cheap labor power and imported inputs' (Dussel Peters 2008: 24), which also explains the negative trade balance and the importance of the automotive and electronic industries as importers of semi-finished products. Value adding activities in Mexico's industries remain minor, and they have even decreased over time. This *maquiladorization* of manufacturing results in poor linkages to other economic sectors, including producer services.[4]

However, it does not render them unnecessary, as we can conclude from the insights gained from written information provided by global service firms in Mexico City and from expert interviews with professionals of these firms. An analysis of the client structure of producer service firms in Mexico City reveals that in the case of publicly traded companies (220 of the 300 biggest firms in Mexico), 91 per cent of the firms (accounting for 95 per cent of the sales) get their auditing services from the Mexico City office of one of the 'Big Four' global accountancy firms (Deloitte, Ernst & Young, KPMG, PricewaterhouseCoopers). Among the Top 100 firms in Mexico, which are listed on the stock exchange, only three have an auditor other than one of the 'Big Four'. Thus, a considerable number of commodity chains obtain at least one producer service from Mexico City. The state-owned oil producer PEMEX, ranked 42nd in the Fortune 500 list, is audited by KPMG, as is the privately-owned cement company CEMEX (3rd in Mexico and 389th worldwide), while the mining company Industrias Peñoles, one of Mexico's major exporters, gets its audit services from Ernst & Young, a firm that also services Teléfonos de México, to which América Móvil (Latin America's biggest mobile phone network provider) belongs. In the automotive industries, Deloitte works for GM, Ernst & Young for Nissan, KPMG for Chrysler, PricewaterhouseCoopers for Volkswagen and Ford, while in financial and insurance services, Deloitte (working for Grupo Financiero BBVA-Bancomer, Grupo Financiero Santander, Grupo Financiero Banorte) and KPMG (Grupo Financiero Banamex, Grupo Financiero HSBC México) have the largest banks as clients. Finally, Wal-Mart, which is responsible for the rapid globalization of Mexico's retail sector, is audited by Ernst & Young. Thus, the question of whether Mexico City is a node, from where producer services are fed into production networks can be answered: for auditing this is clearly the case.

In the case of legal services, available information also suggests that Mexico City is a place from where inputs are supplied to different commodity chains. First, the 'Big Four' accountancy firms also offer legal services. Deloitte, for example, sells legal and tax services to 66 of the 100 biggest firms in Mexico. Second, some of the world's biggest law firms have offices in Mexico City, from where they service mainly foreign companies and Mexican firms with global operations. Raymundo Enríquez, managing partner of the

Mexico City office of Baker & McKenzie, in 2006 the world's sixth biggest law firm (The Lawyer.com 2008), estimates that about 95 per cent of the firm's clients have global reach. Correspondingly, LatinLawyer (2007: 91) states that the 'client list (is) dominated by US and European corporate names'. According to Enríquez, global companies competing for the Mexican market are by far the most important sub-group, while national firms catering to the world market and TNCs carrying out export production in Mexico make up about 20 to 25 per cent of the clients. The Mexican office of Holland & Knight, worldwide the 36th biggest law firm (The Lawyer.com), which operates in Mexico jointly with a long established Mexican law firm (Gallastegui y Lozano), has worked, among others, for PEMEX, Grupo Financiero BBVA-Bancomer, and the conglomerate Grupo Carso, which produces a range of commodities from cigars to autoparts.

One important aspect of servicing global operations of firms is, as all interviewed lawyers confirmed, the legal management of FDI. This includes decisions on the form of business organization of the investing company in Mexico and its internal rules; adapting to the regulatory frameworks that vary across economic sectors and across the 12 free trade agreements Mexico has signed; making decisions on the labour union, with which the company is going to sign the collective bargaining agreement; buying or leasing a plant or a piece of property; dealing with tax issues, royalties and property rights; and attending to migration issues for professionals from the parent company. The importance of the place where FDI is managed is revealed by the discrepancy in Mexico City's share in the ingoing FDI, which is nearly three times larger than the city's contribution to the GNP (INEGI 2008a).[5]

In the fast growing and rapidly globalizing office market of Mexico City, much of the dynamism stems from global firms, be they investors or buyers/tenants of the offices (Parnreiter 2009). The Mexico City offices of global real estate firms supply a number of companies in Mexico that operate at a global level. Among the clients of CBRE are 25 of the Top 50 companies in Mexico (including América Móvil, Wal-Mart, General Motors and Grupo Financiero BBVA-Bancomer), JLL worked with 14 of the Top 50 (for example, General Motors, Grupo Financiero BBVA-Bancomer or Ford), and Colliers International has, among others, Grupo Modelo as a client, a brewery that in recent years successfully went global.

To summarize: there is reliable evidence on forward linkages of global producer service firms in Mexico City to economic sectors, which are strongly linked to the world market via FDI and/or exports. Thus, producer service firms connect to companies within various Global Commodity Chains that either emanate in Mexico (as in the case of petroleum), run through the country (as in the automotive industry), or end there (for example, the products sold in Wal-Mart). Though the information presented is far from all-embracing, there is sound enough evidence to assert that Mexico City is one of those nodes where 'specialized services needed by complex organizations for running a spatially dispersed network of factories, offices, and service outlets' (Sassen 1991: 5) are supplied. Mexico City is therefore *on* the map of both world cities and Global Commodity Chains precisely because it is a place from where global production is made possible through service inputs. The implications of this finding for the second key notion of global city research, namely the command of the world economy, will be discussed in the next sections.

Producer services and the governance of commodity chains

Among the conceptual points that the literature on global cities and on Global Commodity Chains share, the concern for the governance of uneven globalization processes is one of the most important. Sassen's main interest lies in the practices that make globalization feasible, and she identifies producer services as key activities for both 'the production of management *and* control operations' (Sassen 1991: 14; emphasis added). As a consequence of this double perspective, she depicts global cities both as places for the management and the command of the world economy.

Likewise, in Global Commodity Chains research, governance – defined by Gereffi (1994: 97) as the 'authority and power relationships that determine how financial, material and human resources are allocated and flow within a chain' – has been explicitly related to the coordination of transnational production processes *and* to the ability of lead firms to control them. Research deals with power asymmetries between rule-makers and rule-keepers, the origins of different forms of governance and their impacts on the opportunities for upgrading suppliers (thought of mostly as firms in low and middle income countries) (for a review of the literature see Gibbon et al. 2008). In the Global Production Networks literature, Dicken et al. (2001) and Henderson et al. (2002) advocate a more networked perspective on power, which implies less focus on the lead firm and its corporate power, to the benefit of a closer consideration of power, both institutional (wielded, for example, by the state, international institutions or private credit rating agencies) and collective (exercised, for example, by trade unions or small business organizations).

Despite the seemingly mutual interest in the governance and control of globalization processes, the literatures on global cities and on Global Commodity Chains differ in important aspects. First, while the former draws attention to the producer service firms and their inputs into production processes, the latter concentrates on lead firms and their relations to suppliers. In this context it is worthwhile to note that recent studies on the organizational structures of TNCs suggest a shift from vertical control relationships to forms of governance based on internal and external networks of cooperative and lateral relationships (Dicken 2007: 122; Dunning and Lundan 2008: 245). It is, however, barely discussed what role producer service firms play in this shift away from the lead firm. A second difference is that while Sassen stresses the making of global control capabilities instead of corporate power, Global Commodity Chain researchers are more interested in different types of corporate power and their impact on upgrading. Yet, they usually disregard the *modus operandi* of rule-making and rule-keeping in commodity chains. Third, Global Commodity Chain literature is less concerned with the geographies of governance, while for Sassen and Taylor the new places of control constitute the core of their reasoning.

Yet, there is a problem in too straightforwardly equating the management of the world economy with its control. Though Sassen frequently puts the capacity to manage global production on a level with the authority to control it, she does not explicitly describe how the provision of services for the *running* of Global Production Networks actually translates into the capacity to *govern* them.[6] As a consequence, both mechanisms are frequently conflated. However, though there is no doubt that core processes are involved in the management as well as in the command of commodity chains, it is questionable whether all high-wage, high-tech and high-profit services necessary for running global production processes are actually related to decision-making. This question is particularly relevant to global cities in non-core countries, which have a sizeable producer service sector but are normally not considered to host decision-making capacities. Thus, reasoning about the geography of governance in production networks has to consider whether producer service firms actually exercise functions of command and control.

In this context, it is important to distinguish between different services. For example, auditors interviewed in Mexico City agreed that producer service firms in general are increasingly influencing corporate decision-making, though they rejected this notion for the specific service they supply. In the case of law firms, though not all respondents agreed that they themselves influence their clients' decision-making processes, they acknowledged that in general law firms are progressively more involved in this. Luis Cortés, a lawyer at Holland & Knight in Mexico City affirms that:

> Well, not at my level, but the partners of the firm, they have conferences with the clients to plan a deal, to structure a deal. ... (Clients come and say), look, we want to put a plant in this place, how is it convenient for us to structure the business? Thus, the one who takes the decision how things should be done, rather would be here, from the (law) firm. ... That is, the way to do make a deal, to take decisions, if it is not coming from the lawyer's office, I do believe that the one who makes the strategy, it's the partners of the law firm.

Frequently mentioned examples of this pre-structuring of decisions refer to real estate, tax and labour law issues. Bearing in mind Gereffi's definition of governance, it is arguable that some of these fields are less important (for example, the decision about whether to buy or lease a plant), while the choice of the labour union with which an investing foreign company signs the collective bargaining agreement, or decisions on the benefits workers are granted, have an impact on how resources are allocated (or withdrawn) from the 'Mexican segment' of a Global Commodity Chain. Another example of how lawyers might influence decision-making is given by Fernando del Castillo, partner at Santamarina y Steta, a Mexican law firm specialized in corporate practice: 'It is also very usual that lawyers participate in the Board of Directors of big firms. As such, they influence the decisions of the society because they are part of its administration. And this is very usual.'

Though these quotations suggest that producer service firms have a bearing on corporate decision-making, the issue deserves closer investigation. In this regard, the emerging literature on transnational private governance is useful (Djelic and Sahlin-Anderson 2006; Graz and Nölke 2008; Sassen 2006). The argument goes that private actors such as rating agencies, institutional investors and global producer service firms are, supported by national governments, increasingly setting and enforcing standards, which commit other firms to specific ways of doing business. As to accountancy, for example, the big firms are advancing a global harmonization of standards, which means more than a mere technical adjustment of different practices. Rather, it is argued that by advancing a worldwide synchronization of norms, the global auditing firms promote a shift towards a stronger capital market orientation of companies, thus favouring the shareholder at the cost of the stakeholder model (Botzem et al. 2007). This ultimately has an impact on the ways in which surplus is created and distributed. Though it is being discussed that the increasing financialization of non-finance firms has some bearing on the governance of production networks (Milberg 2008; Palpacuer 2008), this insight is not reflected systematically against the backdrop of the rising influence of producer service firms.

Yet, since efforts to create and implement global standards are undertaken in many areas (for example, legal practices, financial markets, real estate markets), it is reasonable to assume that producer service firms have in fact become important influencers in corporate decision-making. A producer service firm's capacity to influence the governance of commodity chains depends, however, on (a) which tasks are decentralized within corporate networks, and (b) which tasks are outsourced, either at the global or at the local level. Because of the newness of the 'decentralization turn', we still lack comprehensive information about which tasks are being accomplished on which level and by which type of firm ('lead' or 'outsourcing' firm). Some authors suggest that both decisions (centralize/decentralize, in-house/ outsource) depend on the characteristics of a company, on the nature of the production, and on the specific function of a task for the company (Dicken 2007; Dunning and Lundan 2008; Merino and Rodríguez Rodríguez 2007). Accounting or finance are more likely to be centrally coordinated, among other things because they represent more sensitive services to a company, while negotiations with organized labour or discussions involving host governments may be delegated to the management of local affiliates.

Mexico City in the geography of governance

So far we know that Mexico City is a place where important services are inserted into Global Commodity Chains. Moreover, in the previous section I offered a general account on the notion that producer service firms influence the creation and distribution of value in production networks. In addition, it provided some admittedly tentative evidence for the assumption that Mexico City's global producer service firms also influence their clients' decision-making processes. Can we conclude, then, that Mexico City has assumed global city functions not only for the management of global production processes, but also for their governance? Or is Mexico City just a subordinate node, where service professionals execute instructions from their respective firm's headquarters? Interviews conducted in Mexico City suggest that the latter is not the case.

Asked about the position of the Mexico City office in their respective firm's global network, all respondents stated that they perceive neither a clear-cut hierarchy between offices nor an only one-way (headquarter–affiliate) communication. This is related, first, to the very structure of the firms. Rather than being just one firm, a global service firm in most cases operates through a network of formally independent firms. Thus, the Mexican 'affiliate' could end the cooperation with the 'global firm' or join another global partner, or the global headquarters could choose another local partner.

A second frequently mentioned reason for rather flat firm structures is the importance of the local offices in the companies' global strategies. Interviews support what is becoming consensus in the literature: for global producer service firms, maintaining a wide net of local affiliates is crucial in accessing foreign markets (Daniels 2007: 116). This is also mirrored in the profiling on the firms' web pages, where they emphasize, as KPMG puts it, to have 'a global network built on profound local roots'. One often stated aspect is the importance of personal relationships with clients. Asked whether business could also be done from Miami, Gerardo Oliver, chief knowledge officer of Ernst & Young replied:

> No. In fact, it is funny, many companies ... have their Latin American headquarters in Miami. But, at the end of the day, they have to create an office in Mexico City because it is not that easy. You have to be here, you have to have the relations with the entrepreneurs, you have to be in the chambers, you have to be at the breakfasts, you have to be at the cocktails. Finally, you have to be here. ... Often clients who know that you are not here they feel that you don't attend them. ... Even if the service is the same, even if people would come from the US every single day, they would feel unattended because they don't have someone who is living the same conditions in which they live in this city.

The importance of having local offices is also derived from the prevalence of intangible knowledge in many business areas. As Herfried Wöss, partner at Wöss & Partners, a Mexican legal firm specializing in corporate law, puts it for the case of the Mexican legal system:

> In Mexico ... there is a philosophical principle that you have to know: the system of islands. You have islands surrounded by water. Now, the law codes look like in France. ... The truth is that some institutions like the summary mercantile procedure work well – but in between them

there is water. Thus, if you are going to structure an infrastructure project, you have to know where are the islands and where is water. ... And this you learn empirically ... There are many *de-facto* mechanisms, you have to know how the system works.

In such a context, the ways in which firm intern knowledge is created and diffused are described as horizontal (see also Beaverstock 2004; Faulconbridge and Muzio 2007). Mexico was, for example, the first Latin American country to open the market to private mobile phone network providers, and the experiences of the Mexican office of Baker & McKenzie acquired in this field was, according to Raymundo Enríquez, a blueprint for Baker & McKenzie worldwide:

In privatizations, for example in Eastern Europe, the same model was followed, to privatize airports, energy, etc. Thus, in having it made in one country allows us to impart this experience to other local offices. And, attention, it is not that a lawyer from London would go to Poland or Hungary; no, the knowledge is communicated to local people.

Arguments that indicate a rather flat organization of global producer service firms are, however, thwarted by the also frequent remark that there is a specific hierarchy in doing businesses, which stems from the client's geography. What in legal, accountancy and real estate services defines the position of the Mexican office *vis-à-vis* other offices is, according to interviewees, the place where a client firm has its headquarters, because it is always the partner with direct contact to the client who is in command. According to Albrecht zu Ysenburg, partner at KPMG in Mexico City, in KPMG 'we don't have global headquarters. ... My global head is always the one from the country from where my client comes. ... There is a lead partner who sends his instructions to all over the world.' Javier Romero Río, partner of Deloitte in Mexico City, similarly states that

We have a list that we call D-1000, like the 1000 companies worldwide which have priority for us. And for this 1000, we have agreed that there is a responsible partner, who is the head of this account, and who has the authority and the responsibility to attend the client and to negotiate whatever project in the name of the 140 firms of Deloitte. ... That is, the hierarchy is not through countries but through the partner who is the head of an account.

Thus, for companies investing in Mexico, the responsible partner (of accountancy, legal or real estate firms) might be in New York, London or Hong Kong, while the Mexican partner cooperates. If a Mexican company goes global, then the Mexican partner is in command, with support from partners in other cities.

It is exactly this structure of the service firms' global networks that helps us to understand the role and reach of Mexico City as a global city. Though at first glance it seems that the networks of producer service firms are rather flat, their organizational model implies that there is the chain of command. Despite the fact that the local cooperation is, as outlined above, seen as being essential to do business, the 'big' strategies are made by the lead partners. Furthermore, it is reasonable to assume that this division of labour also shapes the distribution of value along the chain of producer services – the more lead partners an office has, the more deals it will command, and the more revenues it will capture. Now, the number of lead partners an office of a global service provider can have depends, according to the interviews, by and large on the geography of headquarters of TNCs. Since there are far fewer companies with origins in Mexico that compete successfully in the world market than foreign firms in Mexico, the Mexico City offices of accountancy, legal or real estate firms will not often be in command. Put simply, despite the high grade of autonomy of the Mexico City offices reported in interviews, the economic world order poses serious limitations to the development of governance functions in Mexico City. A geographical analysis of the places where the clients of the Mexican office of Holland & Knight were recruited, reveals the economic subordination of Mexico to the United States. Only 36.2 per cent of the law firm's deals (in total 3531 between 1998 and 2008) originated in Mexico through recruitment by Gallastegui y Lozano, Holland & Knight's partner in Mexico City. The rest was brought through Holland & Knight's offices in Washington (26.5 per cent), Miami (13.3), San Francisco (6.8) and other US cities.

An analysis of the management of FDI supports this nuanced account of the role of producer service firms in Mexico City. Though locally supplied legal services are, according to the respondents, decisive in 'making FDI work', interviewees also indicate limits to the role of local law firms: their involvement diminishes with the experiences an investing company has in Mexico, and with its size, while it increases with the complexity of the transaction. Thus, for a lead firm in the automotive chain with a long record of FDI in Mexico, the management of FDI will comprise mainly routinized tasks that will usually be done in-house by the legal department of the Mexico City office of the lead firm. Only in very specific cases will this firm turn to an external law firm. On the other hand, a German supplier conducting FDI in Mexico for the first time, or a small supplier with no in-house lawyers, will have to rely strongly on Mexico City's legal firms.

In answering the question guiding this section – the position of Mexico City in the geography of governance – I reach the conclusion that the commonsensical assumption that global cities are centres for both the management of the world economy and its command needs not be rejected. There is, however, a need to qualify this notion with regard to non-core cities. First, the influence of producer service firms in Mexico City on the governance of production networks depends both on sector- and on firm-specific factors (namely the geographical origin of the firm), and, secondly, those influences are in general supposed to be weak.

Conclusions

The analysis presented here shows, first, that there are connections between the World City Network and Global Commodity Chains, connections that are created by the flows of auditing, legal and real estate services from firms in Mexico City to companies operating in Mexico. Though these findings are confined to Mexico (City), it is more than likely that similar studies conducted in other cities, where global city formation is under way, would yield similar results. This supports the notion that global cities obtain their centrality because they are service nodes in and for a myriad of commodity chains. Second, the research presented here also indicates reasons why Mexico City is 'on the map' of global cities and Global Production Networks. Access to local knowledge is one frequently mentioned aspect, while another is the felt need to socialize with clients and to share the same urban experiences with one another. Thus, Mexico City is not only a node in various commodity chains, it is necessarily one.

Third, as regards the geography of governance, the analysis presented suggests that it is useful to break up global city functions into the management of the world economy on the one hand, and into its command and control on the other. As regards the former, there is much evidence to support the notion of global city formation in Mexico City, while the command functions results achieved so far point to a need to qualify the argument. Mexico City is by and large the centre of governance for production networks within Mexico and for the few Global Commodity Chains emanating from Mexico. However, as regards influences on value creation and distribution within the 'Mexican segments' of Global Commodity Chains, the – still tentative – results indicate that the scope of influence of both local affiliates of TNCs and of local offices of global producer service firms is rather limited, namely to issues such as taxes or labour laws and unions, where the need for in-depth knowledge of local conditions is required.

In addition to providing qualified evidence for both the management and command functions of global cities, this chapter has also addressed the critique that global city research is, mainly because of its focus on producer services, inadequate for grasping the complexities of urban development in poorer countries. Massey (2007: 35), for example, challenges what she calls the 'Euro-American bias ..., which sets up certain Western cities ... as norms against which others then come to be judged', while Robinson (2006: 93) argues that the attention paid to producer services tends to 'privilege the experience of some cities over those of others'. Because global city research is, according to Robinson, indifferent to the various ways in which cities in poorer countries can be connected to the world economy, 'millions of people and hundreds of cities are dropped off the map of much research in urban studies' (Robinson 2002: 535).

I agree with Massey and Robinson that the diversity of cities is not assessed by the global city literature (though much of what is occurring in many cities in poorer countries cannot be understood without assessing global city formation). Nevertheless, it is important here to be accurate about the argument. Global city research does not deal with the complexities of urban economies or city life, nor is it about the general connectedness of cities to the world economy. Rather, global city research is concerned with the geography of a very specific input into Global Production Networks, namely the means by which their organization and control is made effective. Thus, the 'privileging' of producer services stems from an economic geography perspective rather than from urban studies.

From this follows, first, that most cities around the world are indeed not a direct subject for global city studies because no core activities necessary for running and controlling Global Commodity Chains are located there. This 'dropping-off' results from uneven development, which produces cores and peripheries, and that is why the suggested shift to 'how "global" economic processes affect all cities' (Robinson 2006: 102) would obscure the fact that there are places from which rule-makers operate, and places, where most, if not all people are restricted to being rule-keepers. There is thus a fundamental difference between the role of cities in engendering globalization and the impacts of globalization on cities. Ciudad Juárez in Northern Mexico, for example, has been thoroughly shaped by its function as a production site in the chains of the automotive, computer and electronic industries, though the 'city' had (and has) virtually no hand in the governance of these chains.

This case also challenges Robinson's notion (2006: 102) that the focus on a limited number of cities implies 'defining some cities out of the game, as "excluded from global capitalism"'. Though being 'out of the game' of governing commodity chains, Ciudad Juárez is of course connected and relevant to the global economy. Low-paid work supplied in Ciudad Juárez's manufacturing plants is as vital to the reproduction of global capitalism as is the provision of high-paid producer services, what is explicitly recognized by my contention that the World City Network is built upon ramifications that link global cities to the countless non-global, but yet globalized cities, where production for global markets is carried out. Put differently: global cities are not only mutually constituted, as stressed by Taylor (2004), but also by their connections to Robinson's 'ordinary cities'. Mexico City assumes global city functions, because it helps to articulate low paid production in Mexican cities with the world market.

From this follows my third point. Against the above mentioned critique I maintain that the shift of attention to producer services allows for a more inclusive comprehension of the role of cities in the global South in the world economy, because it helps to grasp the multiple hinges or intermediaries between the few global headquarter cities (often seen as the global command centres) and the countless cities where production for the world market is carried out. Globalization is neither like an oil slick that indifferently covers the whole world, nor is it exclusively organized from a handful of 'supercities'. Mexico City is, as has been shown here, a critical node for the functioning of the world economy, because it is a place from where the articulation of peripheral labour processes in Ciudad Juárez and other Mexican cities that serve as export platforms is made possible through service inputs.

This finding is important because it helps to deepen our understanding of the role of cities in poorer countries in processes of uneven development (or in upgrading), which has not much advanced since Frank's (1966) conceptualization of the Latin American city as a 'bridgehead' for the interests of the dominant centres of the world economy. While in the case of London it might be evident that 'the "global" forces that have their effects in London by no means always have their origins elsewhere' (Massey 2007: 167), it is less clear that cities in poorer countries are also not only affected by globalization. Rather, Mexico City is, just as London is, 'hemmed in, in a kind of spatial trap, as both generator and beneficiary of, and suffering from' (Massey 2007: 92) globalization processes.

Acknowledgements

I thank four anonymous referees for their useful comments. The author is responsible for all views expressed.

Notes

1. I am aware of the conceptual differences between the literatures on Global Commodity Chains, Global Production Networks and Global Value Chains. For the purpose of this chapter, however, these differences are of less importance. The terms 'Global Commodity Chains' and 'Global Production Networks' are used to refer to the cross-border organization of production and consumption. Also, I use the terms 'global city' and 'world city' as synonyms.
2. If not indicated otherwise, data refer to the whole metropolitan area.
3. Headquarter services (*Dirección de Corporativos y Empresas*) are defined in the economic census as services directly related to the corporate management.
4. *Maquiladoras* are in-bond industries, located mainly in the northern border region.
5. In addition, the divergence is partly attributed to a statistical distortion, because companies tend to report FDI where they are headquartered and not where investment is actually realized.
6. Likewise, in the analysis of TNCs (Dicken 2007; Dunning and Lundan 2008), the modalities of decision-making and the role of producer services in it, have also received little attention.

References

Beaverstock, J. V. (2004) 'Managing across borders: knowledge management and expatriation in professional legal service firms', *Journal of Economic Geography*, 4, 157–79.

Botzem, S., M. Konrad and S. Quack (2007) 'Unternehmensbilanzierung und Corporate Governance – die Bedeutung internationaler Rechnungslegungsstandards für die Unternehmenssteuerung in Deutschland. Perspektiven der Corporate Governance', in M. Weiß, D. Sadowski, U. Jürgens and F. G. Schuppert (eds) *Perspektiven der Corporate Governance*, Baden-Baden: Nomos, 358–84.

Brown, E., B. Derudder, C. Parnreiter, W. Pelupessy, P. J. Taylor and F. Witlox (2010) 'World City Networks and Global Commodity Chains: towards a world systems integration, *Global Networks*, 10 (1), 12–34.

Daniels, P. W. (2007) 'A global service economy?', in J. R. Bryson and P. W. Daniels (eds) *The handbook of service industries*, Cheltenham: Edward Elgar, 103–25.

Davis, M. (2006) *Planet of slums*, New York: Verso.

Derudder, B. (2006) 'On conceptual confusion in empirical analyses of a transnational urban network', *Urban Studies*, 43 (11), 2027–46.

Dicken, P. (2007) *Global shift: mapping the changing contours of the world economy*, London: Sage Publications.

Dicken, P., P. F. Kelly, K. Olds and H. W-c. Yeung (2001) 'Chains and networks, territories and scales: towards a relational framework for analysing the global economy', *Global Networks*, 1 (2), 89–112.

Djelic, M.-L. and K. Sahlin-Anderson (2006) *Transnational governance: institutional dynamics of regulation*, Cambridge: Cambridge University Press.

Dunning, J. H. and S. Lundan (2008) *Multinational enterprises and the global economy*, Cheltenham: Edward Elgar, 2nd edn.

Dussel Peters, E. (2008) 'GCCs and development: a conceptual and empirical review', *Competition and Change*, 12 (1), 11–27.

Expansión (various years) *Las 500 empresas más importantes de México*, México DF.

Faulconbridge, J. R. and D. Muzio (2007) 'Reinserting the professional into the study of professional service firms', *Global Networks*, 7 (3), 249–70.

Frank, A. G. (1966) 'The development of underdevelopment', *Monthly Review*, 18, 17–31.

Gereffi, G. (1994) 'The organization of buyer-driven Global Commodity Chains: how retailers shape overseas production networks', in G. Gereffi and M. Korzeniewicz (eds) *Commodity chains and global capitalism*, Westport: Praeger, 95–122.

Gibbon, P., J. Bair and S. Ponte (2008) 'Governing Global Value Chains: an introduction', *Economy and Society*, 37 (3), 315–38.

Graz, J.-C. and A. Nölke (eds) (2008) *Transnational private governance and its limits*, London: Routledge.

Henderson, J., P. Dicken, M. Hess, N. Coe and H. W-c. Yeung (2002) 'Global Production Networks and the analysis of economic development', *Review of International Political Economy*, 9 (3), 436–64.

Hopkins, T. K. and I. Wallerstein (1977) 'Patterns of development of the modern world system: research proposal', *Review*, 1 (2), 111–45.

INEGI (2004) *Censos económicos 2004*, Aguascalientes: Instituto Nacional de Estadísticas, Geografía e Informatica.

INEGI (2008a) 'Banco de Información Económica', Instituto Nacional de Estadísticas, Geografía e Informatica, www.inegi.org.mx, accessed 15 June 2009.

INEGI (2008b) 'Matriz insumo producto', Instituto Nacional de Estadísticas, Geografía e Informatica, http://www.inegi.gob.mx/est/contenidos/espanol/proyectos/scnm/mip03/default.asp?s=est&c=14040, accessed 15 June 2009.

LatinLawyer (2007) *Latin America's leading business law firms 2007*, London: LATINLAWYER.

Massey, D. (2007) *World city*, Malden: Polity Press.

Merino, F. and D. Rodríguez Rodríguez (2007) 'Business services outsourcing by manufacturing firms', *Industrial and Corporate Change*, 16 (6), 1147–73.

Milberg, W. (2008) 'Shifting sources and uses of profits: sustaining US financialization with Global Value Chain', *Economy and Society*, 37 (3), 420–51.

Palpacuer, F. (2008) 'Bringing the social context back in: governance and wealth distribution in Global Commodity Chains', *Economy and Society*, 37 (3), 393–419.

Parnreiter, C. (2002) 'Mexico: the making of a global city?', in S. Sassen (ed.) *Global networks, linked cities*, London: Routledge, 145–82.

Parnreiter, C. (2003) 'Global city formation in Latin America: socioeconomic and spatial transformations in Mexico City and Santiago de Chile', paper presented at the 99th Annual Meeting of the Association of American Geographers, New Orleans 4–8 April, http://www.lboro.ac.uk/gawc/rb/rb103.html.

Parnreiter, C. (2007) *Historische Geographien, verräumlichte Geschichte. Mexico City und das mexikanische Städtenetz von der Industrialisierung bis zur Globalisierung*, Stuttgart: Franz Steiner Verlag.

Parnreiter, C. (2009) 'Global-city-formation, Immobilienwirtschaft und Transnationalisierung. Das Beispiel Mexico City', *Zeitschrift für Wirtschaftsgeographie*, 53 (3), 138–55.

Rabach, E. and E. M. Kim (1994) 'Where is the chain in commodity chains? The service sector nexus', in G. Gereffi and M. Korzeniewicz (eds) *Commodity chains and global capitalism*, Westport: Praeger, 123–43.

Robinson, J. (2002) 'Global and world cities: a view from off the map', *International Journal of Urban and Regional Research*, 26 (3), 531–54.

Robinson, J. (2006) *Ordinary cities: between modernity and development*, London: Routledge.

Sassen, S. (1991) *The global city: New York, London, Tokyo*, Princeton: Princeton University Press.

Sassen, S. (2006) *Territory, authority, rights: from medieval to global assemblages*, Princeton: Princeton University Press.

Sassen, S. (2007) 'Whither global cities: the analysis and the debates', in J. R. Bryson and P. W. Daniels (eds) *The handbook of service industries*, Cheltenham: Edward Elgar, 186–208.

Secretaría de Economía, Dirección General de Inversión Extranjera (2008) 'Reporte de Estadísticas', http://www.si-rnie.economia.gob.mx/cgi-bin/repie.sh/reportes/selperiodo, accessed 15 June 2009.

Short, J. R., Y. Kim, M. Kuus and H. Wells (1996) 'The dirty little secret of world cities research: data problems in comparative analysis', *International Journal of Urban and Regional Research*, 20 (4), 697–717.

Sobrino, J. (2000) 'Participación económica en el siglo XX', in G. Garza (ed.) *La Ciudad de México en el fin del segundo milenio*, México DF: El Colegio de México, 162–9.

Taylor, P. J. (2004) *World city network: a global urban analysis*, London: Routledge.

Taylor, P., P. Ni, B. Derudder, M. Hoyler, J. Huang, F. Lu, K. Pain, F. Witlox, X. Yang, D. Bassens and W. Shen (2009) 'Measuring the World City Network: new developments and results', *GaWC Research Bulletin*, 300, http://www.lboro.ac.uk/gawc/rb/rb300.html, accessed 15 June 2009.

The Lawyer.com (2008) 'The Global 100', http://www.thelawyer.com/global100/2006/tb_1-25.html, accessed 15 June 2009.

UNCTAD (2007) *World investment report 2007: transnational corporations, extractive industries and development*, New York: United Nations.

UNCTAD (2008) 'Handbook of statistics 2008', http://stats.unctad.org/handbook/ReportFolders/ReportFolders.aspx?CS_referer=&CS_ChosenLang=en, accessed 15 June 2009.

World Bank (2008) 'World development indicators quick query', http://ddp-ext.worldbank.org/ext/DDPQQ/member.do?method=getMembers&userid=1&queryId=135, accessed 15 June 2009.

4

City networks and commodity chains: identifying global flows and local connections in Ho Chi Minh City

INGEBORG VIND AND NIELS FOLD

The World City Network (WCN) literature and the Global Commodity Chain (GCC) literature both engage with 'global network phenomena', but they study contemporary globalization processes through very different conceptual, analytical and methodological lenses. That is probably why, for decades, the two research traditions have evolved along separate trajectories with little reference to each other, despite a shared legacy from world-systems theory. In this chapter, we argue that any analytical framework for understanding concrete forms of the intensified incorporation of cities into the world economy needs to go beyond shallow measures of World City Networks based on corporate locations. We seek to combine the World City Network approach with Global Commodity Chain analysis to produce a broader conceptualization of the actual connections and connectivities of global cities. We show how this approach can be applied by discussing the case of Ho Chi Minh City (HCMC), a global city inserted in Global Commodity Chains.

We have structured the chapter as follows. The first part consists of three theoretical sections in which we discuss (1) the limitations of the WCN approach, (2) how the GCC approach may inform the WCN approach and in turn benefit from a more explicit account of the role of (global) cities and producer services, and (3) how an integrative approach can be created. In the second part we investigate how analyses based on the GCC approach may be realigned and integrated with the WCN approach by using two of our own empirical GCC projects from Ho Chi Minh City as illustration. This book provides an opportunity to cross-fertilize our results with insights from the WCN approach. We see this as a tangible and fruitful integration that will enhance, but in no way render superfluous, previous results and methodologies of the two approaches.

World City Networks – with invisible linkages

The literature on global cities (also known as world cities, globalizing cities and global city-regions) is large and covers not only economic aspects but also the social, political, cultural and symbolic dimensions of these cities. We do not attempt to engage with all of this rich tradition here but focus on the World City Network (WCN) approach, that is studies of the *network* of global cities based on empirical data. We narrow our discussion further to those studies that use data on corporate organizations to study city networks.[1] This is where we see most common ground with GCC analysis. There are two distinct types of WCN studies, one type analysing data on TNCs in general, while the other type focuses exclusively on TNCs within advanced producer services (APS). The two types have been associated respectively with John Friedmann and Saskia Sassen, the authors of two foundational texts for the global city literature (see Derudder 2006, 2008).[2]

Friedmann (1986) launched 'The world city hypothesis' as a framework for research on how the integration of cities into the world economy and the functions assigned to them in the new international division of labour affected structural change within them. He suggested that world cities 'are used by global capital as "basing points" in the spatial organization and articulation of production and markets' and that it is possible to discern a 'complex spatial hierarchy' (Friedmann 1986: 71) among them. Friedmann did not prescribe how to measure this hierarchy of cities, but empirical work in this tradition has taken headquarters–subsidiary relations of TNCs to be its main expression. Research by Alderson and Beckfield (2004) is a prominent example of such a WCN study. They analyse data on the headquarters and subsidiaries of 446 of the world's 500 largest TNCs. A city is regarded as powerful if many subsidiaries are controlled from headquarters within it. Measures of the network positions of cities (closeness and betweenness) are based on the matrix of TNC locations. Other city network studies using data on TNC subsidiaries are reported in Rozenblat and Pumain (2007) and Wall et al. (2007), whereas Godfrey and Zhou (1999) refined this type of approach by incorporating regional headquarters.

Saskia Sassen's influential work (2001, first edition published in 1991) aims to explain why the global dispersal of production is accompanied by the increased concentration of certain activities in certain cities – and social polarization in the same cities. Her explanation hinges on advanced producer services, such as finance, law and insurance. The focus is thus on the *practice* of control, rather than on the possession of economic power. APS firms facilitate the global reach of TNCs, as they make the control and management of geographically dispersed production networks possible. They concentrate in global cities because they thrive on their connectivity, information-rich environments, and highly skilled and specialized labour.

The main example of the second type of WCN study is Taylor (2004), for whom APS firms are the 'interlockers' of the World City Network. Numerous other studies, many by authors associated with the globalization and world cities (GaWC, http://www.lboro.ac.uk/gawc/) research network, have been inspired by this approach (for example Beaverstock et al. 2000; Derudder and Taylor 2005; Neal 2008). The global cities are seen as access points to the global economy for producers by virtue of the APS firms: 'the breadth of an APS firm's branch office network defines the breadth of global markets to which its producer clients have direct or effective access' (Neal 2008: 97). In addition to this argument, which draws on Sassen's theory, Jane Jacobs's work on the economy of cities is used to justify assigning the pivotal role to APS firms. Jacobs's thesis is that it is cities, not nation-states, that play the central role in expanding economic life through innovation and diversification. Crucially, development is not the accumulation of old work; it is the addition of new kinds of work (Jacobs 1970). In Taylor's application, APS represent the 'new net-work', critical for economic expansion (Taylor 2007a). This is also explained by an analogy with ecology: a quantitatively unimportant species (like APS firms) may be an 'indicator species' by reflecting the health of an ecosystem and therefore become more interesting than the dominant species (that is large TNCs) (analogy used in Rossi et al. 2007; Taylor 2006; Taylor et al. 2007).

We want to raise some critical points against both types of corporate organization-based WCN analysis. In relation to the TNC-based analyses, our main objection is that legal ownership linkages tell only part of the story of global corporate networks of control and dominance. The exact nature of chain governance is an issue of ongoing debate among the analytical branches that exist within the GCC approach, but a central point of GCC analysis is that lead firms do not only exercise governance in chains through ownership. An example of governance without ownership is buyer-driven chains where commercial capital (retailers and branders) has decisive power over its suppliers (Gereffi 1994). In relation to the APS-based approach, three interrelated issues make it problematic to analyse the network of global cities based on the locations of (a subset of) APS firms. First, the assumption that a TNC needs to go through the networks of APS firms to create its own global network requires qualification: TNCs are often capable of producing many of the services needed for going global internally. Second, APS firms represent only a fraction of 'new work'. Many innovative activities are carried out elsewhere – by TNCs in other industries and by APS firms outside the narrow range of sectors (finance, law, insurance, advertising, management consultancy, accountancy) considered by the WCN approach. APS, elsewhere studied as knowledge-intensive business services, also include engineering consultancy, supply-chain management consultancy, business software solution provision, highly specialized industry-specific services such as sub-component design and many others (Schmitz and Strambach 2008). This also points to an ambiguity. If APS firms are critical because they make global control and command possible (cf. Sassen 2001), then a narrow focus on international finance, trans-jurisdictional law and similar services may be warranted; if APS firms are central because they are indicators of innovation and economic vibrancy (cf. Jacobs 1970), it seems less warranted to include accountancy but not design and niche services. Third, global APS firms, for example the large banks, are engaged in many activities that are neither new work nor targeting the global operations of corporate clients.

The focus of the GaWC research network on APS firms was launched as 'a simple empirical hook in an interesting theoretical area' (Taylor 2000: 29) and has served well as such. It has inspired impressive global-scale data gathering and sophisticated statistical analyses of these novel city-based data. The most recent global data set on APS firms was collected in 2008 and the first analysis of these data was reported in Taylor et al. (2009). However, it is necessary to take a step back and probe the privileged analytical position of APS firms as 'indicator species'. This has not been explored empirically; its underpinnings are refined but assumption-rich.[3]

How can we investigate the actual, real-life economic role and significance of APS firms? How can we go beyond shallow locational and size data from directories and websites? Neither type of WCN study will be able to resolve the question of whether producer services or corporate headquarters are more central for the Global City Network – or, more importantly, what they both mean for what happens in and between cities. If the plea of moving from hierarchies and taxonomies to understanding processes of place-bound globalization is taken seriously, we need to 'move closer' to actual connectivities and flows between cities (Robinson 2005). In the following we introduce GCC analysis as an approach that can contribute towards this.

Global Commodity Chains – with invisible global cities

A commodity chain is the full range of activities carried out by firms and workers to bring a product from conception to final use. This includes activities such as research and development, design, sourcing of inputs, the various stages of production, and marketing. These activities can be contained within a single firm in a single place, but more often, and increasingly so, they are divided among different firms and different places. While the term 'commodity chain' originates from world-system theory in the 1980s, GCC analysis began with a volume edited by Gereffi and Korzeniewicz (1994). We use Global Commodity Chain (GCC) as a common denominator for the different branches that have since developed within this analytical approach: Global Commodity Chain, Global Value Chain (GVC) and Global Production Network (GPN). The different terms do correspond to differences in theoretical and analytical foci, but the commonalities are large enough to justify their common treatment for present purposes (for discussions of and comparisons between GCC, GVC and GPN see Bair 2005; Dicken et al. 2001; Gibbon and Ponte 2005: Chapter 3; Vind and Fold 2007).

GCC analysis has been applied to manufacturing (for example garments, electronics, automotives, surgical instruments, pharmaceuticals) and primary production (for example coffee, cocoa, cotton, fruit, fish) but rarely to the service sector. The main themes of both empirical analyses and theoretical contributions are the nature and forms of chain governance and coordination, especially the links between lead firms and their suppliers (Gereffi et al. 2005; Ponte and Gibbon 2005; Sturgeon 2002) and how these shape upgrading paths and processes, particularly for firms and clusters of firms in developing countries (Gibbon 2001; Humphrey and Schmitz 2002; Palpacuer and Parisotto 2003). Methodologically, the main data for most GCC analyses come from corporate interviews; information is also sought from sources such as trade statistics, the business press and industry organizations.

We believe the GCC approach can inform the WCN approach in two respects. The first is the application of commodity-specific lenses. By moving beyond selecting TNCs based on size criteria, industry-specific analyses will give more 'flesh' to the Global City Network by providing insights into the real-life connections and material links between specific cities. The second is the provision of qualitative information on the practices and strategies of firms, including on the role and significance of APS firms for TNCs in other industries. Fieldwork, including interviews, is needed to collect the type of qualitative and sensitive information that is unobtainable from websites and directories.

69

Conversely, GCC analysis may benefit from cross-fertilization with WCN. Producer services in all their forms – logistical, financial, technical and creative – are 'missing links' in the GCC approach, despite an early call to include the service sector (see Rabach and Kim 1994). Producer services are adequate, or inadequate, in a very tangible way: they may or may not be included in empirical analyses, but they are not considered to be of major theoretical importance for governance structures or upgrading processes. In the GPN framework (a variant of the GCC approach), the chain metaphor is dismissed in favour of the network because 'flows of materials, semi-finished products, design, pro-duction, *financial and marketing services* are organized vertically, horizontally and diagonally in complex and dynamic configurations' (Henderson et al. 2002: 444, emphasis added). However, we are unaware of any empirical studies, inspired by the GPN framework, that account for the role of producer services.

The absence of producer services in GCC analyses is linked to their under-developed spatial dimension. Chain-based analyses of cluster upgrading dynamics and their linkages to global firms and markets (for example Humphrey 2003; Nadvi and Halder 2005; Schmitz 2004) have an obvious spatial dimension, as, more or less by definition, cluster-based firms share the same geographical location. Otherwise, there are typically no references to spatial connections other than company locations within different national territories; the role of (global) cities is not discussed.

Combining commodity chains and city networks

Early on it was noted that ideas on inter-locale linkages from the then emerging GCC approach could inform the conceptualization of 'urban areas as nodes in a multilayered network that comprises the world city system' (Smith and Timberlake 1995: 83). Yet, the literatures on World City Networks and Global Commodity Chains have evolved with little cross-referencing since then. In a recent paper (Brown et al. this book), a group of WCN researchers call for the integration of the WCN and GCC approaches. We share this ambition, but we wish to qualify their contention that the route to an integrative approach goes through the world-systems origin of both approaches.

Central to world-systems analysis is the core/semi-periphery/periphery structure of the capitalist world-economy; WCN researchers repeatedly refer to this thinking. Friedmann (1986) groups his world city hierarchy according to core and semi-peripheral countries (there are none of his world cities in the periphery), and a central book for the WCN approach is entitled *World cities in a world-system* (Knox and Taylor 1995). More recently, Alderson and

Beckfield (2004) compare their rankings of world cities to the world-system; they find that the power and network centrality of cities correspond well to the location of cities in core, semi-peripheral and peripheral countries (the former being more powerful and better positioned). Taylor suggests that a new 'network power is found in non-core cities that have become integral and essential to the servicing of global capital' (Taylor 2004: 199) and that this might become 'part of depolarization processes and an expansion of the semi-periphery' (Taylor 2004: 200). He adds that this new circumstance has 'meagre distributive capacity' (Taylor 2004: 199), but the argument can still be interpreted as a move away from the more rigid assumptions of world-systems thinking. In a later contribution, however, Taylor argues that world-city network-formation is 'contemporary core making', this being accompanied by 'city-yoke formation', that is the peripheralization of places outside the network of dynamic cities. Consequently, we are witnessing 'global economic polarization that reflects global class victory' (Taylor 2007b), a statement that leaves little room for optimism outside the core.

Most accounts, including that by Brown et al. (this book), emphasize the world-systems origin of GCC analysis. However, although the term 'commodity chain' was coined within world-systems analysis, the GCC approach represents a break with core tenets of world-systems thinking, as well as with the language of core, semi-periphery and periphery. The GCC approach has moved 'away from the type of long-range historical and holistic analysis characteristic of the world-systems school ... [and] ... evolved as a network-based, organizational approach to studying the dynamics of global industries' (Bair 2005: 158). While world-systems analysis emphasizes deep structures and systemic tendencies, the GCC approach gives more weight to the role of firms as the organizing agents of capitalism. The GCC approach is an attempt to develop a more dynamic and policy-relevant framework for studying globaliz-ation. In world-systems analysis, commodity chains are studied for their contribution to the reproduction of inequality in the global economy (that is the core-periphery structure); the GCC approach asks rather how 'developing countries [can] leverage participation in these chains to benefit various constituencies, including firms, workers and communities' (Bair 2005: 171).

In the light of the above, it is less obvious that invoking the concepts of core and periphery is useful in integrating the WCN and GCC approaches. In our view, the strengths of the GCC approach stem precisely from its break with structuralist world-systems thinking to engage with economic agents.

A focus on the world-systems origin of both approaches masks their methodological and analytical differences and perhaps explains the hitherto limited success of combining them. We are aware of only two previous explicit attempts at integrating the WCN and GCC approaches. The first is by Parnreiter et al. (2007), who examine the 'missing link' between Global Commodity Chains and global cities in Mexico City and Santiago de Chile. They see APS firms as this missing link, on the assumption that these are 'essential in order to insert firms all over the world into a global division of labor'; the APS firms are promoted from interlockers of World City Networks to interlockers of world cities and Global Commodity Chains. Unfortunately, in their study they assume rather than explore this double interlocking role. They use data on equities and bond issues to link banks to large companies in Mexico and Chile. However, the data are very partial, covering only around half of the top fifty companies in each country. More importantly, this type of data does not illuminate how, or indeed whether, these APS firms are actually essential for firms in Mexico and Chile to access Global Commodity Chains. We cannot know for what purpose financing is raised, to what degree companies finance global operations by other means, or how large their need for financing is compared with other aspects of accessing global networks. The second attempt is by Rossi et al. (2007), who also claim inspiration from the GCC approach in a contribution that analyses data on the locations of APS firms and their clients among (the headquarters of) the largest firms in Brazil. Data stem from an e-mail survey, and the analysis hinges on the APS firms. It is illustrative that six specific types of APS firm (banking, insurance, advertising, accountancy, law and management consultancy) are discussed, but the customers are lumped together into three broad groups (basic, traditional and innovative industries).

The problems of the two studies examined above cannot be resolved through the application of world-systems theory. Both are essentially WCN studies trying to enhance their analysis with reference to GCC analysis. They are important contributions within the WCN approach, as they start to explore the previously neglected theme of linking APS firms and their corporate customers, but their data on the headquarters of the largest companies do not amount to Global Commodity Chain analysis. It is impossible to do this without intensive fieldwork, including corporate interviews; databases or surveys cannot provide the data needed.

However, an integrative approach also calls for a broader perspective than closer scrutiny of the links between APS and their corporate customers in Global Commodity Chains. It is impossible to comprehend the actual form of cities' intensified incorporation in the world economy if flows of importance for the particular forms of globalization processes are excluded, as some prominent practitioners of WCN had previously stated: 'While it could be the producer-services sector that leads the way in binding cities into a global network, it is likely that the industrial sector also constructs connections of control among cities' (Alderson and Beckfield 2006: 902).

GCC analyses provide ample examples of linkages and processes that are important in forming and connecting global cities that are not captured by an analysis hinging on APS firms. Certainly, concentrations of advanced producer services indicate expansion of economic life, but cities may thrive because of other flows and activities. This is obviously the case for many of the so-called 'third-world cities' that are growing on the basis of booming export-oriented industrialization and migration from rural hinterlands and distant regions. If these cities are to be 'put on the map' and incorporated into the analysis of networks of world cities, we need to understand how chain governance structures and upgrading possibilities condition global city processes.

A broader conceptualization to account for actual global city dynamics also entails bringing labour markets and migration (back) into the analysis, as well as extending it into city-regions and hinterlands. Migrant workers and labour market polarization were central themes in Sassen's original formulation of the global city hypothesis, but interest in these issues has since faded in favour of a more business-centred focus in the global city literature (Samers 2002). This is especially true for the WCN approach: its analyses of corporate networks have not been accompanied by discussions of their effects on employment, incomes and migration beyond the small elite group of bankers, lawyers and other APS professionals.[4] Taylor (2007b) is an exception and perhaps marks a realization within the WCN approach that mapping business networks is insufficient to make WCN research relevant. However, the simple dichotomy between the mobility of elite professionals in the World City Network and 'peasant floods' to the slums of mega-cities does not help explain the actual diversity of migration flows to and between global cities.

The offices of global APS firms are typically located in city centres; these are the narrow territorial basis for WCN studies based on APS (Derudder 2006). However, if we are looking beyond APS firms, we also need to look beyond central business districts. We follow Scott (2002) in seeing dynamic regions as the engines of economic expansion, also in the developing world. A region is understood here as an 'area of sub-national extent focused on a central urban agglomeration or agglomerations together with an immediately surrounding hinterland' (Scott 2002: 137). Such a region may coincide with an administrative unit, but more often dynamic city-regions extend beyond the borders of central city governments' jurisdiction.

73

We have now outlined four main tenets that we consider necessary to incorporate into a tentative analytical framework combining GCC and WCN. First, we need to abandon the centre–periphery axiom as the uniting element for the two approaches. Second, we need to understand the structure and dynamics of GCCs that constitute the crucial linkages (in terms of material flows) from globalizing cities to world markets. Third, we need to collect original, fieldwork-based data on actual 'seller–buyer' relationships between APS companies and companies directly involved in these crucial GCCs. Fourth and finally, we need to include labour migration patterns and processes from the rural hinterland of globalizing cities. In the following sections, we elaborate on these findings to illustrate how traditional GCC analyses could be realigned and integrated into the WCN approach. We use two of our own GCC research projects to examine export-oriented manufacturing of electronics and agricultural diversification in the hinterland of Ho Chi Minh City (HCMC).[5] Neither project was originally conceived to understand the dynamics of HCMC in Global City Networks, but we wish to demonstrate how more detailed and qualitative accounts of 'how HCMC is going global' may supplement and integrate with quantitative indicators of 'how global HCMC is'.

Globalizing Ho Chi Minh City – chains in networks

Ho Chi Minh City is the largest city in Vietnam and home to about eight million people. While Hanoi is the capital and centre of political power, HCMC is the country's economic heart and industrial growth pole. HCMC was barred from the global capitalist economy during the time when other Southeast Asian cities industrialized. The city participated in the international division of labour in only a very limited way, exporting products such as work clothes and transistors to the socialist bloc. However, as early as 1987, the attraction of foreign capital and the expansion of international trade became Vietnamese policy objectives, and since then the Vietnamese government has introduced progressive liberalizations of foreign investment regulations (Dixon and Kilgour 2002). In 2007 Vietnam became a member of the WTO, marking its full commitment to an open economy. Vietnam has experienced rapid integration into the global economy, led by HCMC. In 1990, total Vietnamese exports were just US\$ 2.4 billion, in 1996 7.3 billion, and in 2006 they reached 39 billion (General Statistical Office 2008; Tran and Le 1998).

Ho Chi Minh City's nascent global city status has been detected by WCN research based on APS firm locations. In one inventory of world cities, HCMC has 'relatively strong evidence of world city formation' (scoring 3 out of 12)

(Taylor 2000, Table 2). In the most ambitious WCN mapping (Taylor 2004), HCMC also makes it into the lowest connectivity range (20–29 per cent the connectivity of London). As expected, HCMC scores higher than Hanoi (but lower than Bangkok and Kuala Lumpur) in both analyses, but it reveals little about HCMC's actual connections and connectivity.

Our GCC analyses from HCMC extend into industrial zones on the outskirts of the city as well as to the rural hinterland, as these are part of the same vibrant, globalizing city-region (Figure 1). The findings of the two GCC analyses are only briefly reported here as the purpose is to illustrate the integrative potential of existing GCC research (in the subsequent section). Hence, we do not claim to present a full-fledged, integrative GCC/WCN analysis but rather some salient points that serve to illustrate the necessary elements in such an analysis. Only further, specifically designed fieldwork will complete the partial picture we paint here.

Segmentation in export-oriented electronics manufacturing

In 2006, HCMC was responsible for 23 per cent of Vietnamese industrial output; together with the seven other southeastern provinces, the share is close to half (General Statistical Office 2008). HCMC and its neighbouring provinces are also the main destinations for FDI; HCMC alone received more than 2.5 times as much FDI capital as Hanoi in the first five months of 2008 (General Statistical Office 2008). Provincial or city level trade data are unavailable, but it is fair to assume that HCMC is the origin of corresponding shares of exports. Besides oil, Vietnamese exports are dominated by garments and footwear, followed by seafood, wood products and electronics (Table 1). National level data on FDI (Table 2) reveal its predominantly Asian origin.

Before the 1990s, the Vietnamese electronics industry was limited to the assembly of TVs and other consumer applications for the domestic market and an insignificant export of components to the socialist bloc. Since the 1990s, foreign electronics companies have entered, first as joint ventures with Vietnamese state-owned enterprises, and later as wholly-owned foreign enterprises. As a result, the electronics industry in HCMC is now highly segmented. One segment consists of domestically owned and joint venture companies that assemble consumer electronics for the domestic market; they face an uncertain future following trade liberalization under WTO and the ASEAN Free Trade Area. The other segment is rapidly growing; it is wholly owned by foreign, primarily Japanese, transnational companies and produces mainly components for exports.

Figure 1: The Mekong Delta and industrial centres in Ho Chi Minh City

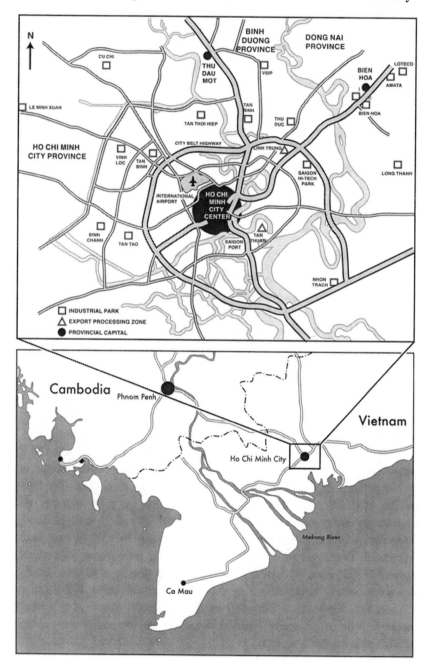

Table 1: Vietnamese exports (million US$)

	2001	2003	2005	2007
Crude oil	n.a.	n.a.	7,390	8,477
Garments	1,975	3,609	4,806	7,784
Footwear	1,587	2,260	3,005	3,963
Seafood	1,816	2,199	2,741	3,792
Wood products	343	608	1,517	2,364
Electronics	709	854	1,450	2,178
Coffee	n.a.	n.a.	725	1,854
Rice	n.a.	n.a.	1,400	1,454
Fruit and vegetables	344	151	234	299
Total	15,029	20,149	32,233	48,387

Before 2005, export of certain products only published by volume (tons)
Source: General Statistical Office (2008)

Table 2: Top countries of origin for FDI in Vietnam, 2007

	Projects	Registered capital (mill. US$)
Republic of Korea	405	4,463
Virgin Islands	56	4,268
Singapore	84	2,614
Taiwan	211	1,736
Malaysia	45	1,091
Japan	154	965
China	115	460
Rest of the world	375	2,259

Source: General Statistical Office (2008)

The role of HCMC in the Global Commodity Chains for electronics is mainly within the segment of basic electronic components (see Vind 2008 for details). It serves as a location for the labour-intensive assembly of parts such as coils, cable assemblies and mini-motors for mobile phones and digital cameras. Assembled components are exported to corporate customers or other subsidiaries of the parent companies, mostly in East and Southeast Asia. The typical activity in Vietnam is manufacturing, with the parent company handling orders and sales. Most of these Japanese companies in Vietnam are not brand name producers of electronics but first-tier suppliers of low-value generics to the brand name companies. With a few exceptions, foreign-owned factories are reproduction factories where mature technology is transferred from the parent company. Quality control and testing of products are generally done in Vietnam and represent the most skill-intensive operations. Apart from packaging materials, most of the inputs needed for production are imported. A lack of local suppliers able to meet global standards is not only a problem for the electronics industry – it is also reported for the larger garment sector, which has been investigated in several GCC studies (Knutsen 2004; Nadvi and Thoburn 2004; Thomsen 2007).

However, despite their restricted labour-intensive operations, the electronics TNCs in HCMC are not footloose in the traditional sense. Several of them have opened two or three plants or plan to do so. The Japanese transnational component manufacturers aim at consistent supplies of simple components and therefore need cheap and efficient labour. These companies seek to develop Vietnam into a complementary location to support their role in the regional production network that supports Japanese brand manufacturers. The Japanese companies in particular are attracted by the absence of the anti-Japanese sentiments they find in China; Vietnam is now the preferred location in Southeast Asia for Japanese electronics companies according to one survey (JETRO 2006). Several companies reported having transferred production capacity from China or expanded in Vietnam instead of China.

Technological spin-offs and skill upgrading are nearly absent and productive linkages to the local economy are weak, apart from the indirect effects of increased wage incomes. The local impact of this particular form of industrialization seems similar to those coming from the more traditional labour-intensive and low-tech garment and footwear industries. Hence, as Vietnam increasingly consolidates its role as a complementary location to China for low-wage dependent industries or segments of industries, the demand for unskilled labour increases steadily.

One of the findings of the GCC study of this industry was that the foreign-owned electronics companies rely more on female migrant workers than the domestic-owned companies. These migrants are perceived to be more amenable and harder working. During the interviews, company managers suggested that residents had become wealthy and therefore shunned the hard factory work. Due to the inflow of migrants, land and housing prices have increased, and resident families can earn incomes by renting rooms to migrants. Migrant workers typically live in crowded shared rooms rented from private house owners, as the industrial zones have no worker housing attached, unlike similar zones in many other countries (Kelly 2002). There is an increasing lack of both unskilled and skilled workers in industrial zones in and around HCMC, and some companies are exercising a strong direct migration pull by going on recruiting trips to rural provinces or by advertising jobs on provincial television. Other companies focus on lowering the typically very high turnover rates of migrant labour by improving conditions, for example by building dormitories for the workers or sponsoring bus transport for migrants to go home for the Têt (lunar New Year) holidays. Not only companies and private recruitment agents are involved in facilitating migration; the labour department of Binh Duong is cooperating with eight rural provinces to attract migrant workers to industrial zones in the province.

Migration and agricultural diversification in the rural hinterland

In the Mekong Delta south of HCMC, agricultural production has been transformed from a previously heavy reliance on rice to a much more diversified production based on various tropical fruits, particularly in the provinces around the northern branch of the Mekong River. The transformation started with a series of reforms in the 1980s and early 1990s. Cooperative ownership gradually gave way to long-term individual user rights to small parcels of land. User rights can now be exchanged, leased, inherited and mortgaged, but some state regulations on land allocation remain. Furthermore, state authorities at the district and provincial levels set production targets for specific commodities (Fforde and de Vylder 1996).

   The reforms resulted in a tremendous boom in rice production due to substantial increases in productivity. As a result, government quotas on the provision of rice to state authorities were relaxed, and farmers started to cultivate different high-value crops on former paddy land. In coastal areas of the Mekong Delta rice farming expanded rapidly, while further inland fruit production grew to such an extent that these areas now constitute about 50 per cent of national output (Marsh and MacAulay 2006; Trang 2004). Domestic demand for fruit has increased over the past decade, reflecting the growth in urban income levels and the increased demand for fresh fruit. The export potential is huge due to booming urban markets in neighbouring China, presently the most important market for fruit exports, and the large consumption of fresh fruit and vegetables in the OECD countries. The Vietnamese government has launched several policy initiatives to boost exports of horticultural products to US$ 1 billion in 2010. 'Speciality fruits' have been selected based on their export potential, and specific areas have been identified to start a localized specialization of the particular fruit. Extension services target these zones with technical support and training courses. Other public initiatives aim to increase the quality and safety of Vietnamese products to comply with standards set on the major OECD markets. These initiatives are supported by the local and foreign supermarket chains that have recently established themselves in Vietnamese cities and demand a similar supply of high-quality fruit (IFPRI 2002).

However, so far these initiatives have yielded only modest results. An important barrier is the chaotic and anarchic way in which farmers have entered fruit production. Farmer practices differ widely, and there is a plethora of varieties that impedes the sourcing of adequate volumes of consistent quality. No kind of contract system has been successfully implemented, as both farmers and buyers, for many good reasons, are unwilling to enter into stable seller–buyer relationships. Numerous wholesalers and collectors operate in the delta's competitive fruit chain, undermining efforts to establish contractual relationships between farmers and exporters or processors, but simultaneously they ensure that substantial volumes of low-quality fruits are available for lower-income urban groups.

Adding to the problems of private companies in sourcing consistent volumes of standardized supplies for export or processing is the growing competition for labour. The concomitant higher wages are a serious problem for the low-profit fruit-processing industry, as well as for export-oriented companies that are dependent on labour-intensive grading of the non-standardized fruit. Farmers are losing family labour and the former availability of cheap rural labour willing to work in the orchards is reduced. Competition exists both with manufacturing industries in HCMC and on home ground. First, migration is fuelled by a strong pull from employment opportunities in the growing export-oriented manufacturing industry. A survey of three villages reveals some indicative figures: between 80 and 95 per cent of out-migration since the mid-1980s took place between 2000 and 2005 and between 60 and 80 per cent of households had at least one member who had left. Migrants are usually between 15 and 35 years of age, single and female (Hoang et al. 2008). Second, new industrial zones are popping up on former paddy fields and near provincial capitals in the delta. So far, it is mostly the garment industry and the growing seafood industry that are expanding or relocating factories to rural areas.[6] The many huge infrastructural projects in the region, mainly in the form of new bridges and highways, also constitute a serious labour drain away from agricultural activities.

HCMC in Asian city networks

Together, the two GCC analyses above produce a partial understanding of the globalization processes that are at play in HCMC and its rural hinterland in the Mekong Delta. Evidence indicates that the GCC for electronics in which HCMC is participating is being 'commanded and controlled' elsewhere, namely in Japanese industrial agglomerations, but we do not know to what extent the parent companies have autonomous power or are governed by the brand name firms that they supply, for example when it comes to deciding the location of subsidiaries. We are also uninformed about the nature and importance of global firms offering various types of producer services in HCMC, for instance we do not know to what extent they are an integral component of the electronics industry: companies interviewed were not asked questions about financing, accountancy or insurance, illustrating the limitations of the GCC approach. However, based on the nature of the Vietnamese operations, it seems likely that the electronics industry demands few advanced producer services in HCMC. On the other hand, the WCN research referred to above has shown that HCMC houses a notable population of global APS firms: what do these firms do in HCMC and who do they service?

To fill the voids, we need a better grasp of the dynamics in the other GCCs 'running through' HCMC, such as garments, footwear and, for the Mekong Delta in particular, seafood. A cursory inspection tells us that TNCs from Taiwan and Korea dominate the GCCs for garments and footwear, adding to indications that HCMC is globalizing primarily within regional networks in East Asia. However, we do not know the role of APS in the GCCs running through HCMC, but the pronounced regional dimension of these chains prompts us to consider whether corresponding Asian circuits for APS exist. These could go unnoticed by WCN analyses, as their identification of *global* APS firms has a Western bias[7] (Robinson 2005): an APS firm is deemed global if it has offices in at least fifteen cities, with at least one city in each of three 'globalization arenas' (Western Europe, Northern America and Pacific Asia).[8] As we have already argued, there is a need to explore the functions and importance of APS firms in GCCs of various industries. This should include probing the existence of differences between the roles of APS firms in the operations of, for instance, US TNCs compared with Japanese (or Korean or Taiwanese) TNCs. GCCs often display distinct characteristics according to the origins of the lead firms; an example is the hierarchical captive networks of Japanese electronics industry versus the modular production networks in the

US electronics industry (Sturgeon 2002). Such differences in chain governance and coordination may correspond to different roles of APS firms.

The developments in the Mekong Delta illustrate how Global Commodity Chains extend into the hinterlands of global cities. Some cities of the developing world are experiencing 'urbanization without industrialization', a situation characterized by rapid urban population growth driven by push effects as migrants leave desperate conditions in the countryside only to arrive in city slums with high unemployment rates (Davis 2006). The picture is far more complex in HCMC with its accelerated industrial growth. The situation in the rural hinterland is also very unlike the 'hollowing out of the rural world' scenario offered by Taylor (2007b). In the Mekong Delta new employment opportunities arise from agricultural diversification, industrialization and infrastructure development – although this is not without problems for the labour demand in the agricultural sector and the efforts to promote competitive export-oriented fruit production. The complex relationship between causes and 'thresholds' for urban-directed labour migration vs. the opportunities for income increase and diversification for those remaining in the rural hinterland determines the scope of labour market frictions in rapidly industrializing city regions. A better understanding of these balances would improve the understanding of the industrial dynamics and be of considerable value for labour market regulation and physical planning, both urban and regional.

Finally, having suggested the existence and importance of an East-Asian city network for globalizing HCMC we wish to point to two other dimensions that serve to stress the East-Asian connections of globalizing HCMC. These are observable in the development of the urban landscape and are of significant importance for HCMC's position in the Global City Networks. Skylines, property development and global city ambitions are closely related in East Asia; the region's cities are home to a disproportionately large share of the world's 'top 25 skylines' (Knox 2007) and 'urban mega-projects' (Olds 2001). There are not yet any skyscrapers of landmark quality in HCMC, but two kinds of urban development linked to globalization processes in East Asia are very visible. These are industrial and export-processing zones, which receive most of the FDI in electronics and many other manufacturing industries; and the building of new urban areas to accommodate city growth and the demands of expatriate staff of TNCs, as well as affluent Vietnamese (for example those with careers in companies successfully participating in globalization).

As for the industrial zones, the most successful ones have been developed with foreign partners. The oldest is Tan Thuan EPZ, dating from 1991 and located next to the container port in HCMC, which Taiwanese investors developed in a joint venture with a state-owned corporation. Notable also is the Vietnam-Singapore Industrial Park in Binh Duong, just north of the provincial border with HCMC. This is part of Singapore's Regionalization 2000 strategy of creating little enclaves of a Singaporean business climate combined with the lower costs of Southeast Asian countries (Perry and Yeoh 2000). There are also Linh Trung EPZ (Chinese partner), Long Binh Techno Park (Japanese partner) and AMATA (Thai partner).

As for the urban development projects, the two major ones are both advertised as new city centres – Saigon South and Thu Thiem. The Taiwanese group behind the Tan Thuan EPZ is developing Saigon South and is located close to it. The plan for Saigon South comprises residential areas, a golf course, an international exhibition centre, the private Franco-Vietnamese Hospital, office buildings and shopping centres. Much of this is already in place. The international schools in the area reflect the major nationalities of the expatriate community: there is a Korean, a Japanese and a Taiwanese school. Saigon South's terraced houses and condos are well beyond the economic means of migrant factory workers. The Thu Thiem New Urban Area is being developed on 700 hectares of the Thu Thiem peninsula, located across the Saigon River from the city centre. The area is only partially built-up, much of it being swamp and waterways. Previously, it was linked to the centre only by ferries, but in early 2008 the first of several new bridges was opened. Sasaki Associates, a US consultancy, has developed the master plan for the area, and an international design competition is now being held for central public spaces in Thu Thiem, including an 'iconic pedestrian bridge' (Investment & Construction Authority for Thu Thiem New Urban Area 2008). The geographical set-up (a new centre across the river from the old) is similar to Shanghai's Lujiazui district in the Pudong area, which has been massively developed to provide a whole new skyline for the city (Olds 2001).

In connection with this East-Asian redesign of the urban landscape, the fresh food supply system to HCMC has been restructured. The process started after the turn of the century, emulating auctioning and quality-control practices, logistical systems and the physical structure of wholesale markets in major East-Asian cities, particularly in China and Taiwan. The numerous and widely spread wholesalers previously located within the city boundaries have now been relocated to three big market places on the outskirts of the city, though near industrial zones and the future residential growth centres.

Conclusion

We have argued that the World City Network and Global Commodity Chain literatures can inform each other, but that an integrative framework is needed to explore empirically the assumption of the WCN approach that APS firms are the critical agents in connecting (producers in) cities. The qualitative methodologies and industry-specific analyses of the GCC approach can inform such an exploration. Moreover, we suggest that the relevance of an integrative approach hinges on a broader conceptualization of the global connections of cities and the impacts of these. Corporate networks are relevant units of analysis, but analysis must extend to their impacts on labour markets, migration and hinterlands to address how global forces and dynamics shape urban realities across the world. Other dimensions of these globalizing processes may warrant closer scrutiny because they are indicative of city networks being constituted by other activities such as the design, financing and construction of industrial parks and new urban areas.

Global City Networks are dynamic, as are Global Commodity Chains; the connections of cities and regions are not fixed. To understand the dynamics of how network positions are created, sustained or eroded, it is necessary to explore what goes on in cities below the top echelons of New York, London and Tokyo – and Hong Kong and Singapore in Southeast Asia. Cities not (yet) in prominent positions in the World City Network must be included. HCMC is one such city. A dynamic understanding of how HCMC is positioned will help us understand how cities come to occupy their network positions. It also directs our attention to the possible existence of important regional dynamics within World City Networks parallel to the regional organization of many Global Commodity Chains.

Notes

1. We largely sidestep other measures of networks, including infrastructural connections (for example Choi et al. 2008) and political organizations (for example Taylor 2005).
2. In an attempt to clarify the terminology, Derudder (2006) argues that 'world city' implies a concentration of corporate headquarters (economic power) in the tradition of Friedmann, while 'global city' connotes a concentration of advanced producer services in the tradition of Sassen. The distinction should not, however, be exaggerated: Friedmann (1986) included advanced producer services as one of the expanding sectors that drive world city growth. In practice, in most of the literature, including the present chapter, the terms are used interchangeably.

3. Much empirical research has explored the globalization of APS firms, also in qualitative terms (for example Beaverstock 2007; Beaverstock et al. 1999; Faulconbridge and Muzio 2007). However, research on the globalization strategies of APS firms and their tendency to concentrate in global cities is not the same as research on the (assumed critical) role of APS firms in linking (producers in) these cities.

4. The absence of these issues is a major point in the critique of the WCN approach for failing to grasp the material realities and importance of 'third-world cities' (Robinson 2002).

5. The analyses build on data gathered through fieldwork in the HCMC region and the Mekong Delta. For the electronics study, interviews were conducted with managers of electronics companies and with representatives of industrial zones, business associations, provincial authorities and other relevant institutions in HCMC, Binh Duong and Dong Nai Provinces. The majority of electronics companies are located in these three provinces. As for the study into agricultural diversification, interviews were carried out with cooperatives and wholesalers in four of the major fruit-producing provinces of the Mekong Delta. In addition, representatives from exporting and processing companies, and of business associations in HCMC, were interviewed.

6. Several interviewees in the electronics study believed the growing labour shortage was caused by former or prospective migrants finding jobs nearer to home.

7. The Western bias of the WCN approach remains even if the interlocking network concept has also been applied to analysis of so-called Islamic financial services, most recently by Bassens et al. (2009).

8. These arenas are identified based on 'previous experiments in this field' (Taylor 2004: 65); the two works cited as such are studies of London and US law firms (Beaverstock et al. 1999, 2000).

References

Alderson, A. S. and J. Beckfield (2004) 'Power and position in the world city system', *American Journal of Sociology*, 109, 811–51.

Alderson, A. S. and J. Beckfield (2006) 'Reply: whither the parallel paths? The future of scholarship on the world city system', *American Journal of Sociology*, 112, 895–904.

Bair, J. (2005) 'Global capitalism and commodity chains: looking back, going forward', *Competition & Change*, 9, 153–80.

Bassens, D., B. Derudder and F. Witlox (2009) 'Setting "other" standards: on the role, power and spatialities of interlocking Shari'a boards in Islamic financial services', *GaWC Research Bulletin*, No. 309 (www.lboro.ac.uk/gawc).

Beaverstock, J. V. (2007) 'World city networks "from below"', in P. J. Taylor, B. Derudder, P. Saey and F. Witlox (eds) *Cities in globalization: practices, policies and theories*, London: Routledge, 52–71.

Beaverstock, J. V., R. G. Smith and P. J. Taylor (1999) 'The long arm of the law: London's law firms in a globalizing world-economy', *Environment and Planning A*, 31, 1857–76.

Beaverstock, J. V., R. G. Smith and P. J. Taylor (2000) 'Geographies of globalization: United States law firms in world cities', *Urban Geography*, 21, 95–120.

Brown, E., B. Derudder, C. Parnreiter, W. Pelupessy, P. J. Taylor and F. Witlox (2010) 'World City Networks and Global Commodity Chains: towards a world-systems' integration', *Global Networks*, 10, 12–34.

Choi, J. H., G. A. Barnett and B.-S. Chon (2008) 'Comparing World City Networks: a network analysis of Internet backbone and air transport intercity linkages', *Global Networks*, 6, 81–99.

Davis, M. (2006) *Planet of slums*, London: Verso.

Derudder, B. (2006) 'On conceptual confusion in empirical analyses of a transnational urban network', *Urban Studies*, 43, 2027–46.

Derudder, B. (2008) 'Mapping global urban networks: a decade of empirical world cities research', *Geography Compass*, 2, 559–74.

Derudder, B. and P. Taylor (2005) 'The cliquishness of world cities', *Global Networks*, 5, 71–91.

Dicken, P., P. Kelly, K. Olds and H. W-c. Yeung (2001) 'Chains and networks, territories and scales: towards a relational framework for analysing the global economy', *Global Networks*, 1, 89–112.

Dixon, C. and A. Kilgour (2002) 'State, capital, and resistance to globalisation in the Vietnamese transitional economy', *Environment and Planning A*, 34, 599–618.

Faulconbridge, J. R. and D. Muzio (2007) 'Reinserting the professional into the study of globalizing professional service firms: the case of law', *Global Networks*, 7, 249–70.

Fforde, A. and S. de Vylder (1996) *From plan to market: the economic transition in Vietnam*, Boulder: Westview.

Friedmann, J. (1986) 'The world city hypothesis', *Development and Change*, 17, 69–83.

General Statistical Office (2008) *Homepage of General Statistical Office* (www.gso.gov.vn).

Gereffi, G. (1994) 'The organization of buyer-driven Global Commodity Chains: how US retailers shape overseas production networks', in G. Gereffi and M. Korzeniewicz (eds) *Commodity chains and global capitalism*, Westport: Praeger, 95–122.

Gereffi, G. and M. Korzeniewicz (eds) (1994) *Commodity chains and global capitalism*, Westport: Praeger.

Gereffi, G., J. Humphrey and T. J. Sturgeon (2005) 'The governance of Global Value Chains', *Review of International Political Economy*, 12, 78–104.

Gibbon, P. (2001) 'Upgrading primary production: a Global Commodity Chain approach', *World Development*, 29, 345–63.

Gibbon, P., and S. Ponte (2005) *Trading down: Africa, value chains, and the global economy*, Philadelphia: Temple University Press.

Godfrey, B. J. and Y. Zhou (1999) 'Ranking world cities: multinational corporations and the global urban hierarchy', *Urban Geography*, 20, 268–81.

Henderson, J., P. Dicken, M. Hess, N. Coe and H. W-c. Yeung (2002) 'Global production networks and the analysis of economic development', *Review of International Political Economy*, 9, 436–64.

Hoang Xuan Thanh, Dinh Thi Thu Phuong, Nguyen Thu Huong and C. Tacoli (2008) *Urbanization and rural development in Viet Nam's Mekong Delta: livelihood transformations in three fruit-growing settlements*, London: International Institute for Environment and Development.

Humphrey, J. (2003) 'Globalization and supply chain networks: the auto industry in Brazil and India', *Global Networks*, 3, 121–41.

Humphrey, J. and H. Schmitz (2002) 'How does insertion in Global Value Chains affect upgrading in industrial clusters?', *Regional Studies*, 36, 1017–27.

IFPRI (2002) *Fruit and vegetables in Vietnam: adding value from farmers to consumers*, Washington: IFPRI.

Investment & Construction Authority for Thu Thiem New Urban Area (2008) *Thu Thiem New Urban Area Design Competition* (thuthiemcompetition.com).

Jacobs, J. (1970) *The economy of cities*, New York: Random House.

JETRO (2006) 'JETRO releases its latest survey of Japanese manufacturers in ASEAN and India' (www.jetro.go.jp/en/news/releases/20060330657-news).

Kelly, P. F. (2002) 'Spaces of labour control: comparative perspectives from Southeast Asia', *Transactions of the Institute of British Geographers*, 27, 395–411.

Knox, P. L. (2007) 'World cities and the internationalization of design services', in P. J. Taylor, B. Derudder, P. Saey, and F. Witlox (eds) *Cities in globalization: practices, policies and theories*, London: Routledge, 72–86.

Knox, P. L. and P. J. Taylor (eds) (1995) *World cities in a world-system*, Cambridge: Cambridge University Press.

Knutsen, H. M. (2004) 'Industrial development in buyer-driven networks: the garment industry in Vietnam and Sri Lanka', *Journal of Economic Geography*, 4, 545–64.

Marsh, S. P. and T. G. MacAulay (2006) 'Land reform and the development of commercial agriculture in Vietnam: Policy and issues', *Australian Agribusiness Review*, 10, 1–18.

Nadvi, K. and G. Halder (2005) 'Local clusters in Global Value Chains: exploring dynamic linkages between Germany and Pakistan', *Entrepreneurship and Regional Development*, 17, 339–63.

Nadvi, K. and J. T. Thoburn (2004) 'Vietnam in the global garment and textile value chain: impacts on firms and workers', *Journal of International Development*, 16, 111–23.

Neal, Z. P. (2008) 'The duality of world cities and firms: comparing networks, hierarchies, and inequalities in the global economy', *Global Networks*, 8, 94–115.

Olds, K. (2001) *Globalization and urban change: capital, culture and Pacific Rim mega-projects*, Oxford: Oxford University Press.

Palpacuer, F. and A. Parisotto (2003) 'Global production and local jobs: can global enterprise networks be used as levers for local development?', *Global Networks*, 3, 97–120.

Parnreiter, C., K. Fischer and K. Imhof (2007) 'The missing link between Global Commodity Chains and global cities: the financial service sector in Mexico City and Santiago de Chile', *EURE – Revista Latinoamericana de Estudios Urbano Regionales*, 33, 135–48.

Perry, M. and C. Yeoh (2000) 'Singapore's overseas industrial parks', *Regional Studies*, 34, 199–206.

Ponte, S. and P. Gibbon (2005) 'Quality standards, conventions and the governance of Global Value Chains', *Economy and Society*, 34, 1–31.

Rabach, E. and E. M. Kim (1994) 'Where is the chain in commodity chains? The service sector nexus', in G. Gereffi and M. Korzeniewicz (eds) *Commodity chains and global capitalism*, Westport: Praeger, 123–43.

Robinson, J. (2002) 'Global and world cities: a view from off the map', *International Journal of Urban and Regional Research*, 26, 531–54.

Robinson, J. (2005) 'Urban geography: world cities, or a world of cities', *Progress in Human Geography*, 29, 757–65.

Rossi, E. C., J. V. Beaverstock and P. J. Taylor (2007) 'Transaction links through cities: "decision cities" and "service cities" in outsourcing by leading Brazilian firms', *Geoforum*, 38, 628–42.

Rozenblat, C. and D. Pumain (2007) 'Firm linkages, innovation and the evolution of urban systems', in P. J. Taylor, B. Derudder, P. Saey and F. Witlox (eds) *Cities in globalization: practices, policies and theories*, London: Routledge, 130–56.

Samers, M. (2002) 'Immigration and the global city hypothesis: towards an alternative research agenda', *International Journal of Urban and Regional Research*, 26, 389–402.

Sassen, S. (2001) *The global city: New York, London, Tokyo*, Princeton: Princeton University Press.

Schmitz, H. (ed.) (2004) *Local enterprises in the global economy: issues of governance and upgrading*, Cheltenham: Edward Elgar.

Schmitz, H. and S. Strambach (2008) 'The organisational decomposition of the innovation process: what does it mean for the global distribution of innovation activities?', *IDS Working Paper*, No. 304 (www.ids.ac.uk).

Scott, A. J. (2002) 'Regional push: towards a geography of development and growth in low- and middle-income countries', *Third World Quarterly*, 23, 137–61.

Smith, D. A. and M. Timberlake (1995) 'Cities in global matrices: toward mapping the world-system's city system', in P. L. Knox and P. J. Taylor (eds) *World cities in a world-system*, Cambridge: Cambridge University Press, 79–97.

Sturgeon, T. J. (2002) 'Modular production networks: a new American model of industrial organization', *Industrial and Corporate Change*, 11, 451–96.

Taylor, P. J. (2000) 'World cities and territorial states under conditions of contemporary globalization', *Political Geography*, 19, 5–32.

Taylor, P. J. (2004) *World city network: a global urban analysis*, London: Routledge.

Taylor, P. J. (2005) 'New political geographies: global civil society and global governance through World City Networks', *Political Geography*, 24, 703–30.

Taylor, P. J. (2006) 'The rise of "global" advertising from 1990', *GaWC Research Bulletin*, No. 195 (www.lboro.ac.uk/gawc).

Taylor, P. J. (2007a) 'Cities within spaces of flows: theses for a materialist understanding of the external relations of cities', in P. J. Taylor, B. Derudder, P. Saey, and F. Witlox (eds) *Cities in globalization: practices, policies and theories*, London: Routledge, 287–97.

Taylor, P. J. (2007b) 'World city network and planet of slums: access and exclusion in economic globalization', *GaWC Research Bulletin*, No. 239 (www.lboro.ac.uk/gawc).

Taylor, P. J., M. Hoyler, D. M. Evans and J. Harrison (2007) 'Balancing London? A preliminary investigation of the "Core Cities" and "Northern Way" spatial policy initiatives using multi-city corporate and commercial law firms', *GaWC Research Bulletin*, No. 224 (www.lboro.ac.uk/gawc).

Taylor, P. J., P. Ni, B. Derudder, M. Hoyler, J. Huang, F. Lu, K. Pain, F. Witlox, X. Yang, D. Bassens and W. Shen (2009) 'The way we were: command-and-control centres in the global space-economy on the eve of the 2008 geo-economic transition, *Environment and Planning A*, 41, 7–12.

Thomsen, L. (2007) 'Accessing Global Value Chains? The role of business state relations in the private clothing industry in Vietnam', *Journal of Economic Geography*, 7, 753–76.

Tran, C. N. and A. D. Le (1998) 'Technological dynamism and R&D in the export of manufactures from Viet Nam', in D. Ernst, T. Ganiatsos, and L. Mytelka (eds) *Technological capabilities and export success in Asia*, London: Routledge, 267–324.

Trang, T. T. T. (2004) 'Vietnam's rural transformation: information, knowledge and diversification', in D. McCargo (ed.) *Rethinking Vietnam*, London: Routledge, 110–25.

Vind, I. (2008) 'How do linkages with local suppliers affect the impact of TNCs on development? The case of electronics in Vietnam', in E. Rugraff, D. Sanchez-Ancochea, and A. Sumner (eds) *Transnational corporations and development policy*, Basingstoke: Palgrave, 225–46.

Vind, I. and N. Fold (2007) 'Multi-level modularity vs. hierarchy: global production networks in Singapore's electronics industry', *Danish Journal of Geography*, 107, 69–83.

Wall, R., B. van der Knaap and W. Sleegers (2007) 'Towards network sustainability: between corporate network analysis and development indicators', Final report for the Netherlands Environmental Assessment Agency, Erasmus University Rotterdam.

5

Cities, material flows and the geography of spatial interaction: urban places in the system of chains

MARKUS HESSE

My aim in this chapter is to develop a better conceptual understanding of the role of cities in the context of Global Commodity Chains (GCC) or value chains. I shall therefore focus on cities as places (and stakeholders), rather than on urban system analyses or city hierarchies. I aim to cross-fertilize two approaches or subjects of analysis: the chain as the complex arrangement of interwoven economic activities on the one hand, and the city as site, place or scalar configuration in which material processes – the creation of value alongside the chain – are embedded on the other hand. Each of these two different strands of research and debate has developed separately rather than in conjunction, and their material dimension appears somehow abstract, if not widely neglected.

The starting point of this discussion is the relationship between places and flows, which has been the subject of geographical studies for decades. More recently, this relationship has altered as a result of technological and socio-economic change. The rise of global economic exchange, the establishment of Global Production Networks as well as trade and travel are bringing about new geographies of urban places, both in terms of urban system at large scale (Taylor 2003) and of urban structure and urban land use (Hesse 2008); these forces put pressure on urban policy to adapt to the emerging logic and imperative of flows, for example by providing accessibility and infrastructure. There is also a certain dependence of cities on connectivity, which becomes increasingly important for inter-urban competition (Savitch and Kantor 2002). In this context, I relate to a hypothesis expressed by Castells (2002), arguing that 'the space of flows dominates the space of places'. However, the question of stability or change in urban contexts remains undecided, since forces of urban concentration and dispersal, and of deterritorialization and re-embedding are often observed simultaneously.

I shall further apply this conceptual question to cities and their potential part in a global chain. In particular, I examine how these related issues have been dealt with in the past in urban theory and GCC research. Hence, I do not primarily focus on related networks and infrastructures *per se*, but attempt rather to 'read' and analyse urban development through the perspective of connectivity and accessibility. In looking at the basic association between places and flows, I do not confine the discussion to *world* cities or *global* cities as such, but emphasize urbanization and the role of urban places in more generic terms. Regarding the existing work on GCCs, I concentrate on the development of material flows in the context of physical distribution. Although authors from different scientific backgrounds have researched cities and urban studies are by definition interdisciplinary, here I shall focus primarily on contributions from urban geographers. This makes it possible to clarify the issues of the methodological discussion by connecting them to some of the fundamental debate that has been held within that discipline.

My argument is threefold. First, GCC discourses need to consider the issue of material flows more precisely, particularly because of the role that physical distribution and logistics management play in determining the extent, origin, destination, volatility and governance of the chains. Second, the analysis of chains should be connected more strongly to cities and urban places, since they all have different means to attract, manage and redirect flows in such networks, which, in turn, shape the overall performance of the chains. Only the *assemblage* of the two – of city and region on the one hand and of the chain on the other – provides a complete understanding of the subject under enquiry. Third, due to technological and organizational changes, the relationship between cities and flows is subject to ongoing transformations that have considerable impacts on both places and flows. It could be argued that places neither dominate flows nor that flows tend to determine places, but that the two are intertwined in a complex relationship that is constantly reproduced in the context of global exchange.

Against this background, the chapter is organized as follows. First, to better understand the interplay of place and flows (of site and situation), I discuss some of the classical approaches in human geography, namely Ullman's (1954) idea of spatial interaction regarding central places and transport places. Second, I confront urban development and spatial interaction with globalization and the changing socio-economic framework, particularly the emergence of GCC. Third, as a result of spatial reorganization (Janelle 1969), a related shift from 'centrality' to 'intermediacy' is discussed, particularly regarding the emergence of 'gateways' and 'hubs' as outcomes of the changing role of urban places in the context of flows. To provide empirical evidence, the impact of global supply chains on site and situation is applied to the case of seaports and port cities, not least a good example for chain insertion. To address the situatedness of places related to flows and chains, Sheppard's (2002) concept of '*positionality*' is discussed in the last section. This approach could help place cities in the context of an organizationally complex, functionally fragmented and spatially stretched economic system.

Places and flows, site and situation

Cities and urban regions have always been significant nodes for the exchange of people and commodities, ideas and innovation. Trade and merchandising, wholesale and retail distribution have been closely connected with urban places and urban development. Cities have been central places by definition, and often gateways for providing goods and services to more distant hinterlands. The classical function of the city as a centre of goods transshipment was acknowledged in traditional urban theory. Weber (1921: 61) argued that the 'regular exchange of goods' was one of the basic characteristics of cities, distinguishing a city from towns or other settlements. Christaller's (1933) central place theory was instrumental in this respect, in that it explained the size, significance and spatial distribution of cities or settlements against the background of their function to provide goods and services and thus the management of flows. The ability of the city to concentrate people and workforce, ideas and interactions can be considered as derived from connectivity. With respect to these changes, the theory of the multi-nuclear city developed by Harris and Ullman (1945: 9–15) emphasized the foundation of the city as a generic transport focus, emerging from the demand for 'break of bulk' and related services. This generic urban significance of the system of goods exchange was particularly fostered by interregional trade that made some cities become nodes within a large-scale network of commodity and money flows.

The main question of interest here is how flows and physical space interact, and in how far this relationship has been changed lately. In his contribution on 'geography as spatial interaction', Edward Ullman stressed the basic role of the interplay of site and situation. In his words, site refers to 'local, underlying areal conditions'. Situation refers to 'the effect of one area on another area. It logically focuses on the connection between areas' (Ullman 1954: 13). His view evolved from a critical assessment of the discipline as being obsessed by the gravity model and its emphasis on areas and territories, rather than on behaviour, situation and interrelation. A comparable emphasis on such issues had emerged in other disciplines as well, for example in the social or human ecology strands of the social sciences, as they were developed by McKenzie, Hawley and others (see Smith 2005). The main assumption made by Ullman was that establishing connections between certain areas would be just as important as establishing the character of the areas themselves, thus taking into account the 'relations and flows of all kinds among industries, raw materials, markets, culture, and transportation' (Ullman 1953: 56).

The innovative element in his framework was to consider the two subjects – site and situation – as inevitably linked: he concluded that hardly any single place is (economically or socially) independent and exists on its own, but is interwoven in a network of interaction and interdependency. This view became generally accepted in human geography long before the discourses on world cities and globalization emerged. The medium that once connected such places was transport. Ullman and others consequently focused on the effects of trade and transport on areal differentiation, both in terms of the sheer size of a system of exchange and of the emerging regional specialization. He noted three factors that determine the degree of spatial interaction: (i) complementarity as an outcome of areal differentiation, (ii) intervening complementarity or 'opportunities' between places, and (iii) distance including transport cost and time (Ullman 1954: 18). Ullman's legacy in this regard is no longer to separate site from situation (or the other way round), but to integrate them in a systematic way. This is particularly helpful when interpreting the functional specialization of certain places (notably cities) in the context of transport flows and chains.

The association of locational fix and mobility is still valid today, when urbanization and localization effects are being held responsible for the sustained power of the city. As Scott (2008: 760–1) has put it recently, the essence of the contemporary city is the dense spatial concentration of human activity, principally ascribed to two mutually reinforcing developments – the locational clustering of units of capital and labour, and increasing return effects that endow the emerging agglomeration with multiple competitive advantages and social benefits. As a consequence, it might seem that the link between urbanization and accessibility is stronger than ever. The functionality of flows appears to be a prime location factor for cities in the changing framework of the network economy or network society. 'Cities and urban regions become, in a sense, staging posts in the perpetual flux of infrastructure mediated flow, movement and exchange' (Graham 2000: 114). However, on closer examination, accelerated globalization and the increasing interrelation of value-added processes at different spatial scales have changed the historical continuum of urban development significantly.

Globalization, commodity chains and material flows

Globalization has triggered fundamental socio-economic and socio-cultural changes across the globe. This seems to be undisputed, even considering the many different definitions and understandings of globalization (Dicken 2003: 7; Held et al. 1999: 3) and the open question of whether it represents something new or if it is just an extension of ongoing, historical trends (Hirst and Thompson 1999). One major issue in this debate is its impact on urban and regional development. Initial interest focused on the formation of world cities (Friedmann 1986) or global cities (Sassen 2001) and thus emphasized selected locations that have developed certain abilities to serve as the most competitive urban centres. This applied to places such as the prototypical global cities of New York, London and Tokyo or the hubs of global air travel like Chicago, Frankfurt, Los Angeles and Paris. Thanks to strong business performance and amenities, they are able to meet the needs of global service firms and the associated business milieux.

Consequently, such cities were ranked at the top of the increasingly popular hierarchies of the new urban system (Beaverstock et al. 2002; Derudder and Witlox 2008). Other authors stressed the process of globalizing cities, that is, the impact of globalization on cities in general, regardless of their size and significance (Amin and Thrift 1994; Marcuse and van Kempen 2002; Smith 2001). Only a few of these cities may profit from globalization and serve as relevant nodes in the system of global exchange, for example in labour market issues (Palpacuer and Parisotto 2003). Others, like many old industrialized regions, have lost most of their industrial base and struggle with resurgence.

Regarding the specific interrelations between the global 'system' of trade, production networks and chains, and local or regional places, a large body of research has been devoted to studying Global Commodity Chains (GCC) or Global Value Chains (GVC). The related concepts were introduced in the context of world-system analysis, then further developed and reinvigorated in political economy (Bair 2005, 2008, 2009; Gereffi et al. 1994). When considering the 'chain', different layers have to be taken into account: the value chain as a whole, representing interfirm relations in economic space, the commodity chain as the issue most frequently emphasized, including institutions and governance, and the logistics or supply chain comprising material flows and physical distribution. These three are in many ways interrelated. Yet, there are still gaps in GCC research. One applies to their core spatial dimension (Leslie and Reimer 1999); another regards the nature of chains and flows as material artefacts, derived from not least physical exchange between territorially distanciated units (Ciccantell and Smith 2009).

In some ways related to GCC, the discourse on Global Production Networks (GPN) has significantly broadened our understanding of globalization, for example by challenging the conventional idea of the contradiction between the 'global' and 'regional'. According to Coe et al. (2004: 469), GPN represent a close interrelationship rather than a dichotomy between global and regional processes. In this context, the authors have conceptualized regional development as 'a dynamic outcome of the complex interaction between territorialized relational networks and Global Production Networks within the context of changing regional governance structures' (Coe et al. 2004: 469). Due to the advance of information and communication technologies and the successful handling of complex organizational processes, GPN indicate that economic globalization is reaching a degree of global integration not known before. Furthermore, 'production networks are inherently dynamic; they are always, by definition, in a process of flux – in the process of becoming – both organizationally and geographically' (Coe et al. 2008: 272).

At the global level, both GCC and GPN developments seem to have two properties in common. First, the related processes trigger a complex, even though often overlooked relationship between different locations at various spatial scales, where material space (place) still plays a vital role in terms of accessibility, flexibility, labour supply, or power and politics (Hudson 2001). Space is becoming crucial because of the impacts of agglomeration, economies of scale and congestion. Second, this fundamental role of physical flows in the context of globalization, networks and chains has been overlooked in related research (Hesse and Rodrigue 2006). Even the proponents of GPN openly admit that a material dimension is missing in current debates:

> social scientists – including, remarkably, economic geographers ... seem to assume that, with the development of the time–space shrinking technologies of transportation and communication, the problem of actually moving materials, components and finished products has been solved. In fact, with the vastly increased complexity and geographical extensiveness of production networks, and the need to coordinate and integrate extraordinarily intricate operations as

rapidly and efficiently as possible, the logistics problem is absolutely central.

(Coe et al. 2008: 276)

Given the limitations of both accounts, the dimension of material flows needs to be integrated further into GPN- and GCC-related research. This is particularly justified since, as a result of global interrelations, networks and chains are taking 'place' in concrete locales. The notion of what a city may represent in the global economy has changed significantly in the context of the emerging flows. Amin and Thrift (2002: 67) have stressed that cities are no longer perceived 'as a bounded, punctuated economic site, but as sites within spatially stretched economic relations'. Instead, they see them as assemblages of more or less distanciated economic relations with different intensities at different locations. According to the authors, 'economic activity is now irremediably distributed. Even when economic activity seems to be spatially clustered, a close examination will reveal that the clusters rely on a multiplicity of sites, institutions and connections, which do not just stretch beyond these clusters, but actually constitute them' (Amin and Thrift 2002: 52). Consequently, they 'replace the idea of the city as a territorial economic engine with an understanding of cities as sites in spatially stretched economic relations' (Amin and Thrift 2002: 63). This argument stands in contrast with the statement by Scott (2008) mentioned above, yet it seems to be in line with the emerging notion of 'flow' and mobility in contemporary urban studies and social theory (Graham and Marvin 2001; Urry 2007). It also confirms relational approaches in economic and social geography that consider the development of place as increasingly embedded in relation rather than fixity, in routes rather than roots. The ability of urban places to act as a spatial fix in an environment of increasing flows is being questioned.

Cities in the system of chains and flows

Spatial reorganization, centrality vs. intermediacy, gateways and hubs

The emergence of complex interdependencies of the local and the global as a result of large-scale network architectures challenges the traditional notion of the city as a distinct, territorially fixed economic entity and thus stands in contrast to theories of clusters, embeddedness and localized milieux. Whereas empirical evidence does not support the assumption of a general 'footloose-ness' of the economy, the way global networks and flows are being operated reveals an increasing degree of disconnection from traditional urban and economic network topologies (Hudson 2004). As a result, both site and situation are likely to change. Will the city, once prime market place and site of economic exchange, become transformed to a mere terminal, providing the transshipment of commodities from A to B? Will cities face the risk of becoming disadvantaged just by changes in the orchestration of global commodity flows or in the routing of global passenger flows?

Such processes are the outcome of a changing relationship between site and situation, which was once also conceptualized as 'spatial reorganization' (Janelle 1969: 348), meaning that places adapt both the locational structure and the characteristics of their social, economic and political activities to changes in time–space connectivity. This ability depends on different factors, such as accessibility, transport innovations, time–space convergence, centralization and specialization and also spatial interaction. It is assumed that improvements in accessibility may result in growth of the area, in centralization and spatial specialization. As a consequence, the degree of interaction will increase, at least as far as the negative effects of agglomeration will not supersede its economic benefits. In the less recognized part of their seminal paper on 'The nature of cities' (compared with the theory of the multi-nuclear city), Harris and Ullman were also aware of the power that connectivity and flows may yield over urban areas. They distinguished between cities that are *central places* and those that evolve into *transport places*, which are specialized in offering transport and wholesale services, thanks to their strategic location on transport channels (Harris and Ullman 1945: 8–9). Transport places thus destroyed the symmetry of central places. However, based on accessibility and technological standards of that time, their potential was determined by physical conditions, particularly by topography, trade routes and infrastructure.

As a conceptual development of transport places, Burghardt (1971) discussed *gateway cities*, which he defined as 'an entrance into (and necessarily an exit out of) some area. The entrance tends to be narrow and will probably be used by anyone wishing to enter or leave the tributary area behind. The city is in command of the connections between the tributary area and the outside world' (Burghardt 1971: 269). According to the author, entrance into an extended hinterland is one of the essentials of the gateway concept. The contrast between gateway city and central place appears to be essential (Bird 1973). From an historical point of view, Burghardt (1971: 272) distinguished several phases of gateway performance. Initially, the gateway city grows rapidly because it profits from its sudden importance for serving a particular hinterland. Depending on the future development of the hinterland, the gateway city will either be reduced to a central place (in the case of a productive hinterland development), or maintain its position for serving the tributary area. In this perspective, the prospects of gateway and hinterland are inversely related. The final phase will consist of an approximation of central place distribution of cities and a hierarchy of centres in which gateways may play a distinct yet no longer dominant role.

The problem of gateway cities is that their competitive advantage is being challenged by decreasing transport costs and the extension of services into the hinterland, often making a gateway somewhat obsolete. The old rationale for an emerging gateway city was well-grounded in the physical environment, in particular transport conditions or in barriers to overcome, such as borders. Yet, as technology and transport have changed, so have the characteristics of a city or region as a gateway. In particular, this applies first to the issue of difference, for example between specific topographic situations or between land and sea, which has been largely overcome by transport infrastructure, technology or communication. Second, the critical state of gateways is being reinforced by changes in the political setting, not only through privatization and deregulation, but simply due to new political geographies. In the aftermath of 1989–90, vanishing borders and the resulting processes of market deregulation and liberalization helped make the traditional use of gateways (as a means to overcome physical, political or fiscal differences) more and more superfluous. As a result, traditional gateway locales are often situated in a restricted setting of place, infrastructure and access, and the usual attempts to expand infrastructure or facilities may be limited. Consequently, facilities that require a friction-free materials flow will be newly established, with their locations strategically adjusted – often at places that are farther away from the old gateway. A case in point in this respect is given by mushrooming satellite container-ports such as the one in Gioia Tauro, in southern Italy. As a result of its start-up, goods flows in the Mediterranean have been rerouted, at the expense of seaports at the North Range (Slack and Frémont 2005). Thus, the problems of adapting to a changing environment – due to land or access constraints, or physical barriers – and the related locational dynamics challenge the idea of a gateway.

Peter Taylor suggests that '"gateways" can be easily by-passed using new communication technologies and therefore it is too soon to predict simple hierarchical enhancement since all cities are partially "released" from national bounds through global networking' (Taylor 2007). Against the background of the dissolution of the core properties of a gateway, Fleming and Hayuth (1994) proposed the corresponding terminology of *intermediacy*, based on their study of *transport hubs*. By definition, intermediate places or hubs are neither central place nor gateway, but are located in between other places. They specialize in relation to them, mostly based on connectivity, and emerged as intermediate places primarily thanks to a strategic location along a transport axis or with respect to market areas. This is often applied to the network of air carriers (see Zook and Brunn 2006), where the hub principle has gained increasing prominence since the 1980s and 1990s, both regarding passenger flows (major hubs being for example Houston, Texas or Atlanta, Georgia) and air freight (with newly emerging hubs for example in Memphis, Tennessee or Louisville, Kentucky). Current container throughput ports have also made this concept popular. Intermediacy is particularly given when external relationships are becoming more important than the regionally based economic activity. Strategic location in relation to other places – both in terms of space and time – is the most important property of intermediate areas. However, the authors contend that intermediacy can be quite a 'transitory and artificial' characteristic (Fleming and Hayuth 1994: 18).

The concepts of spatial interaction, gateway and intermediacy can be understood as early attempts to overcome a rather Euclidian understanding of geographical space, with the gravity model as the basic rationale for exploring and interpreting spatial activity and differentiation. Under present-day conditions, things have changed further. Places seem to become involved in flows no longer by location and by centrality, at least not sufficiently. Rather, places have to provide an appropriate organizational setting, due to the spatio-temporal organization of chains, beyond the immediate physical implications and requirements of the management of flows (infrastructure, facilities, space). This requires a spatio-temporal capacity that was already coined 'organization space' (Easterling 1999). Easterling assumes that contemporary urban developments such as transport interchanges, ports, airports, malls and economic franchises can best be understood as dynamic sites for organizing logistical processes – 'The primary means of making space consist of a special series of games for distributing spatial commodities' (Easterling 1999: 113). She also points out that the critical architectures of these spaces are not visible, but are woven into their extended technical and information systems and often hidden infrastructure networks: 'the real power of many urban organizations lies within their relationships between distributed sites that are disconnected materially, but which remotely affect each other – sites which are involved, not with fusion or holism, but with adjustment' (Easterling 1999: 113). These processes of newly adjusting site and situation can be prototypically observed in the case of seaports.

How places cope with mobility: the case of seaports

Seaports, the 'frontline soldiers' of globalization (Ducruet and Lee 2006), represent an excellent case of the changing role of urban places in concert with flows, and not only because their function as both central place and gateway or hub is widely investigated. Ports themselves have recently been under pressure of substantial changes, both regarding the management of flows and the corresponding role of the urban:

> Ports, historically, were created as regional or national gateways to serve and promote the economic development of their respective regions or countries. With the globalization of the world economy and the world-wide restructuring of production and distribution, seaports are frequently reassessing their own role in a global system. Ports are becoming cogs in the wheel mobilized by a world economic system.
>
> (McJunkin 1990, cited in Fleming and Hayuth 1994: 12)

In the light of globalizing supply chains and the emergence of a worldwide network of logistics services, it appears that the flow of goods and the associated handling operations are no longer tied to one particular place and its specific setting, but tend to become mobilized in the context of global networks. Shipping lines or global terminal-operator conglomerates have gained new freedom in selecting ports and locations for their operations (Slack 1993). This may have a similar effect as the decline of the shipbuilding or food processing industries has had in the 1970s and 1980s, when these industries left the port locales and spread toward remote places. As a consequence of the complex reorganization of logistics chains, the port may lose its advantage of proximity, agglomeration and related economies of scale.

Traditional gateways such as container ports are becoming nodes within a network, severing the strong ties to the hinterland and repositioning the port, depending on strategic decisions made by focal players who control large components of the chains (Olivier and Slack 2006; Robinson 2002). Since the classical function of the gateway is being challenged by a deterritorial-ization of processes, and mainports may face the risk of losing their monopoly on providing transport and distribution services for their hinterlands, the strong connection between port and territory is weakened. The more global players take command and control of the chains, the more the role of port authorities becomes questioned. As Kreukels (2003: 26) has put it, ports are particularly 'spatially embedded' – but not necessarily physically and in spatial proximity, but in organizational proximity and via corresponding networks. Thus network building is no longer based on physical space, on infrastructure and interfaces, but on information and organization.

The relationship between port and city has been investigated empirically by Ducruet and Lee (2006), framing the interplay of site and situation in the particular context of centrality and intermediacy as mentioned above. They compared the development of city population and port between 1970 and 2005 and measured the related concentration effects, using a database of 653 port cities worldwide. Depending on the degree of centrality, cities were categorized as a coastal town, urban port or general city (in the case of low intermediacy), as an outport, cityport or maritime city (in the case of medium intermediacy), and as a hub, gateway or port metropolis in the event of high intermediacy. Based on the concentration index assigned to regional areas, the findings reveal a puzzle of simultaneous phenomena – urban constraint and spatial growth, port expansion and competition, congestion and lack of space, uneven industrial growth and geopolitical change. First, individual trajectories of port cities appear highly differentiated, with (i) major general cities experiencing a decline of port and gateway functions (for example Chicago, Boston, Baltimore or Toronto); (ii) port cities that stabilized this function, although it is becoming less important for the regional economy (for example Seattle-Tacoma, Marseille, Lisbon); and (iii) port cities that experienced a continuous increase in concentration (for example Los Angeles/Long Beach, Hamburg, Shanghai). Most of the latter have a 'very peculiar situation favouring intermediacy, but the lack of space is altering their trajectory as hub or hinterland ports' (Ducruet and Lee 2006: 119). Other port cities have (iv) regained competitiveness, that is by extending hinterland connections or developing strategies and institutional changes, for example Incheon (Korea), New York/New Jersey or Rotterdam.

Second, there were some general conclusions drawn from the empirical assessment:

> The correlation between city size and port traffic is increasing until 1990, and declines since then. It is assumed that containerisation has spread among the existing urban hierarchy. ... Because of limiting factors such as lack of space for port expansion and rising handling costs, container traffics have developed in non-urban locations for facilitating the concentration of shipping lines, allowing the formation of hub-feeder networks and backed by new port policies throughout the

world. Thus, the relationship between urban and port hierarchy is put in question.

(Ducruet and Lee 2006: 114)

The authors also advocate that, on an average basis, general cities and hubs – the two extreme poles in the spectrum of the port–city relationship – tend to be relatively stable, whereas the unstable situation of hubs with high growth variations represents the 'inadequacy' of logistics and urban development. This is explained with the absence of a sufficient economic base and local community effects that might stabilize traffic throughput. However, port–city evolution seems to be a gradual phenomenon rather than a matter of sudden disruption, and even though highly urbanized port cities have seen their port function decline over time, 'many of them have managed to overcome the difficulties of port competition and urban growth, thanks to efficient planning policies and exceptional locational advantages' (Ducruet and Lee 2006: 120). Important differences between these cases, according to the authors, are also explained by different temporalities. The 'success' of port cities is increasingly dependent on the management of a sustaining equilibrium between different temporalities, functions and scales. Particularly important is the difference between the long-term temporality of cities, the short-term temporality of maritime networks and the medium-term temporality of ports.

If the framework conditions have changed, and site and location no longer guarantee the significance of a certain place in the context of flows, when, how and to what extent can certain stakeholders become embedded into the chain – be it corporations, a set of corporations or certain economic sites (such as seaports), or even cities? Spatial interaction based on chain-like configurations is neither grounded on a sole territorial rationale, such as proximity, nor can it be achieved by the mere extension of physical infrastructure, as it was most common until recently. Cities have to rearrange site and situation to become part of the chain(s). This could be the case for 'insertion' – the way territorial units can become part of the organizational space of firms (Dicken and Malmberg 2001: 359). 'Insertion' is understood by the authors either directly (place as 'the geographic locus of particular functions') or indirectly ('through customer–supplier relationships with other firms'). The template for such a strategy is given by multilocational firms with the potential 'to manipulate geographic space and to use territory as an intrinsic part of their competitive strategy' (Dicken and Malmberg 2001: 359). It can be argued that cities have to behave like organizational units and try to catch a certain position in the chain, thus gaining access to added value, to positive labour market effects or to markets. Such a proactive strategy had been framed by Savitch and Kantor (2002) in the context of competitive bargaining processes. Port cities have long been pursuing such a role by providing land and infrastructure, labour markets, localized assets and the advantages of agglomeration.

This is the point where we return to the issue mentioned earlier – the question of how places and even cities – not just firms – can become part of the chain. In the GPN and GCC context, different forms of chain involvement are discussed, namely regarding value creation, enhancement and capture by firms (Humphrey and Schmitz 2002). The authors compare their approach to chains with clusters and networks. In the case of supply chains and physical distribution, the increasing significance of (global) flows can also be a starting point for regional development – in a system of complex interactions between territorialized relational networks and Global Production Networks. In this respect, two benefits are provided by an efficiently working distribution system: first, it allows regional agents to participate in the operation of competitive structures of industry or services; second, the distribution sector itself promises to generate regional impacts as an industry of its own. This will be even more so as this sector tends to become 'structural', rather than derived from external demand (see Rodrigue 2006).

Hall and Robbins (2007) and also Jacobs and Hall (2007), to whom this particular point explicitly refers, applied the concept of chain involvement to economic sites such as seaports. They introduced insertion, integration and dominance. Once actors seek to *insert* themselves in supply chains, this offers them access to critical resources such as technology, market access, capital, knowledge or expertise. Thus, insertion is the necessary precondition for any transport hub to become a site of economic activity. However, insertion can become a complex and unstable goal, since many sites and agents are subject to rising competition. Second, actors inserted in supply chains may seek to *integrate* activities within the supply chains in order to reduce overall costs and provide services more efficiently. This often occurs by way of vertical and horizontal integration, in order to extend control over the chain and to reduce transport and transaction costs. Third, actors operating in supply chains look for *dominance*, that is the ability or power to extract value from localized (logistics) activities, for example by assuring control over scarce resources or assets or by further exploiting economies of scale (Jacobs and Hall 2007: 329).

Related strategies can be observed empirically in the case of most of the global agents in the maritime business: terminal operators, shipping lines, the often privatized port authorities. The same applies to cities in this respect. However, one crucial point for urban development is that cities are complex, highly context-dependent agents. The differences between corporate and municipal strategies are substantial. City governments are prime local agents (often associated with local firms), whereas a seaport is a national, not city-bound, agent. The two different milieux are quite distinct in their ability to cope with institutional and spatial fragmentation. The limited local scale of the city is part of the tensions with the national scale of the port. In the light of such limitations, Hall and Robbins (2007: 224) have addressed certain strategies – not only for ports, but also for port cities – to position themselves in the context of the chain. Regarding the particular opportunities of cities to act, this applies mainly for improving infrastructure conditions, for organizing backhaul cooperation and developing transport industry cluster-strategies. Improving such local impacts of global flows is a case for governance – the collective term for the coordination of policies, strategies and measures undertaken across different spatial scales and among a variety of agents (Gereffi et al. 2005).

Positionality: placing cities in the global context

Historically, the management of flows took 'place' in the vicinity of urban and metropolitan areas. As a result, the city developed as a market place, based on a distinct relationship between site and situation. The territorially defined space generated a certain demand for movement, thus place dominated the organization of flows. This remains the case in cities and urban regions since they are central places. However, the relationship between place and flows has changed further, with flows having an increasing impact on place and location. Under the conditions of globalization, cities are subject to processes of disembedding as well as of reterritorialization, so they may lose or gain from the rerouting of flows. As a result, the question is whether the city becomes an intermediate (a kind of terminal for the throughput of commodities), rather than a central place in the very sense of this definition?

This question recalls the proposition by Manuel Castells that the 'space of flows' might determine the 'space of places' – in other words, site would no longer determine situation, but the seamless organization of flows would be decisive for the site. Site and situation would thus tend to coalesce, mobility would become a constitutive framework condition for urban development, not only a byproduct of exchange. This is not yet the case, except for some very rare, extreme cases. Laboratories like Dubai have revealed how agents successfully combined capital, labour, land and a favoured position on the global scale to develop aggressively both site and situation. Not coincidentally, one of the recently developed areas in Dubai is labelled 'logistics city', and it was DP World, the worldwide operating Dubai shipping company that brought the management of global flows to perfection (Jacobs and Hall 2007). Other examples may include the export processing zones in China, where positionality and accessibility (situation) created new spaces of production and distribution (sites). On the contrary, cases like so-called 'Airport Cities', as once predicted to emerge by John Kasarda ('Aerotropolis'), are far from being a fact. They represent extreme concepts or exaggerations of the city, rather than generic urban formations. Port-city relationships seem to evolve from path dependence and gradual evolution, rather than rupture, as Ducruet's and Lee's (2006) data suggest.

To search for more generic conclusions, I draw on Sheppard's (2002) account of the times and spaces of globalization. He argues that, in a flow-oriented economy, 'place, scale and networks have been deployed ... as geographic tropes for discussing globalization, sidelining a fourth trope: "positionality"'. This term is developed in order to capture the 'shifting, asymmetric, and path-dependent ways in which the future of places depend on their interdependencies with others' (Sheppard 2002: 308). The early understanding of spatial interaction is advancing towards the relative notion of places in networks. Positionality helps to overcome the excessively essentialist understandings of place in relation to flows. According to Sheppard, positionality consists of three elements: first, it is a relational construct, including the conditions of possibility for an agent depending on her or his position with respect to others. This relational impact is visible in the case of the global agents of the maritime economy, where some corporations such as DP, Hutchison Ports or Eurogate have been extremely successful in placing themselves on the landscape of global competition, depending on their position in the chain (Notteboom 2002). In so doing, the locales of their engagement are becoming 'archipelagos' in an increasingly uneven economic environment, based particularly (though not exclusively) on excellent accessibility. This implies that other places may fall behind those archipelagos. Second, it becomes clear that positionality involves power relations, regarding the uneven distribution of influence along the chain and the situated nature of related knowledge. In this respect, chain management may have serious impacts on territorially bounded units such as cities. These impacts might not only originate from focal firms such as buyers (retailers) or producers (manufacturers), as research on the governance of commodity chains has revealed, but from shippers and distributors who are orchestrating the flows as well! As logistics not only relates to space, but increasingly evolves from the sophisticated management of time, space- and time-transcending technologies thus make some places economically closer to the rest than others. Third, positionality is enacted in ways that both reproduce and challenge its pre-existing conditions. Again, it is the issue of path-dependency rather than rupture that characterizes the relationship between cities and flows. In a majority of cases, historical trajectories come into play that determine current developments (for example the position of the large metropolises), contrasting with the apparent notion of change that is perceived in the context of the management of flows.

In territorial terms, positionality includes more than just distance or location. According to Sheppard, it often laps across space and thus cannot be read off easily from conventional topographic or cartographic images of relative location. It seems evident that the status of cities is increasingly determined by their position within transnational networks, rather than by place-bound characteristics such as size, corporate headquarters or dominant economic activity (Sheppard 2002: 324) – even if they are not yet dominated by the issue of flows (see above). I suggest that, to achieve a successful positionality that allows for chain insertion, integration or dominance, cities have to establish a creative *assemblage* of *site* and *situation*. Neither space and infrastructure alone nor the exclusive management of information flows may provide the desired output, but they may provide the successful insertion into supply chains and the sustainable orchestration of flows – based on a favoured positionality within chain and network.

As a consequence of globalization and rising flows, cities and regions have recently started to search for positionality with the aim of becoming a 'hub'. This applies particularly to old industrialized regions rather than to world cities or global cities. However, such strategies face risks and uncertainties. Problems could occur as a result of the predicted decline of natural resources in general and of oil in particular. As most of the circulation industries are highly dependent on cheap oil, it is an open question whether business models such as air cargo services can be extended into the future. The volatility of the flows and the increasing freedom of powerful agents to rearrange and reroute the stream of commodities obviously constitutes a second problem. Examples for this can be found in the maritime economy and the air traffic business. 'Unlike many infrastructure systems, routes between airports are temporary, intangible manifestations of supply and demand relationships. Depending on global or domestic economic conditions and regional demand, these paths can appear, disappear, expand or contract. Simply put, links lack permanence in this system' (Grubesic et al. 2009: 274). Hence, the locational bundling or

107

clustering of economic activity seems to be limited if based on the volatile flow of materials. Given the delicate and constantly changing relationship between cities and flows, it is doubtful if the interplay of site and situation can easily be translated into policy strategies and recipes.

References

Amin, A. and N. Thrift (eds) (1994) *Globalization, institutions, and regional development in Europe*, Oxford: Oxford University Press.

Amin, A. and N. Thrift (2002) *Cities: reimagining the urban*, Cambridge: Polity Press.

Bair, J. (2005) 'Global capitalism and commodity chains: looking back, going forward', *Competition and Change*, 9, 153–80.

Bair, J. (2008) 'Analysing economic organization: embedded networks and global chains compared', *Economy and Society*, 37, 339–64.

Bair, J. (ed.) (2009) *Frontiers of commodity chain research*, Stanford: Stanford University Press.

Beaverstock, J. V., M. A. Doel, P. J. Hubbard and P. J. Taylor (2002) 'Attending to the world: competition, cooperation and connectivity in the World City Network', *Global Networks*, 2, 111–32.

Bird, J. (1973) 'Of central places, cities and seaports', *Geography*, 58, 105–18.

Burghardt, A. F. (1971) 'A hypothesis about gateway cities', *Annals of the Association of American Geographers*, 61, 269–85.

Castells, M. (2002) 'Local and global: cities in the network society', *Tijdschrift voor Economische en Sociale Geografie*, 93, 548–58.

Christaller, W. (1933) *Die zentralen Orte in Süddeutschland. Eine ökonomisch-geographische Untersuchung über die Gesetzmäßigkeit der Verbreitung und Entwicklung der Siedlungen mit städtischen Funktionen*, Darmstadt: Wissenschaftliche Buchgemeinschaft, reprinted 1968.

Ciccantell, P. and D. Smith (2009) 'Rethinking Global Commodity Chains: integrating extraction, transport, and manufacturing', *International Journal of Comparative Sociology*, 50, 361–84.

Coe, N., M. Hess, H. W-c. Yeung, P. Dicken and J. Henderson (2004) 'Globalizing regional development: a Global Production Networks perspective', *Transactions of the Institute of British Geographers*, 29, 468–84.

Coe, N., P. Dicken and M. Hess (2008) 'Global Production Networks: realizing the potential', *Journal of Economic Geography*, 8, 271–95.

Derudder, B. and F. Witlox (2008) 'Mapping World City Networks through airline flows: context, relevance, and problems', *Journal of Transport Geography*, 16, 305–12.

Dicken, P. (2003) *Global shift*, London: Guilford.

Dicken, P. and A. Malmberg (2001) 'Firms in territories: a relational perspective', *Economic Geography*, 77, 345–63.

Ducruet, C. and S.-W. Lee (2006) 'Frontline soldiers of globalisation: port–city evolution and regional competition', *GeoJournal*, 67, 107–22.

Easterling, K. (1999) *Organization space: landscapes, highways, and houses in America*, Cambridge, MA: The MIT Press.

Fleming, D. K. and Y. Hayuth (1994) 'Spatial characteristics of transportation hubs: centrality and intermediacy', *Journal of Transport Geography*, 2, 3–18.

Friedmann, J. (1986) 'The world city hypothesis', *Development and Change*, 17, 69–83.

Gereffi, G., M. Korzeniewicz, and R. Korzeniewicz (1994) 'Introduction', in G. Gereffi and M. Korzeniewicz (eds) *Commodity chains and global capitalism*, Westport, CT: Praeger, 1–14.

Gereffi, G., J. Humphrey, and T. Sturgeon (2005) 'The governance of Global Value Chains', *Review of International Political Economy*, 12, 78–104.

Graham, S. (2000) 'Introduction: cities and infrastructure networks', *International Journal of Urban and Regional Research*, 24, 114–19.

Graham, S. and S. Marvin (2001) *Splintering urbanism: networked infrastructures, technological mobilities and the urban condition*, London: Routledge.

Grubesic, T., T. Matisziw, and M. Zook (2009) 'Spatio-temporal fluctuations in the global airport hierarchies', *Journal of Transport Geography*, 17, 264–75.

Hall, P. V. and G. Robbins (2007) 'Which link, in which chain? Inserting Durban into global automotive supply chains', in J. Wang, D. Olivier, T. Notteboom and B. Slack (eds) *Ports, cities, and global supply chains*, Aldershot: Ashgate, 221–31.

Harris, C. D. and E. L. Ullman (1945) 'The nature of cities', *The Annals of the American Academy of Political and Social Science*, 242, 7–17.

Held, D., A. McGrew, D. Goldblatt and J. Perraton (1999) *Global transformations: politics, economics and culture*, Stanford: Stanford University Press.

Hesse, M. (2008) *The city as a terminal: logistics and freight transport in an urban context*, Aldershot: Ashgate.

Hesse, M. and J.-P. Rodrigue (2006) 'Global Production Networks and the role of logistics and transportation', *Growth and Change*, 32, 499–509.

Hirst, P. and G. Thompson (1999) *Globalization in question: the international economy and the possibilities of governance*, Cambridge: Polity.

Hudson, R. (2001) *Producing places*, New York: Guilford Press.

Hudson, R. (2004) 'Conceptualizing economies and their geographies: spaces, flows and circuits', *Progress in Human Geography*, 28, 447–71.

Humphrey, J. and H. Schmitz (2002) 'How does insertion in Global Value Chains affect upgrading in industrial clusters?', *Regional Studies*, 36, 1017–27.

Jacobs, W. and P. V. Hall (2007) 'What conditions supply chain strategies of ports? The case of Dubai', *Geoforum*, 68, 327–42.

Janelle, D. (1969) 'Spatial reorganization: a model and concept', *Annals of the Association of American Geographers*, 59, 348–64.

Kreukels, A. (2003) 'Wie verankern sich Häfen im Raum?', *DISP*, 154, 26–7.

Leslie, D. and S. Reimer (1999) 'Spatializing commodity chains', *Progress in Human Geography*, 23, 401–20.

Marcuse, P. and R. van Kempen (eds) (2000) *Globalizing cities: a new spatial order?*, Oxford: Blackwell.

Notteboom, T. (2002) 'Consolidation and contestability in the European container handling industry', *Maritime Policy and Management*, 29, 257–69.

Olivier, D. and B. Slack (2006) 'Rethinking the port', *Environment and Planning A*, 38, 1409–27.

Palpacuer, F. and A. Parisotto (2003) 'Global production and local jobs: can global enterprise networks be used as levers for local development?', *Global Networks*, 3, 97–120.

Robinson, R. (2002) 'Ports as elements in value-driven chain systems: the new paradigm', *Maritime Policy and Management*, 29, 241–55.

Rodrigue, J.-P. (2006) 'Challenging the derived transport-demand thesis: geographical issues in freight distribution', *Environment and Planning A*, 38, 1449–62.

Sassen, S. (2001) *The global city: New York, London, Tokyo*, Princeton: Princeton University Press.

Savitch, H. V. and P. Kantor (2002) *Cities in the international marketplace*, Princeton: Princeton University Press.

Scott A. J. (2008) 'Inside the city: on urbanisation, public policy and planning', *Urban Studies*, 45, 755–72.

Sheppard, E. (2002) 'The spaces and times of globalization: place, scale, networks, and positionality', *Economic Geography*, 78 (3), 307–30.

Slack, B. (1993) 'Pawns in the game: ports in a global transportation system', *Growth and Change*, 24, 579–88.

Slack, B. and A. Frémont (2005) 'Transformation of port terminal operations: from the local to the global', *Transport Reviews*, 25, 117–30.

Smith, D. A. (2005) 'The new urban sociology meets the old: rereading some classical human ecology', *Urban Affairs Review*, 30, 432–57.

Smith, M. P. (2001) *Transnational urbanism: locating globalization*, Oxford: Blackwell.

Taylor, P. (2003) *World City Network: a global urban analysis*, London: Routledge.

Taylor, P. J. (2007) 'Cities within spaces of flows: theses for a materialist understanding of the external relations of cities', in P. J. Taylor, B. Derudder, P. Saey and F. Witlox (eds) *Cities in globalization: practices, policies and theories*, London: Routledge, 287–97.

Ullman, E. L. (1953) 'Human geography and area research', *Annals of the Association of American Geographers*, 43, 54–66.

Ullman, E. L. (1954) 'Geography as spatial interaction', reprinted in 1980 in E. L. Ullman and R. R. Boyce (eds) *Geography as spatial interaction*, Seattle: University of Washington Press, pp. 13–27.

Urry, J. (2007) *Mobilities*, Cambridge: Polity Press.

Weber, M. (1921) *Wirtschaft und Gesellschaft. Teilband 5: Die Stadt.* Max Weber Gesamtausgabe, edited by W. Nippel. Tübingen: Mohr Siebeck, (Reprinted 1999).

Zook, M. A. and S. D. Brunn (2006) 'From podes to antipodes: positionalities and global airline geographies', *Annals of the Association of American Geographers*, 96, 471–90.

6

Integrating world cities into production networks: the case of port cities

WOUTER JACOBS, CESAR DUCRUET AND PETER DE LANGEN

Since the mid-1990s, a large body of research has emerged that deals with processes of economic-geographical globalization and the formation of Global Production Networks, Global Value and Commodity Chains (Coe et al. 2004; Dicken et al. 2001; Ernst and Kim 2002; Gereffi and Korzenwiecz 1994; Gereffi et al. 2005; Henderson et al. 2002; Kaplinsky 2004). The aim of this research is to conceptualize and understand the processes of industrial restructuring and the deregulation of national markets that has taken place since the late 1970s and resulted in a new spatial division of labour. Feenstra (1998: 31) summarizes this process as 'the integration of world trade and disintegration of production'.

During the same period, a different strand of research has emerged that focuses on the formation of *world* or *global cities* (Beaverstock et al. 2000; Knox and Taylor 1995; Sassen 1991; Taylor 1997, 2004). This research stream analyses how city hierarchies and urban systems are linked worldwide through corporate networks of advanced producer services (for example banks, insurance companies and law firms) that control flows of capital and information. The focus is on how the dynamics of urban hierarchies are related to the overall restructuring of the world economy (Friedmann 1986). Both schools (hereafter referred to as GCC-GVC-GPN and WCN) provide different but complementary analyses of the globalization of the economy.

Few studies have attempted to integrate both bodies of research conceptually and empirically. Such integration seems necessary as it allows us to provide a more complete picture of the structure and evolution of the global economy. In this contribution to the book, we argue that port cities are an excellent area in which to investigate empirically the interaction between Global Commodity Chains and advanced producer services.

In this chapter we explore to what extent specific maritime and port-related advanced producer services are concentrated in world cities in general and in port cities in particular. Theoretically, the embeddedness of port cities in

111

global networks needs further understanding. Interactions between (maritime) port activities that facilitate global commodity flows and other types of economic activities, most notably advanced producer services, are relevant to this area of research. Practically, port cities compete to attract port-related firms. Attracting APS may be a good strategy for port cities to upgrade their economies and strengthen the position of ports in a particular commodity chain.

Our aims in this chapter are twofold. First, we intend to integrate the respective conceptual frameworks of GCC-GVC-GPN and WCN. Second, we develop a method that allows us to investigate empirically the role and position of port cities in both Global Commodity Chains and World City Networks. We have structured the chapter as follows. In the next section, we look at the similarities and differences between GCC-GVC-GPN and WCN and discuss the role of port cities as a location where both advanced producer services and Global Commodity Chains come together. We present an analytical framework and a research method in section three and our empirical results in section four. We end with conclusions and future directions of port city research.

Integrating world cities and Global Production Networks

Rather than providing a complete overview of the conceptual evolution of GCC-GVC-GPN and World City Network research, we compare them conceptually and methodologically and address how an integrative approach could advance the study of the global economy (for a complete review, see Coe et al. 2008; Hess and Yeung 2006 on GCC-GVC-GPN; Brenner and Keil 2006; Derudder 2006 on WCN).

World City Networks and Global Production Networks

Both approaches analyse the dynamics and geography of the global economy. They start from the premise of a new globalized division of labour and industrial organization (cf. Fröbel et al. 1980), which resulted from a variety of factors such as changing economic policies,[1] and the cost reduction of new communication and transport technologies. This perspective draws inspiration from Castells's (1996) global transformation from a 'space of places' to a 'space of flows', although both approaches explicitly recognize that the world has become both (Derudder and Taylor 2005; Henderson et al. 2002; for a similar statement see Hesse in this book).

Hence, although the concept of network is their core unit of analysis, the respective interests of the WCN school (international connectedness of cities through corporate networks) and of the GPN-school (territorial embeddedness of – social – networks involved in global commodities) remain somewhat different in nature and scope. The widely used WCN approach put forth by Sassen (1991) and Taylor (2004) looks at networks as the intra-firm links of advanced producer services in different locations. WCN neither takes into account relations between these types of firms and other actors nor pays attention to historical and institutional contexts that may partly explain interactions among firms and the structure of city networks. The GPN approach takes a more sophisticated and theoretical stand by emphasizing the *relational* character of networks (Dicken et al. 2001). Understanding networks as such requires the identification of different network actors, their social relationships and power configurations, as well as the structural outcomes of these interactions.

As a result, the methodological approach differs. The WCN school draws on large data sets of location patterns of the world's leading advanced producer service providers. The GPN approach as mentioned by Hess and Yeung (2006) is essentially a heuristic approach with an underdeveloped methodological foundation (Dicken 2004). As a result, GPN research tends to be qualitative with a strong preference for interviews with key actors. As Hess and Yeung (2006: 1201) put it, 'it falls short of delivering a rigorous analysis that can give "the big picture" of GPNs on a global scale.' The WCN-approach provides the big picture on a global scale but often at the expense of a deeper understanding of the historical, institutional and strategic conditions that influence the formation of cities and city networks. Nevertheless, we agree with them that researchers on GPNs should incorporate more explicitly quantitative data and relevant statistical tools into their analytical apparatus.

GCC-GVC-GPN is conceptually more comprehensive in scope than WCN. It is important to distinguish between GPN and GCC/GVC. According to Coe et al. (2008: 2), GCCs/GVCs are considered linear structures with sequential stages in the production–distribution–consumption chain through which value is added, whereas GPN 'strives to go beyond such linearity to incorporate all kinds of network configuration'. This implies that the GPN approach also includes non-linear linkages and social relationships (for example with state agencies or advanced producer services) that are active at different stages within the chain and that are not necessarily directly involved in the actual physical flow of the commodity at stake. Moreover, GPN is more comprehensive in the sets of actors and types of relationships it includes. GCC/GVC primarily focuses on the governance of inter-firm relationships, whereas GPN encompasses both intra- and inter-firm relationships and actors such as the state, NGOs and international regulatory agencies. Furthermore, GPN pays attention to specific types of relationships (such as public or private partnerships) or social network formations (for example business associations).

Towards an integrated approach

Recently, the WCN school has started to develop a relational approach. Beaverstock et al. (2002) see the formation of World City Networks as the outcome of the interaction between two communities: territorial (city and state) and functional-economic (firm and sector). This approach explicitly recognizes the role and influence of sector-specific institutions, multi-scalar governance arrangements and state-enforced regulations on the formation of inter-urban connections. As such, they have brought World City Network analyses more in line with the GPN framework by including other actors as well as institutional and sector-specific features. More specifically, this contribution recognizes that cities are both embedded within networks (in this case of international operating advanced producer services) and within territorial contexts. Thus, despite little evidence about the specific role of APS within commodity chains and Global Production Networks, the afore-mentioned studies have fostered integration between WCN and GPN frameworks towards a more accurate picture of the 'nexus of interconnected functions, operations and transactions through which a specific product or service is produced, distributed and consumed' (Coe et al. 2008: 2).

An important step to integrate WCN and GPN is acknowledging the non-linear relations that exist at certain places and at certain stages within the production chain (Coe et al. 2008). Conceptually, the GPN approach can incorporate linkages between producers, transporters and industrial suppliers on the one hand and advanced service providers on the other. Such an approach demands that we analyse the sector specificity of advanced producer services.[2] In every production network, there is a need for advanced producer services (see also Brown et al. this book; Lühti et al. this book). Some provide specialized services for specific industries (for example maritime freight transport) or clusters of related industries (for example energy). Are these APS located in direct proximity of the nodes in the production chain, or do they arrange such transactions in proximity of other service activities located in 'world cities'?

Such an analysis can provide insights for strategic policy. The GPN approach argues that successful regional economic development depends to a large degree on strategic coupling (Coe et al. 2004), which refers to the capacity of local actors to couple critical regional assets with extra-local actors involved in global flows. The location of specialized APS in a region can accommodate insertion of local industries in Global Commodity Chains.

The case of port cities

Despite their role in the worldwide distribution of goods (almost 90 per cent of world trade volumes are transported by ship), seaports have not received much attention in both bodies of research. Their position as transport hubs and production centres has been largely ignored by researchers on Global Commodity Chains or production networks.[3] On the other hand, WCN has largely ignored the significance of commodity flows and the role of APS in relation to these flows. However, attention to ports is relevant in WCN and GPN research for several reasons.

First, recent contributions in WCN have looked at the connectedness of world cities by investigating telecommunication, corporate networks (Rimmer 1999), airport traffic statistics (Derudder and Witlox 2005), and Internet connections (Choi et al. 2006). These contributions have looked at the importance of crucial physical infrastructure in the global transfer of both people and information as a proxy for world city connectedness. It is argued that inter-city linkages can be studied along the flows of people, information and commodity (Derudder and Taylor 2005; Smith and Timberlake 1995). WCN-analysis has largely ignored the physical flow of commodities. Further attention to seaports is relevant in this respect (see also Hesse this book).

Second, ports are important transport nodes in the global supply chains of specific commodities in which value is created (Jacobs 2007; Robinson 2002; Wang et al. 2007) but have hardly been analysed from the GCC-GVC-GPN perspective. Qualitative case studies from Carbone and De Martino (2003) and Hall and Robbins (2007) have analysed the attempts of the ports of Le Havre (France) and Durban (South Africa) respectively, to become integrated with international automotive chains of Renault and Toyota, but conceptual studies are limited. Recent contributions (Jacobs and Hall 2007; Wang and Olivier 2006) have started to integrate ports conceptually with the work on Global Production Networks and supply chains, but these studies are still in a premature phase.

Third, many ports have developed into a geographical concentration of related economic activities (cf. Langen 2003), including manufacturing facilities such as petro-chemical refineries, specialized suppliers of, for example, machine tools, maintenance firms and logistics service providers. In addition, many Global Commodity Chains move through seaports: liquid bulk (for example oil and gas), dry bulk (for example ore and coal), food (grain, corn, soya, fruits) and other kinds of consumer goods shipped in containers. Ports are a good example of what Humphrey and Schmitz (2002: 1018) call 'export-oriented clusters that are inserted into global value chains', but have seldom been analysed. Fourth, WCN generally neglects the sector-specificity of advanced producer services. By focusing on port cities and port related activities, we can contribute to the development of WCN by focusing on advanced producer services specializing in the maritime and transport related industries. Our approach is summarized in Table 1.

Table 1: World port-city network analysis

Ports	Research focus	Cities
GCC-GVC-GPN	**Conceptual**	World City Networks
Intra and inter firm network of producers and suppliers	**Unit of analysis**	Intra firm network of advanced producer services
Specialized manufacturing Stevedoring Wholesale & trade Transport Logistics & warehousing Offshore	**Types of activities / sectors**	Financial services Insurance Legal services Consultancy – R&D Engineering ICT
Containers Liquid bulk (crude oil, LNG, chemicals) Agri-bulk (grain, corn, soya, fruits) Break bulk (ore, coal, scrap) RoRo (automotive) General cargo (forestry, iron, steel products)	**Specialization**	Merchant banking Ship finance Maritime insurance & brokerage (Hull, P&I, Charterers Liability) Maritime law & arbitration Maritime education & research Software
Throughputs Added value Employment	**Variables**	Urban size Office locations Land rents, wage levels
Geographical pattern →	**World port city networks**	**← Geographical pattern**

World port city networks: a framework for analysis

The main activity of ports is enabling the transfer of goods from ships to other transport modes and vice versa. This generally requires temporary storage. Port-related activities such as wholesale, warehousing, logistics and transport are attracted to the direct proximity of ports due to reduced transaction and transport costs. In addition, some ports have also developed into major sites of production and manufacturing because of industries' dependency on the import of raw materials. For example, ports such as Rotterdam, Antwerp, Houston and Singapore host extensive petro-chemical refineries and storage facilities. The concentration of industrial activity attracts utility and energy companies as well as other local suppliers of components and machinery.

The relationships between port and city changed considerably during the second half of the twentieth century (Levinson 2006).[4] Ports have become increasingly disconnected from cities. Spatially, the increased intensity of port-industrial activity, in combination with urban growth, lack of available land for further expansion, and environmental constraints have led to the move of port facilities away from city centres (see Bird 1963; Hall 2007; Hoyle 1989). Institutionally, the devolution of local government control on the port's management (see Brooks and Cullinane 2007; Jacobs 2007) further eroded port–city relationships. Economically, this relationship resulted from reduced dependence of ports on the urban labour market as well as the reduced dependence of cities on ports for local economic growth.[5]

The degree to which port activities and advanced producer services (APS) are interdependent is unknown. While most evolutionary models depict stages of spatial and functional separation between port and urban activities (Ducruet and Lee 2006), there is a recognition of the less visible port–city relationship in the service sector (Amato 1999). The location pattern of APS tends to follow the urban hierarchy rather than the hierarchy of port throughputs, as seen in the cases of Canada (Slack 1989) and Australia (O'Connor 1989). O'Connor (1989) distinguishes three main types of locations: (1) port cities that provide basic services dealing with daily physical operations, (2) maritime industrial cities that manage long-term contracts and host more diverse functions (for example banking), and (3) international cities from where the global maritime shipping sector is managed. These studies, however, are not based on a sound empirical assessment of the extent to which maritime APS are located in port cities. Port economic impact studies rarely detail which activities among APS are influenced in their location by port functions.

The location of maritime APS is the result of two opposing forces. First,

APS firms derive benefits from co-location with firms in port-industrial complexes, as physical proximity fosters the exchange of ideas and the building of trust. For example, an insurance company that specializes in marine terminals, vessels or storage facilities will have lower transaction costs and be able to monitor market demands closely if located in the port city. Second, APS located in a world city benefit from qualified labour as well as from relations with other APS firms. For instance, insurance products can be easily offered to port users from a world city at a distant location, with face-to-face contacts limited to occasional meetings in which representatives are flown in. For example, Lloyd's of London, the world's leading marketplace in maritime shipping insurances, forms the core of a highly spatially concentrated cluster in the City of London that facilitates international business relations in shipping, arbitration and insurance (Bennett 2001).

The extent to which port cities attract APS firms differs. Some ports are serviced completely by APS firms located elsewhere, while other port cities will attract more APS firms. Figure 1 shows our framework to empirically classify port cities in this respect. It shows the position of a port city in the world city hierarchy (in terms of specialized advanced producer services) on the horizontal axis and the volumes of commodities passing through the port on the vertical axis. *Load centres* are well positioned in GPN-GCC-GVCs because of heavy physical infrastructure, variety of transport (gateway) functions, regular shipping calls, large throughput volumes and substantial market share within a given port range (Hayuth 1981; Notteboom 1997). Agglomeration economies remained limited due to geographical remoteness or to the lock-in effect of pre-existing urban centres (Fujita and Mori 1996). On the other hand, *service centres* have important ranks in the hierarchy of WCNs thanks to successful agglomeration economies, although the initial advantage of water transport is no longer dominant. For such places, functions related to the physical transfer of goods are often limited due to lack of space, congestion, environmental concerns and the development of more sophisticated activities or central place functions.

In *port cities* and *world port cities,* urban and port functions coexist in relative harmony and interdependence. Port cities may attempt to evolve into load centres, service centres, or world port cities. On the one hand, general spatial processes related to the cyclical development of transport nodes, such as agglomeration or congestion, may be sufficient in some cases to explain the trajectory of port cities. On the other hand, specific territorial contexts, policies, and firm-specific factors and strategies may modify the general trend. For instance, following the collapse of the Socialist block in the early 1990s, important shipping line headquarters shifted from London to Hamburg (Ducruet 2006).

Figure 1: Analytical framework and port city typology.

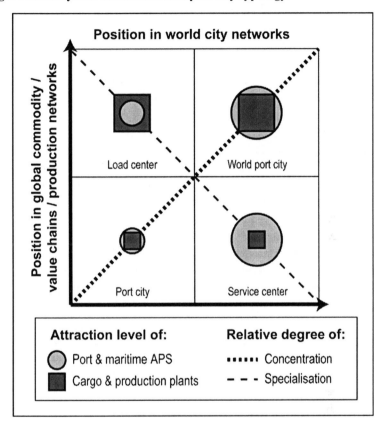

Source: realized by authors based on Ducruet and Lee (2006)

Based on the world shipping register[6] dataset, we map the location of the world's maritime advanced producer services. The choice of this database is motivated by its larger content and easier access compared with other maritime directories such as Lloyd's maritime directory or Fairplay's world shipping register. Among all activities included in the database presented in Appendix 1, the following port and transport related APS are discerned – insurance and law, consultancy and surveying, and maritime organizations.[7] The database covering approximately 9000 establishments of around 650 firms was refined by eliminating double counts and the few establishments without location infor-mation, resulting in a total of about 6500 establishments. Although we recognize that this dataset is incomplete, we believe that it is a valid representation of the spatial distribution of specialized APS activity. For these APS firms, we have located their headquarters and counted the number of (inter) national links in the form of intra-firm networks for every port city. We then compare these data with the conventional list of world cities as developed by the Globalization and World Cities Research Network (GaWC) (see Beaverstock et al. 1999; Derudder and Taylor 2005; Taylor et al. 2009). However, we have decided not to make a ranking by assigning rather arbitrary scores as in earlier WCN contributions. Instead, we stick to a simple headquarters–subsidiary approach (Alderson and Beckfield 2004; Rozenblat and Pumain 2007).

Next, we link these data with port throughput figures as an indication of position within commodity chains. This information is publicly available through websites, annual reports and port statistics on a national level. However, we were unable to obtain information on the added value of the port throughputs. These data are only available in individual cases, and the definition and calculation method of added value greatly differs from one port to another. The precise location of APS and throughput was maintained whenever possible based on jurisdictional limits of the port area. For instance, Los Angeles and Long Beach remain apart because they represent two different port jurisdictions. Although New York as a metropolis spreads across two different US states with marine terminals in New Jersey, there is only one port authority. By combining both data sources, we can see how port cities are positioned within the global flow of commodities and within the corporate networks of specialized advanced producer services.

Empirical results

The global picture of maritime and port-related APS

When we look at the global picture of maritime related APS, one of the clearest findings is the dominant position of London. In terms of maritime law and insurance (see Figure 2), for example, London has twice as many establishments and headquarters than New York, the second city on the list. In addition, London is set apart in terms of international links, especially with Hong Kong, Singapore, New York and Tokyo. Much of London's central and dominant position can be explained by historical and institutional factors. Most international contracts between shipowners, insurance companies and third parties have been based upon English law ever since 'Britannia rule[d] the waves'. History might also explain the strong establishments and connectedness of former British crown colonies Hong Kong and Singapore. These port cities are intensively connected with London but do not share significant relations with each other or with the rest of Asia.

Figure 2: Global network of P&I and maritime law offices

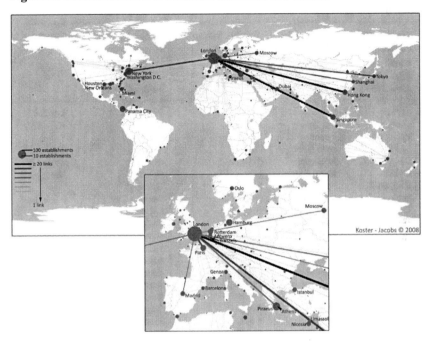

Source: derived from world shipping register 2008.

The position of Asian world cities within the protection and indemnity (P&I, marine insurance) and maritime law networks matches closely the conventional GaWC list (Taylor et al. 2009). As seen in Table 2, Singapore, Tokyo and Hong Kong are the leading cities in terms of APS in general as well as in this specific niche market. However, some cities that did not rank high in the GaWC research, such as Houston, Rotterdam, Panama City, Piraeus, Hamburg and Antwerp, clearly emerge as prime locations. This seems to prove the influence of a major seaport on the international connectedness of cities in terms of specialized advanced producer services. In the extreme cases of Panama City and Piraeus, this can be explained by the presence of crucial infrastructure or a flexible business environment for shipping (for example flag of convenience) in Panama and of a high concentration of ship owners in Piraeus. Our data also show the relatively strong position of some cities that do not have a seaport, such as Madrid, Moscow and Paris. This may be attributed to the dominance of the city in the national urban hierarchy and/or to centralist features of maritime related public administration.

Table 2: Ranking of world cities according the GaWC (2008) compared with port-city APS

The GaWC ranking of world cities 2008 (Taylor et al. 2009)	The ranking of port related APS cities	World cities of GaWC not included in top 40 port related APS city ranking	Port related APS cities not included in top 40 world cities GaWC ranking 2008	Overlap
ALPHA ++	London	Milan	Piraeus	London
London	Singapore	Warsaw	Rotterdam	New York
New York	Piraeus	Budapest	Hamburg	Tokyo
ALPHA +	New York	Zurich	Antwerp	Singapore
Hong Kong	Rotterdam	Toronto	Genoa	Shanghai
Paris	Hong Kong	Chicago	Houston	Hong Kong
Singapore	Hamburg	Sao Paulo	Dubai	Paris
Sydney	Panama City	Vienna	Panama City	Madrid
Tokyo	Houston	Caracas	Oslo	Brussels
Shanghai	Tokyo	Prague	Limassol	Washington
Beijing	Dubai	Amsterdam	New Orleans	Buenos Aires
ALPHA	Shanghai	Santiago	Valetta	Sydney
Milan	Antwerp	Rome	Alexandria	Istanbul
Madrid	Madrid	Taipei	Vancouver	Jakarta
Seoul	Mumbai	Dublin	Seattle	Auckland
Moscow	Limassol	Lisbon	Durban	Athens
Brussels	Oslo	Beijing	Cape Town	Miami
Toronto	Paris	Kuala Lumpur	Rio de Janeiro	Seoul
Mumbai	New Orleans	Stockholm	Manila	Mumbai
Buenos Aires	Istanbul	Mexico City		Bangkok
Kuala Lumpur	Genoa	Frankfurt		Moscow
ALPHA -	Sydney			
Warsaw	Miami			
Jakarta	Moscow			
Sao Paulo	Washington			
Zurich	Buenos Aires			
Mexico City	Valletta			
Dublin	Seoul			
Amsterdam	Jakarta			
Bangkok	Alexandria			
Taipei	Brussels			
Rome	Rio de Janeiro			
Istanbul	Athens			
Lisbon	Cape Town			
Chicago	Vancouver			
Frankfurt	Seattle			
Stockholm	Manila			
Vienna	Bangkok			
Budapest	Durban			
Athens	Auckland			
Prague				
Caracas				
Auckland				
Santiago				

Figure 3 presents the total picture of all maritime APS in our database (P&I and law, consultants and surveyors, and maritime organizations). The graph represents the hierarchy of cities by a measure of betweenness centrality within the intra-firm networks, which is defined by the number of possible shortest paths running through every node in the graph. The position of cities in the graph thus echoes their respective proportion of exclusive linkages with other cities and their relative importance in terms of decision functions. For example, London hosts 71 headquarters that control 479 establishments in 350 different cities. Most of these cities are only connected to a London-based headquarter, as seen in the number of smaller dots forming the tributary gravitational area of London in Figure 3. With reference to the GaWC results, London can be said to be the world's maritime cluster nucleus.

Figure 3: Graph of intra-firm links among cities connected through maritime APS (Derived from World Shipping Register, based upon TULIP software)

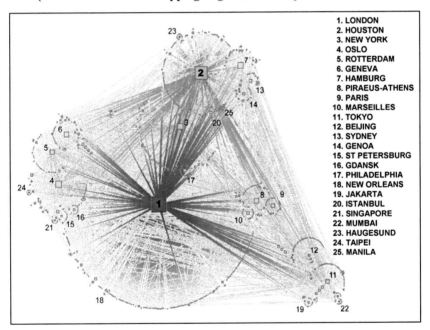

1. LONDON
2. HOUSTON
3. NEW YORK
4. OSLO
5. ROTTERDAM
6. GENEVA
7. HAMBURG
8. PIRAEUS-ATHENS
9. PARIS
10. MARSEILLES
11. TOKYO
12. BEIJING
13. SYDNEY
14. GENOA
15. ST PETERSBURG
16. GDANSK
17. PHILADELPHIA
18. NEW ORLEANS
19. JAKARTA
20. ISTANBUL
21. SINGAPORE
22. MUMBAI
23. HAUGESUND
24. TAIPEI
25. MANILA

At the same time, other regional cores such as Houston, New York, Oslo and Rotterdam also possess a dedicated network of subsidiaries while being strongly connected with London. Thus, the hierarchy of cities is closely related with the number of establishments under control. Compared with Figure 2, which is based on absolute scores, Singapore and Hong Kong are less important because most of their establishments are controlled from external headquarters. Smaller cities such as Haugesund (Norway), St Petersburg (Russia), and Gdansk (Poland) score better, because they act as subcluster nuclei in the Scandinavian and Baltic regions respectively. Shanghai may have many connections with other leading APS centres in absolute terms, but in relative terms it acts as a regional location for foreign-based companies. The Chinese network gravitates around Beijing due to its role as political and administrative centre. Another important dimension in the graph is the closeness of some clusters that are in reality geographically distant from each other. In Figure 3 for instance, Haugesund is located in the vicinity of the Houston cluster, probably due to the focus on oil products. In the next section, we look at how the centres of specialized maritime advanced producer services perform in terms of the physical flows of commodities.

Relation with commodity flows

Total annual throughput volume per port (in metric tons) is used as a measure of port activity.[8] Total volume was preferred to container volume because total tonnage includes the wide variety of cargoes introduced in Table 1, while containers remain a 'black box' of which the content of shipments is not known.

There is no straightforward relation between APS establishments and throughput tonnage (we do not observe noticeable correlations, cf. Table 3). While larger ports have generally more APS than smaller ports, cities with more APS by no means have more cargo throughput.

Table 3: Correlations between maritime APS and port tonnage

Method	Throughput ranking		APS ranking	
RAW DATA	Top 10 ports	0.431	Top 10 APS	-0.077
	Top 20 ports	0.310	Top 20 APS	0.129
	Top 30 ports	0.308	Top 30 APS	0.266
	Top 50 ports	0.444	Top 50 APS	0.367
	All ports	**0.309**	**All APS**	**0.299**
LOG DATA	Top 10 ports	0.288	Top 10 APS	0.053
	Top 20 ports	0.150	Top 20 APS	0.263
	Top 30 ports	0.278	Top 30 APS	0.359
	Top 50 ports	0.158	Top 50 APS	0.336
	All ports	**0.304**	**All APS**	**-0.113**

Figure 4: Port traffic volume and importance of maritime APS establishments

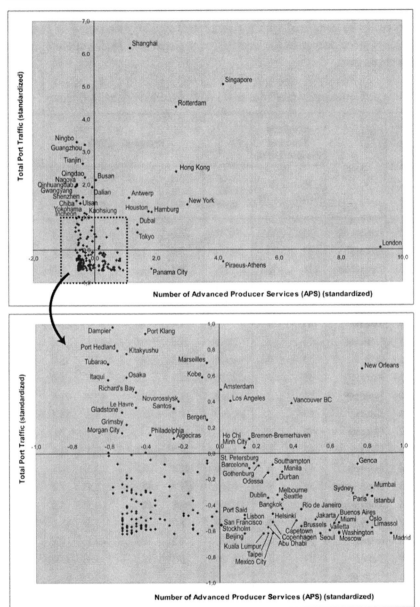

Sources: derived from world shipping register, 2008; Eurostat, 2008; AAPA, 2008; port authorities.

In order to plot port cities in the framework given in Figure 1, we standardize the data using z-scores to compare the distributions. Figure 4 provides an overview of the position of port cities on the two dimensions and can easily be compared with the conceptual typology presented in Figure 1. Table 4 goes deeper in the analysis of regional and local variations in the European case.

Table 4: Commodity traffic at main APS concentrations in Europe

Rank	City	Advanced Producer Services (APS)		Port traffic (2006)					
		No. Establ.	No. HQs	Total (000' tons)	Solid bulk (%)	Liquid bulk (%)	General cargo (%)	Ro-ro (%)	Con-tainers (%)
1	London	386	71	51,911	26.6	36.8	7.2	17.4	12.0
2	Piraeus	187	14	19,959	1.9	1.3	0.4	26.9	69.5
3	Rotterdam	128	10	353,576	24.2	49.0	2.8	3.0	20.9
4	Hamburg	97	8	115,529	24.9	12.3	2.0	0.3	60.5
5	Antwerp	68	2	151,704	16.9	24.9	12.0	3.6	42.6
6	Madrid	60	7	-	-	-	-	-	-
7	Limassol	56	8	3,533	11.1	0.0	12.1	7.4	69.3
8	Oslo	55	8	6,410	26.7	31.9	5.3	19.9	16.3
9	Paris	55	6	22,256	81.1	2.9	11.5	0.6	3.8
10	Istanbul*	53	5	7,834	6.3	0.0	49.8	11.8	27.7
11	Genoa	53	3	40,619	6.8	45.7	3.3	15.3	28.9
12	Moscow	49	5	-	-	-	-	-	-
13	Valletta	47	0	1,992	27.7	48.8	6.4	11.1	5.7
14	Brussels	41	0	4,200	52.8	28.8	15.5	0.0	2.8
15	Copenhagen	35	4	6,896	33.7	43.0	2.5	5.8	15.0
16	Southampton	35	2	40,557	5.6	69.6	0.3	3.8	20.6
17	Helsinki	35	0	11,669	8.9	3.8	7.5	48.1	31.7
18	Odessa	34	2	28,009	0.2	46.1	40.1	0.6	13.2
19	Dublin	34	1	20,796	9.9	19.5	1.5	43.0	26.0
20	Gothenburg	32	2	39,912	0.6	52.5	0.2	30.1	16.6

Source: realized by authors based on Eurostat (2008) and port authorities' websites.
*Traffic shares for Istanbul are calculated on quay length due to lack of data.

Figure 4 shows that there are only a few true world port cities, namely locations that are both leading nodes in commodity flows and centres of specialized maritime APS. The *world port cities* are Singapore, Rotterdam, Hong Kong, Hamburg, Houston, New York, Dubai, Tokyo, Antwerp and Shanghai. To a lesser extent, we can identify cities such as New Orleans, Vancouver, Amsterdam, Bremen-Bremerhaven, Los Angeles and Ho Chi Minh City. As mentioned, London is a special case, since it dominates in APS establishments, but its port does not handle much traffic. The *service centres* are port cities with strong positions within APS networks but not within the physical flows of goods. Some of these maritime centres do not have a port at all,[9] most notably Mexico City DF, Madrid, Kuala Lumpur, Beijing, Taipei, Seoul and Moscow. Leading service centres are Piraeus, Panama City, Genoa, Istanbul, Limassol and Oslo. Some other service centres have a more balanced profile due to the larger throughput volumes: Southampton, Barcelona, Manila, Genoa, Gothenburg, and St Petersburg.

Our data also clearly identify *load centres*, or port cities with a strong position in commodity flows but with a weak position in advanced producer services. One group is dominantly Asian. The Asian profile of the world's load centres is not a surprise, given the rise of manufacturing in China and Southeast Asia, resulting in tremendous traffic growth since the 1970s. Another explanation for why these port cities score weak on APS is evolutionary: they have only developed during the 1990s as growth poles with a strong dependency on established urban areas for advanced services. Load centres such as Ningbo (China), Chiba (Japan) and Shenzhen (China) may use APS located in service centres or in their respective world port cities of Shanghai, Tokyo and Hong Kong.

Another type of load centre is composed of dedicated terminals near mining regions, as in Australia (for example Dampier, Port Hedland) or Brazil (for example Tubarao, Itaqui) for exporting specific commodities. A third group are gateways to inland urban concentrations located at the head of mass freight corridors, such as Port Klang (Kuala Lumpur), Le Havre (Paris) and Santos (Sao Paulo). The final group consists of port cities that do not excel in advanced producer services or handle enormous traffic volumes. These port cities are often second-order cities in their national urban system (for example Valencia, Liverpool, Trieste and Constanta) that handle relatively limited cargo throughputs. In evolutionary terms, these port cities may have dropped down the hierarchy of cargo throughput and/or APS due to a variety of factors such as congestion, lack of space and changing trade patterns, as seen in the cases of Liverpool and Baltimore.

A more detailed picture may be obtained from the comparison of rank in the APS hierarchy and distribution of commodity shares in total port traffic by port city (Table 4). Northern range port cities such as Rotterdam, Hamburg and Antwerp rank high as locations of APS due to the presence of a strong port cluster embedding local and global industries with the port function. The higher share of roll on, roll off (ro-ro or automotive goods) traffic in some national capitals (for example Helsinki, Dublin, Piraeus and Oslo) reflects the importance of passenger traffic and short-sea shipping rather than automotive chains. The specialization in container traffic shows the importance of the distribution and logistics function of some port cities such as Hamburg and Antwerp, which create value locally through warehousing and other ancillary services. The importance of container traffic in the south (for example Piraeus and Limassol) is better explained by transshipment activities that do not create much added value locally, because containers are simply shifted from one vessel to another across the terminal.

These data suggest the absence of a direct relation between traffic specialization and rank in APS hierarchy. Ports exert various functions on different scales, responding to the need of the local, regional and international economy. Commodity specialization illustrates only partially local industry specialization and insertion in particular value chains. Nevertheless, it is interesting to measure to what extent the activity of an entire port depends on a certain commodity, because traffic itself is a unique measure of the insertion of ports into Global Production Networks.

Conclusions

On the basis of our conceptual analysis, we developed a topology of locations that are firmly inserted in international physical commodity chains and that serve as centres of specialized advanced producer services. It is clear that there is a weak relation between commodity flow patterns in ports and APS firm localization in port cities. This is probably because these two different activities, although they historically and spatially co-evolved within port cities, are fuelled by different logics. Specialized APS tend to agglomerate near other APS service providers along the (global) urban hierarchy instead of in the proximity of the commodity flows that move through ports. This is certainly the case for London and for other world cities such as New York, Singapore and Hong Kong. The concentration of maritime APS firms within non-port cities such as Madrid, Moscow and Paris supports this argument: these specialized APS agglomerate on the basis of something other than commodity flows, like proximity to political-administrative units, APS services in general or proximity to customers (for example headquarters of shipowners). This seems to suggest a spatial division of labour in which port-maritime advanced services are spatially disconnected from the global flow of commodities that it supports.

On the other hand, we can identify some specific cases such as Rotterdam, Houston and Hamburg where the concentration of physical flows coincides with the location of specialized APS functions, despite the relatively low ranking of these cities in conventional WCN rankings. This suggests co-location benefits of maritime APS with economic activities in Global Commodity Chains. The development of the position of port cities in specialized APS networks is influenced by these opposing forces. This inconclusive statement calls for more empirical research in which the following methodological issues should be taken into account. We were not able, due to the lack of more detailed data on commodity-specific APS, to identify location patterns of APS specialized in a particular commodity chain. For example, the port cities of Rotterdam, Singapore and Houston have a dominant position within the commodity chains of crude oil and may thus be home to many APS specialized in oil/energy. In addition, we were unable to identify the urban economic impact of being a maritime APS centre. The question remains of how many jobs maritime APS generate within specific port cities or how much value is added by APS along the chain. However, our results indicate that some port cities attract more APS than predicted by their position in the WCN hierarchy. Further exploration of the influence of local port clusters on the international position of port cities within WCN and GPN hierarchies is needed. A third point of attention is the time factor. In this study we have presented a static global picture, but it would be interesting to identify how certain patterns evolve over time. For example, the contemporary strong position of Dubai in terms of APS must be related to the emirate's rapid urban economic growth over the last two decades.

Future research should take into account these points of attention. Further studies that focus on a particular commodity and a specific local context should shed more light on the role of specialized advanced producer services within Global Production Networks. This should be done by case-specific analysis in which both local APS and port-transport related activities are confronted with their degree of inter-firm interaction and the local spillover that occurs in terms of employment, value creation and knowledge diffusion. It will also allow us to include specific institutional features into the analysis as well as to assess the role of strategic policy and government agencies in shaping the development paths of port cities in the global economy. Some methodological issues may be addressed, such as an analysis based on morphological and/or functional criteria defining port cities based on port jurisdictions or functional economic areas. Traffic data in this study should be complemented with container traffic, as it constitutes the most valuable cargo passing through seaports. In addition, research may benefit from further application of social network analysis through graph visualization and the use of clustering techniques to highlight the cliquishness of port cities within geographical and/or functional regions of the world.

Appendix 1: Overview of world shipping register data

Activity	Number of establishments
Bunkerer	652
Consultants, surveyors	**3,122**
Marine Equipment	10,738
Maritime organization	**2,949**
Other	2,480
Owner, manager	106,369
P&I, insurance, law	**2,851**
Pilotage	103
Port agent	5,615
Port authority	3,727
Port service	5,667
Ship broker	2,189
Ship chandler	836
Ship builder, repairer	8,940
Towage, salvage	789
TOTAL	146,749

Acknowledgements

The authors would like to thank Hans Koster for his contribution to data collection and cartography. The authors are thankful for the insightful comments by three anonymous reviewers. An earlier draft of this manuscript had been made available as Research Bulletin 298 on the Globalization and World Cities Research Network (GaWC) website. The usual caveats apply.

Notes

1. We recognize that both schools have drawn inspiration from works that date back farther. In the case of WCN, reference is often made to Geddes (1924) and Hall (1966), who have used the term 'world city' in a different historical context. In the case of GPN, much inspiration is drawn from Granovetter (1985) on the 'social embeddedness' of rational economic behaviour. Here, we primarily refer to Castells (1996) as a shared source to summarize the importance of 'networks', both in the metaphorical and material sense, that underpin the economic geography of the global economy and its conceptualizations (see Dicken et al. 2001).

2. Note that our approach to the sector-specificity of APS firms differs from that of Beaverstock et al. (2002). Our focus is on the inter-sectoral specialization of APS (for example the insurance of ships instead of real estate) as opposed to the specific structure of certain sectors where certain APS activities take place (for example the insurance sector). Our approach is more in line with that of Jane Jacobs (1969).

3. As mentioned by Coe et al. (2008: 6). 'In fact, with the vastly increased complexity and geographical extensiveness of production networks ... the logistics problem is absolutely central. We need to understand it. And, yet it is virtually ignored outside the specialist technical world of supply chain management.'

4. Port cities are historically commercial centres with considerable geo-economic and political power. During the 1600s, a banking system emerged in cities such as Venice, Amsterdam and London around the commodity trade through these seaports (O'Connor 1989). Over the last two centuries the location of these financial and trade-related economic activities has become more dispersed.

5. Port regions often struggle to upgrade and diversify their economy. Recent studies confirm that industrial port regions underperform in terms of traffic growth compared with port regions where the service sector is relatively strong (Ducruet 2009). Furthermore, de Langen (2007) shows that the growth of cargo volumes in US ports does not automatically lead to good regional economic performance (see also Grobar 2008).

6. Available at http://e-ships.net/ accessed between May and September 2008.

7. WCN usually also discern other types of APS such as ICT, banking, marketing and accountancy. We have not included these types in our study for two reasons. First, we believe that there is limited sector-specific specialization among these types of APS. Second, these types are not included in the world shipping register database.

8. Data were extracted from Eurostat, the Association of American Port Authorities, and from various port authorities' websites.

9. The traffic of these inland cities was counted as zero.

References

Amato, D. (1999) 'Port planning and port/city relations', *The Dock and Harbor Authority*, July-December, 45–8.

Alderson, A. S. and J. Beckfield (2004) 'Power and position in the world city system', *American Journal of Sociology*, 109, 811–51.

Beaverstock, J. V., P. J. Taylor and R. G. Smith (1999) 'A roster of world cities', *Cities*, 16 (6), 445–58.

Beaverstock, J. V, R. G. Smith and P. J. Taylor (2000) 'World City Network: a new metageography?', *Annals of the Association of American Geographers*, 90 (1), 123–34.

Beaverstock, J. V., M. A. Doel, P. J. Hubbard, and P. J. Taylor (2002) 'Attending to the world: competition, cooperation and connectivity in the World City Network', *Global Networks*, 2 (2), 111–32.

Bird, J. (1963) *The major seaports of the United Kingdom*, London: Hutchinson.

Bennett, P. (2001) 'Mutual risk: P&I insurance clubs and maritime safety and environmental performance', *Marine Policy*, 25 (1), 13–21.

Brenner, N. and R. Keil (eds) (2006) *The global cities reader*, London: Routledge.

Brooks, M. and K. Cullinane (eds) (2007) *Devolution, port governance and performance*, Dordrecht: Elsevier.

Brown, E., B. Derudder, C. Parnreiter, W. Pelupessy, P. J. Taylor and F. Witlox (2010) 'World City Networks and Global Commodity Chains: towards a world systems integration, *Global Networks*, 10 (1), 12–34.

Carbone, V. and M. De Martino (2003) 'The changing role of ports in supply-chain management: an empirical analysis', *Maritime Policy and Management*, 30 (4), 305–20.

Castells, M. (1996) *The rise of the network society. The information age: economy, society and culture*, Oxford: Blackwell.

Coe, N. M., M. Hess, H. W-c. Yeung, P. Dicken and J. Henderson (2004), 'Globalizing regional development: a global networks perspective', *Transactions of the Institute of British Geographers*, 29, 468–84.

Coe, N. M., P. Dicken and M. Hess (2008) 'Global Production Networks: realizing the potential', *Journal of Economic Geography*, 8 (3), 271–95.

Choi, J. H., G. A. Barnett and B. S. Chon (2006) 'Comparing World City Networks: a network analysis of Internet backbone and air transport intercity linkages', *Global Networks*, 6 (1), 81–99.

Derudder, B. (2006) 'On conceptual confusion in empirical analyses of a transnational network', *Urban Studies*, 43 (11), 2027–46.

Derudder, B. and P. J. Taylor (2005) 'The cliquishness of world cities', *Global Networks*, 5 (1), 71–91.

Derudder, B. and F. Witlox (2005) 'An appraisal of the use of airline data in assessing the World City Network: a research note on data', *Urban Studies*, 42 (13), 2371–88.

Dicken, P. (2004) 'Geographers and globalization: (yet) another missed boat?', *Transactions of the Institute of British Geographers*, 29 (5), 5–26.

Dicken, P., P. F. Kelly, K. Olds and H. W-c. Yeung (2001) 'Chains and networks, territories and scales: towards a relational framework for analysing the global economy', *Global Networks*, 1 (2), 89–112.

Ducruet, C. (2006) 'Port–city relationships in Europe and Asia', *Journal of International Logistics and Trade*, 4 (1), 13–35.

Ducruet, C. (2009) 'Port regions and globalization', in T. E. Notteboom, C. Ducruet, and P. W. de Langen (eds) *Ports in proximity: competition and cooperation among adjacent seaports*, Aldershot: Ashgate.

Ducruet, C. and S. W. Lee (2006) 'Frontline soldiers of globalization: port-city evolution and regional competition', *GeoJournal*, 67 (2), 107–22.

Ernst, D. and L. Kim (2002) 'Global Production Networks, knowledge diffusion and local capability formation', *Research Policy*, 31 (8/9), 1417–29.

Feenstra, R. C. (1998) 'Integration of trade and disintegration of production in the global economy', *Journal of Economic Perspectives*, 12 (4), 31–50.

Friedmann, J. (1986) 'The world city hypothesis', *Development and Change*, 17 (1), 69–83.

Fröbel, F., J. Heinrichs and O. Kreye (1980) *The new international division of labour*, Cambridge: Cambridge University Press.

Fujita, M. and T. Mori (1996) 'The role of ports in the making of major cities: self-agglomeration and hub-effect', *Journal of Development Economics*, 49 (1), 93–120.

Geddes, P. (1924) 'A world league of cities', *Sociological Review*, 26, 166–7.

Gereffi, G. and M. Korzeniewicz (eds) (1994) *Commodity chains and global capitalism*, Westport: Praeger.

Gereffi, G., J. Humphrey and T. Sturgeon (2005) 'The governance of Global Value Chains', *Review of International Political Economy*, 12 (1), 78–104.

Grobar, L. M. (2008) 'The economic status of areas surrounding major US container ports: evidence and policy issues', *Growth and Change*, 39 (3), 497–516.

Granovetter, M. (1985) 'Economic action and social structure: the problem of embeddedness', *American Journal of Sociology*, 91 (3), 481–510.

Hall, P. (1966) *The world cities*, London: Heinemann.

Hall, P. V. (2007), Seaport, urban sustainability and paradigm shift, *Journal of Urban Technology*, 12, 87–101.

Hall, P. V. and G. Robbins (2007) 'Which link in which chain? Inserting Durban into global automotive chains', in J. J. Wang, D. Olivier, T. E. Notteboom and B. Slack (eds) *Inserting port cities in global supply chains*, Aldershot: Ashgate, 221–31.

Hayuth, Y. (1981) 'Containerisation and the load centre concept', *Economic Geography*, 57 (2), 160–76.

Henderson, J., P. Dicken, N. M. Coe and H. W-c. Yeung (2002) 'Global Production Networks and the analysis of economic development', *Review of International Political Economy*, 9 (3), 436–64.

Hess, M. and H. W-c. Yeung (2006) 'Whither Global Production Networks in economic geography? Past, present and future', Guest editorial, theme issue on Global Production Networks, *Environment and Planning A*, 38 (7), 1193–204.

Hesse, M. (2010) 'Cities, material flows and the geography of spatial interaction: urban places in the system of chains', *Global Networks*, 10 (1), 75–91.

Hoyle, B. S. (1989) 'The port-city interface: trends, problems and examples', *Geoforum*, 20 (4), 429–35.

Humphrey, J. and H. Schmitz (2002) 'How does insertion in Global Value Chains affect upgrading in industrial clusters?', *Regional Studies*, 36 (9), 1017–27.

Jacobs, J. (1969) *The economy of cities*, New York: Vintage.

Jacobs, W. (2007) *Political economy of port competition: institutional analyses of Rotterdam, southern California and Dubai*, Nijmegen: Academic Press Europe.

Jacobs, W. and P. V. Hall (2007) 'What conditions supply chain strategies of ports? The case of Dubai', *GeoJournal*, 68 (4), 327–42.

Kaplinsky, R. (2004) 'Spreading the gains from globalization. What can be learned from value-chain analysis?', *Problems of Economic Transition*, 47 (2), 74–115.

Knox, P. and P. J. Taylor (eds) (1995) *World cities in a world system*, Cambridge: Cambridge University Press.

Langen, P. W. de (2003) *The performance of seaport clusters*, Rotterdam: ERIM.

Langen, P. W. de (2007) 'The economic performance of seaport regions', in J. J. Wang, D. Olivier, T. E. Notteboom and B. Slack (eds) *Ports, cities and global supply chains*, Aldershot: Ashgate, 187–202.

Levinson, M. (2006) *The box: how the shipping container made the world smaller and the world economy bigger*, Princeton: Princeton University Press.

Lüthi, S., A. Thierstein and V. Goebel (2010) 'Intra-firm and extra-firm linkages in the knowledge economy: the case of the emerging mega-city region of Munich', *Global Networks*, 10 (1), 114–37.

Notteboom, T. E. (1997) 'Concentration and the load center development in the European container port system', *Journal of Transport Geography*, 5 (2), 99–115.

O'Connor, K. (1989) 'Australian ports, metropolitan areas and trade-related services', *The Australian Geographer*, 20 (2), 167–72.

Rimmer, P. J. (1999) 'The Asia-Pacific Rim's transport and telecommunications systems: spatial structure and corporate control since the mid-1980s', *Geojournal*, 48 (1), 43–65.

Robinson, R. (2002) 'Ports as elements in value-driven chain systems: the new paradigm', *Maritime Policy and Management*, 29 (3), 241–55.

Rozenblat, C. and D. Pumain (2007), 'Firm linkages, innovation and the evolution of urban systems', in P. J. Taylor, B. Derudder, P. Saey and F. Witlox (eds) *Cities in globalization: practices, policies and theories*, London: Routledge, 130–56.

Sassen, S. (1991) *The global city: New York, London, Tokyo*, Princeton: Princeton University Press.

Slack, B. (1989) 'Port services, ports and the urban hierarchy', *Tijdschrift voor Economische en Sociale Geografie*, 80 (4), 236–43.

Smith, D. A. and M. Timberlake (1995) 'Cities in global matrices: toward mapping the world-systems' city system', in P. L. Knox and P. J. Taylor (eds) *World cities in a world-system*, Cambridge: Cambridge University Press, 79–97.

Taylor, P. J. (1997) 'Hierarchical tendencies amongst world cities: a global research proposal', *Cities*, 14 (6), 323–32.

Taylor, P. J. (2004) *World City Networks: a global urban analysis*, London: Routledge.

Taylor, P. J., P. Ni, B. Derudder, M. Hoyler, J. Huang, F. Lu, K. Pain, F. Witlox, X. Yang, D. Bassens and W. Shen (2009) 'Measuring the World City Network: new developments and results', *GaWC Research Bulletin*, 300.

Wang, J. J. and D. Olivier (2006) 'Port-FEZ bundles as spaces of global articulation: the case of Tianjin, China', *Environment and Planning A*, 38 (8), 1487–503.

Wang, J. J., D. Olivier, T. Notteboom and B. Slack (eds) (2007) *Ports, cities and global supply chains*, Aldershot: Ashgate.

7

Intra-firm and extra-firm linkages in the knowledge economy: the case of the emerging mega-city region of Munich

STEFAN LÜTHI, ALAIN THIERSTEIN AND VIKTOR GOEBEL

Globalization has entailed a reorganization of spatial development processes on the global, European, national and regional scales. New forms of hierarchical and network development and functional differentiation between cities can be observed (Friedmann 1986; Sassen 2001). Scott (2001) and, lately, Hall and Pain (2006) argue that cities cannot be separated from their regional hinterlands as they often compose a functional division of labour in terms of different kinds of services and value chains among firms. Hence, the traditional hierarchical model of a core city dominating its urban hinterland is becoming increasingly obsolete. Instead, a process of selective decentralization of particular urban functions, and the simultaneous recon-centration of others, has led to the emergence of polycentric mega-city regions (Kloosterman and Musterd 2001; Lüthi et al. 2008; Thierstein et al. 2008). This emerging urban form is spread out over a large area containing a number of cities more or less within commuting distance, and one or more international airports that link the region with other parts of the world (Hoyler et al. 2008b).

Different attempts have been made to handle these extended urban regions analytically, and a variety of research projects and publications concerned with polycentricity at the city-regional scale has been realized (for example ESPON 2004; Hall and Pain 2006; Hoyler et al. 2006; Hoyler et al. 2008a; Thierstein et al. 2006). Furthermore, a number of labels have been used to denote the identified new metropolitan form (Hoyler et al. 2008b); for instance polycentric urban regions (Kloosterman and Musterd 2001), global city-regions (Scott 2001) or – as in this chapter – mega-city regions (Hall and Pain 2006). The main objective of this chapter lies in the exploration of the mega-city region hypothesis through combining the World City Network research with a value chain approach. By analysing the two main pillars of the knowledge economy – advanced producer services (APS) and high-tech firms – we first look at how multi-location firms from the knowledge economy develop their intra-firm networks internationally. Second, we look for the partners with which these firms have working relationships along individual chains of value, and in which these extra-firm linkages are located. A case study in the greater Munich area provides the empirical basis drawing on both quantitative and qualitative research methods.

The chapter is structured in three main sections. The first section focuses on the concept of mega-city regions by discussing two associated theoretical approaches: World City Network and value chain models. In the second section we present the research concept and the main findings of our case study about the emerging mega-city region of Munich. And finally, in the third section, we conclude by synthesizing the main findings and proposing an agenda for further research activities.

Theoretical background

In this chapter, the emergence of polycentric mega-city regions is understood as a spatial phenomenon that results from two interdependent processes – World City Networking and value-added relations between knowledge intensive enterprises. In this respect, it is possible to differentiate between two streams of theoretical thinking, namely World City Network models and value chain models. Unfortunately, these literatures have developed quite independently and with little cross-referencing. In the following sections, the main arguments of the World City Network and the value chain models will be discussed with a view to showing their differences and similarities and relating them to the concept of emerging mega-city regions.

World City Network models

Much of world city research has been related to the emergence of a globally networked knowledge economy in which advanced producer services (APS) firms play a predominant role (Sassen 2001). In this respect, Saskia Sassen's global city approach is an important contribution. It provides a new geography of centrality in which city centres or central business districts form the heart of the global urban network. The functional centrality of these global cities leads to an increasing disconnection of city centres from their broader hinterlands or adjacent metropolitan region. The reason for this disconnecting process lies, according to Sassen, in the location strategies of APS firms as spearheads of the rising global knowledge economy. These enterprises are increasingly located just within the city centres of economic regions and connect these places directly with other city centres in the world.

In contrast to Saskia Sassen's global city approach, John Friedmann, with his concept of a world city, argues that the territorial basis of world cities comprises not only the central city but also the whole economic space of the surrounding region. Therefore, world cities are often polycentric urban regions containing a number of historically distinct cities that are located in more or less close proximity. This fundamental difference between John Friedmann's world cities and Saskia Sassen's global cities are well described by Derudder (2006: 2034):

> Sassen's focus on centrality leads her to conceptualising 'global cities' as focal points that operate separately from their hinterlands. Friedmann's focus on the relative concentration of power, in contrast, implies that a 'world city' may consist of multiple cities and their hinterlands that may themselves be subject to urbanisation processes.

Furthermore, John Friedmann describes the rise of a transnational urban network as a major geographical transformation of the capitalist world economy whose production systems are increasingly internationalized. This reconfiguration results in a new international division of labour whose main agents are multinational enterprises with complex spatial organizational structures. It is the presence of these multinational enterprises that makes world cities into geographical places of great economic power (Friedmann 1986).

Another heuristic framework about network cities is provided by Manuel Castells's highly influential concept of a space of flows. He (Castells 1996: 412) describes it as follows:

> Our societies are constructed around flows: flows of capital, flows of information, flows of technology, flows of organizational interactions, flows of images, sounds and symbols. ... Thus, I propose the idea that there is a new spatial form characteristic of social practices that dominate and shape the network society: the space of flows.

Castells argues that the new spatial logic is determined by the pre-eminence of the space of flows over the space of places. By space of flows he refers to the system of exchange of information, capital and power that structures the basic processes of societies, economies and states between different localities, regardless of localization.

While Friedmann and Castells offer a heuristic and theoretical framework on why globalization requires a networked conception of cities, with his World City Network approach Peter Taylor (2004) provides an empirical instrument for analysing inter-city relations in terms of the organizational structure of the global economy. With his team at Loughborough University – the Globalisation and World Cities Study Group (GaWC) – he analyses inter-city relations using a methodology in which relationships between cities are not measured directly. Instead, he uses a proxy by analysing the internal structures of large APS firms and revealing the relationships between head offices and other branches located all over the world. In this way he focuses on the distribution of branch offices of individual companies and assumes connectivity of locations by emphasizing the existence of a network in line with the idea of potential knowledge exchange between the branch offices.

However, as Thierstein et al. (2008) argue, this kind of approximation does not tell the whole story of the nature and quality of business activities between those different locations. Knowledge exchange and business activities arise not only through branch office networks, but also and primarily from the division of labour between different companies. In many cases, outsourcing strategies with respect to single activities are more efficient and lead to higher quality products and services. Many firms concentrate on their key competencies, which are produced in-house, while activities that do not belong to the core business are outsourced to other companies. Even networks between competitors open the opportunity for formal and informal knowledge exchange within the same field of business. To grasp these networks fully, it is necessary to analyse not only the connectivity within a single firm but also the value chain relations between different enterprises and sectors.

Furthermore, to tap the full potential of the World City Network approach, we propose to apply it not only to APS firms but also to high-tech enterprises. High-tech enterprises are also part of the knowledge economy. To understand the geographies of globalization processes in the knowledge economy, one has to account simultaneously for both the APS and the high-tech sectors because both of them are integral parts of mega-city region development. Krätke for example argues that in both the APS and high-tech sectors, which constitute the key sectors of an increasingly knowledge-based and innovation-driven economy, an ongoing process of selective spatial concentration in urban agglomerations and metropolitan regions leads to the development of strong cluster potentials, which raise the productivity and innovation capacity of these regional economic centres and contribute to an increase of work-places, particularly in these branches of industry (Krätke 2007: 4).

All in all, we argue that a value chain approach is well able to provide a complementary asset to World City Network models and helps to understand the changing nature of international trade and spatial industrial organization.

Value chain models

Studies from a range of disciplines show that the value chain approach has become much more prevalent and elaborate in the past ten years. Its argumentation starts form the notion of a value-added chain, as developed by international business scholars who have focused on the strategies of firms in the global economy. In its most basic form, a value-added chain is 'the process by which technology is combined with material and labour inputs, and then processed inputs are assembled, marketed, and distributed. A single firm may consist of only one link in this process, or it may be extensively vertically integrated' (Kogut 1985: 15). Hence, the key questions in this literature are which activities and technologies a firm keeps in-house and which should be outsourced to other firms, and where the various activities should be located (Gereffi et al. 2005).

A rich literature has evolved to explain how global industries are organized and governed (Coe et al. 2008a). Three sets of terminology have become especially prominent. An early, but still very active body of research exists on Global Commodity Chains (GCC), a term that Gary Gereffi has popularized in a large number of publications since 1994. The GCC framework pays particular attention to the powerful role that large retailers and highly successful branded merchandisers have come to play in the governance of global production and distribution.

In the last decade, however, transnational giants have changed quite dramatically, outsourcing many activities and developing strategic alliances with competitors. They have become less vertically integrated and more network-oriented (Wildemann 2003). As a consequence of these structural changes researchers at the Institute of Development Studies in Sussex have developed a second approach: the Global Value Chain (GVC) framework. In contrast to the GCC framework, the GVC approach attempts to delineate the varying governance structures both within and between different sectors (Coe et al. 2008a). Thereby, the value chain is understood as providing the full range of activities that firms and workers do to bring a product or a service from its conception to its end use and even beyond (Gereffi et al. 2005).

The third approach, finally, is the Global Production Network (GPN) framework, initially developed by researchers in Manchester (Henderson et al. 2002). GPNs can be defined as the globally organized nexus of interconnected functions and operations through which goods and services are produced, distributed and consumed (Coe et al. 2004). Thereby, the process of embeddedness, both territorially and within business networks is of great importance. Henderson et al. (2002) argue that the mode of territorial embeddedness or the degree of a GPN firm's commitment to a particular location is an important factor for value creation, enhancement and capture.

Although the GCC, GVC and GPN frameworks enable a focus on worldwide networks of production processes, there are some shortcomings that must be addressed by future research activities. First, the study of the actual geographies of value chains has remained relatively underdeveloped (Brown et al. this book). Coe et al. (2004) even argue that the Global Commodity Chain approach still remains preoccupied with the nation-state as the main geographical scale of analysis (for example OECD 2008; Tokatli et al. 2008). A second, more specific limitation in value chain research is that the empirical scope of analysis has mainly been concerned with a small number of primary commodities and industrial sectors (for example Hassler 2003; Palpacuer and Parisotto 2003; Pilat et al. 2008; Rothenberg-Aalami 2004) and pays little attention to APS enterprises. A third shortcoming, finally, is the fact that value chain research has an underdeveloped set of tools for the operationalization of the conceptual framework. There appears to be a strong preference for a qualitative interview-based approach at the expense of quantitative research methods (Jacobs et al. this book).

Even though there is little or no cross-referencing between the World City Network and the value chain literatures, they display a remarkable conceptual overlap. They both depict fundamental spatial models of flows (Brown et al. this book) and take economic globalization and the spatio-economic behaviour of firms as the holistic starting point of their analysis (Jacobs 2008). Besides these similarities, there are two major differences between them. The first concerns the information flow in firm networks. World city research focuses in particular on *intra-firm* networks of APS firms, whereas value chain models concentrate on *extra-firm* relationships and the global division of labour, value and power within the supply chains of goods (Jacobs 2008). The second difference concerns the geographical scale of investigation. Whereas the

World City Network focuses mainly on the *city* as a spatial analytical entity, the value chain model often remains preoccupied with the nation state as the geographical scale of analysis.

Emerging mega-city regions

Mega-city regions are not a completely new phenomenon. Jean Gottmann originally made similar observations as long ago as 1961 in his pioneering study of *Megalopolis: the urbanized Northeastern seaboard of the United States* (Gottmann 1961). A few years later, Sir Peter Hall (1966) observed that next to the traditional 'highly centralized giant city' there exists a 'polycentric type of metropolis'. This polycentric metropolis consists of 'a number of smaller, specialized, closely-related centres' and should be understood as 'a perfectly natural form, which has evolved over a period of history quite as long as the single metropolitan centre' (Hall 1966: 9). However, the most recent rediscovery of the concept has been in eastern Asia, in areas like the Pearl River Delta and Yangtze River Delta regions in China, the Tokaido (Tokyo-Osaka) corridor in Japan, and Greater Jakarta (Hall 1999; Scott 2001). Peter Hall and Kathy Pain emphasize its large-scale nature and developing polycentric structure by defining mega-city regions as:

> a series of anything between ten and 50 cities and towns physically separated but functionally networked, clustered around one or more larger central cities, and drawing enormous economic strength from a new functional division of labour. These places exist both as separate entities, in which most residents work locally and most workers are local residents, and as parts of a wider functional urban region connected by dense flows of people and information carried along motorways, high-speed rail lines and telecommunications cables.
>
> (Hall and Pain 2006: 3)

This definition is based on Friedmann's world city concept, which argues – in contrast to Saskia Sassen's global cities – that the territorial basis of world cities comprises not only the central city but also the entire economic space of the surrounding region. On a wider spatial scale, such polycentric systems are interlinked with other city regions forming European and global knowledge networks, as proposed by Peter Taylor's (2004) concept of the World City Network. The key point of this conception is that mega-city regions are not solely defined by simple attributes such as demographic size or physical settlement structures but as socio-economic relational processes linking regions to other cities and towns on different geographical scales.

Different attempts have been made to analyse the polycentric structure of emerging mega-city regions in Europe and Germany (for example, Krätke 2007; Krätke and Brandt 2009; Kujath 2005; Kujath and Schmidt 2007). One of the most recent empirical research activities is the INTERREG IIIB Study POLYNET – on the sustainable management of European polycentric mega-city regions (Hall and Pain (2006) provide a comprehensive illustration of the POLYNET results). POLYNET aimed to investigate the polycentricity of the following eight mega-city regions in northwest Europe and their current state of functional division of labour – Southeast England, the Paris region, central Belgium, the Dutch Randstad, Rhine-Main, RhineRuhr, northern Switzerland, and Greater Dublin (Hall 2007). With its seminal research project, POLYNET introduced a new way of looking at polycentric urban structures and hierarchies adopting Peter Taylor's World City Network approach on the mega-city region scale (Taylor et al. 2008). The study started from the premise that business service firms offer a strategic lens through which to examine intercity relations within and beyond larger urban regions, building theoretically on Saskia Sassen's (2001) identification of advanced producer services as crucial actors and outcomes of globalization and localization processes, on Manuel Castells's (1996) notion of a 'space of flows', and on Peter Taylor's (2004) concept of a 'World City Network' (Hoyler et al. 2008a). The POLYNET study advanced the theoretical debate on large polycentric urban regions on the basis of new empirical evidence from northwestern Europe. Its main conclusion is that polycentricity emerges as a scale-dependent phenomenon based on the coming together of various business service networks of different organizational architectures and scalar reach (Hoyler et al. 2006). The mega-city region, in its various guises, is becoming a more general phenomenon in advanced economies (Hoyler et al. 2008b).

The emerging mega-city region of Munich

In the following section – referring to the theoretical discussion above and to the argument of Thierstein et al. (2008) concerning the combination of the World City Network model with a value chain approach – we present our research concept and the main findings of a case study carried out in the greater Munich area. We thus extend the POLYNET approach by two important dimensions: first, we investigate not only APS enterprises but also high-tech firms, which form another important pillar of the knowledge economy, and not only in Germany. Second, we extend the analysis by also looking at extra-firm networks of knowledge-intensive enterprises along their individual chains of value added.

Main hypotheses

Starting from the theoretical and conceptual considerations discussed above, we propose three central hypotheses with respect to the greater Munich area. Referring to the mega-city region definition of Peter Hall and Kathy Pain (2006), the first hypothesis suggests that there is an emerging mega-city region of Munich defined as physically separated but functionally networked socio-economic space:

> *Hypothesis 1:* Secondary cities in proximity to Munich and Munich itself are linked together by interlocking networks of APS firms, defining the greater Munich area as an emerging polycentric mega-city region.

The second hypothesis suggests that knowledge-intensive business operations and flows are associated with a hierarchical polycentric pattern of urban development. The central question concerns the extent to which the functional urban hierarchy within the greater Munich area is associated with different sectors and scales of knowledge-intensive activities:

> *Hypothesis 2:* There is a steep functional urban hierarchy within the greater Munich area, with Munich as primary city in relation to international intra-firm connectivities; in terms of regional intra-firm connectivities, however, this functional urban hierarchy is less pronounced.

The third hypothesis understands the greater Munich area as a spatial system of socio-economic added value interconnecting different value chains of knowledge-intensive enterprises. Under these conditions, there is an elevated potential for the development of new products and services requiring upstream and downstream inputs and customers:

> *Hypothesis 3:* Extra-firm linkages of APS and high-tech firms tend to concentrate in the greater Munich area, which, as a consequence, is evolving into a high-grade localized system of value chains.

The study area

Munich is one of the most competitive metropolitan areas in Germany. Several companies operating at the global scale – such as Siemens, BMW and Allianz – have their headquarters or major offices in or around Munich. Universities and research institutions with excellent reputations contribute to a highly qualified labour market. In many rankings based on economic indicators and soft location factors Munich is the leading city in Germany. However, as in many other European cities, the greater Munich area is faced with urban sprawl, increasing traffic and criss-cross commuting patterns as well as increasing prices for real estate, especially in the core of the agglomeration (Lüthi et al. 2007).

The spatial expansion of economic networks over recent decades led to the emergence of a functional space of economic interrelations within the greater Munich area. It is important to recognize that this greater Munich area is not a clearly defined region but a spatial concept approximating a functional space of economic interrelations. Analysing this functional space is an explicitly explorative project involving a field that has hitherto received little attention in Germany. Notable exceptions are the POLYNET case studies on RheinRuhr (Knapp and Schmitt 2008; Schmitt and Knapp 2006) and Rhine-Main (Hoyler et al. 2008a).

However, for the quantitative analysis of our case study, it was necessary to decide on a working definition that delimits the greater Munich area in a pragmatic way. To define the outer borderline of the study region, we calculated the area that can theoretically be reached within a one-hour car journey from Munich city centre. This corresponds approximately to a radius of 70 km. This methodology is based on the GEMACA (Group for European Metropolitan Areas Comparative Analysis) approach using commuter data as functional criteria for the delimitation of metropolitan areas (GEMACA 1996). Within this 60-minute travel-to-work radius, the main analytical building blocks are constituted by nine functional urban areas (FUAs), as defined by the ESPON research project 111, with potential for polycentric development in Europe (ESPON 2004). These are München, Kaufbeuren, Garmisch-Partenkirchen, Rosenheim, Landshut, Freising, Regensburg, Ingolstadt and Augsburg (Figure 1). FUAs are defined as having an urban core of at least 15,000 inhabitants and over 50,000 in total population; the definition of the rings is based on 45-minute isochrones. Further details of the FUA delineation can be seen in the Annex Report D of the ESPON Project 111 (Schürmann 2004).

Figure 1: Area of the case study

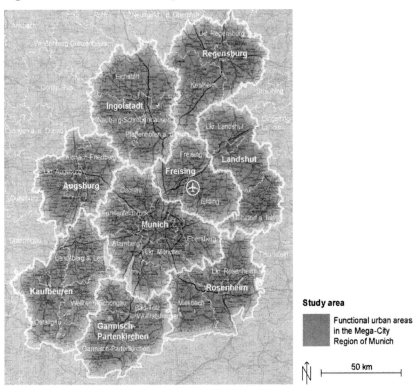

Study area

■ Functional urban areas in the Mega-City Region of Munich

⊢———— 50 km ————⊣

Source: authors' illustration.

Sampling strategy

In this case study, we analyse the location behaviour of knowledge-intensive enterprises focusing particularly on APS and high-tech firms. The sampling strategy follows a top–down approach in two steps. In the first step, the APS and high-tech sectors are operationalized on the basis of the international NACE (nomeclature générale des activités économiques) classification. For the APS sector, we basically adopted the operationalization used in the POLYNET study (Hall and Pain 2006) to effectuate direct comparisons. The empirical operationalization of the high-tech sector, however, is based on the Oslo manual of the OECD (OECD 2005) (Table 1).

In the second step, the sample of knowledge intensive firms whose intra-firm and extra-firm networks are analysed is defined. The firms have to meet four criteria: first, they have to belong to a knowledge-intensive economic

147

sector as defined above. Second, they have to belong to the largest knowledge-intensive firms in the mega-city region of Munich, measured my means of employment size. Third, they have to be multi-branch enterprises with at least one office location in the study area. Having met these conditions, firms are finally selected on the basis of the availability of information on their office networks. The result of this process was a basic set of 164 APS firms and 155 high-tech enterprises.

Table 1: Studied sectors, NACE codes in brackets

Advanced Producer Services (APS)	high-tech
accounting (7412)	chemistry & pharma (24)
insurance (66, 672)	machinery (29)
banking & finance (65, 671)	computer (30)
management & IT-consulting (72, 7413, 7414, 7415)	electrical machinery (31)
law (7411)	telecommunication (32)
logistics (3p & 4p) (6024, 611, 612, 621, 622, 631, 632, 634, 64)	medical & optical instruments (33)
design & architecture (742)	vehicle construction (34, 35)
advertising & media (744, 221, 921, 922, 924)	

Source: authors' compilation.

In identifying APS and high-tech firms within the emerging mega-city region of Munich, the data set from Hoppenstedt has been used. Hoppenstedt is one of the largest business data providers in Germany. Its database includes over 245,000 profiles of German companies, their branches and the major industrial associations in Germany. In order to take all FUAs and all branches adequately into account, we gathered additional information about important knowledge-intensive enterprises by checking websites of local and regional bodies and business associations.

148

The interlocking network model

The analysis of intra-firm networks is based on the methodology of the Globalisation and World Cities Study Group (GaWC) as used for the POLYNET study (Taylor et al. 2008). This approach estimates city connectivities from the office networks of multi-location multi-branch enterprises. The basic premise of this method is that the more important the office, the greater its flow of information will be to other office locations. The empirical work comprises two steps.

In a first step, we developed a so-called 'service activity matrix'. This matrix is defined by FUAs in the lines and knowledge-intensive firms in the columns. Each cell in the matrix shows a service value (v) that indicates the importance of an FUA to a firm. The importance is defined by the size of an office location and its function. By analysing the firms' websites from September 2006 to February 2007, all office locations are rated at a scale of 0 to 3. The standard value for a cell in the matrix is 0 (no presence) or 2 (presence). If there is a clear indication that a location has a special relevance within the firm network (for example headquarter, supra-office functions) its value is upgraded to 3. If the overall importance of a location in the firm-network is very low (for example small agency) the value is downgraded to 1.

In the second step, we used the interlocking network model established by Taylor (2004) to estimate connectivities between FUAs within and beyond the emerging mega-city region of Munich. The primary outputs of the interlocking network analysis are network connectivities, a measure that estimates how well connected a city is within the overall intra-firm network. There are different kinds of connectivity values. The connectivity between two FUAs (a, b) of a certain firm (j) is analysed by multiplying their service values (v) representing the so-called *elemental interlock* (r_{abj}) between two FUAs for one firm:

$$r_{abj} = v_{aj} * v_{bj} \qquad (1)$$

This approach seems reasonable when the following assumptions are made (see Derudder and Taylor 2005: 74–5). First, offices generate more flows within a firm's network than to other firms in their sector. This is inherently plausible in a context where protecting global brand image through providing seamless service is the norm. Second, the more important the office, the more flows are generated and these have a multiplicative effect on inter-city relations. The first part of this assumption is very plausible again. The second part reflects (i) the fact that larger offices with more practitioners have the capacity to create more potential dyads, and (ii) the hierarchical nature of office networks where larger offices have special functions like control and provision of specialized knowledge.

To calculate the total connectivity between two FUAs, one has to summarize the elemental interlock for all firms located in these two FUAs. This leads to the *city interlock* (r_{ab}):

$$r_{ab} = \sum r_{abj} \qquad (2)$$

Aggregating the city interlocks for a single FUA produces the *interlock connectivity* (N_a). This describes the importance of an FUA within the overall intra-firm network.

$$N_a = \sum r_{ai} \quad (a \neq i) \qquad (3)$$

Finally, if we relate the interlock connectivity for a given FUA to the FUA with the highest interlock connectivity, we gain an idea of its relative importance in respect to the other FUAs that have been considered.

The value chain approach

Extra-firm relationships have been analysed by means of an internet-based survey running from April to May 2007. The survey combines relational data on firm locations with the degree and importance of working interrelationships along individual firms' chain of value. The empirical analysis is based on 1800 APS and high-tech firms of the emerging mega-city region of Munich, whereas 258 enterprises have completed the survey satisfactorily. Hence, the rate of return is 14.3 per cent. The distribution of the numbers of companies questioned varies widely across the branches under study. With 15 per cent, companies in the area of machinery were the most frequent participants, followed by companies in management consulting and electrical machinery with 13 per cent. Companies in chemistry and pharmaceuticals, third and fourth party logistics, banking and finance, advertising and media, design and architecture, vehicle construction and the telecommunication sectors participated between 4 and 10 per cent. At 1 per cent and 2 per cent, accounting, computer, medical and optical instruments, insurance and law companies form the smallest groups.

The web survey comprised three sections. In the first section information is gathered about the firm's business location and the spatial range where they source inputs for their products from. In the second, the firms are asked to localize and assess the importance of their extra-firm relations to other APS and high-tech firms. And finally, in order to relate the extra-firm relationships to a stylized value chain, the responding firms have to localize their business activities along the individual value chain elements of 'research & development', 'processing', 'marketing', 'sales & distribution' and 'customers'. With this procedure, we obtained a comprehensive picture about the spatial value chain patterns of APS- and high-tech firms in the mega-city region of Munich on the global, European, national and regional scale.

Networks of knowledge in the emerging mega-city region of Munich

Let us now take a closer look at the empirical results. This will be done along the three hypothesis suggested above. First, we show how interlocking intra-firm networks of APS firms define an emerging polycentric mega-city region of Munich. Based on these intra-firm networks, we then present the functional urban hierarchy within the mega-city region referring to different geographical scales. And third, referring to the extra-firm analysis, we present the extent to which the mega-city region of Munich can be seen as a localized system of value chains.

The greater Munich area as an emerging polycentric mega-city region
The increasing importance of network economies has introduced new thinking about space, place and scale that interprets regions as unbounded, relational spaces. From a relational point of view, regions can be defined by their linkages and relations within and beyond their territorial boundaries (Pike 2007). The linkages of the knowledge economy in the greater Munich area are facing pronounced structural change due to the reorganization of its value chain, the emergence of new economic players and the outsourcing tendency within the APS and high-tech sector. This has implications for the spatial division of labour and the spatial organization of intra-firm networks. Figure 2 shows the spatial patterns of the intra-firm connectivity between APS firms on the regional scale. The thickness of the lines illustrates the total connectivity between two FUAs. These connectivity values are related to the highest interlock connectivity of the study area, which is the connection between Munich and Regensburg. This high value is because many APS firms have relatively important and therefore highly-rated locations in the cities of both Munich and Regensburg.

Figure 2: Intra-firm connectivity between APS firms at regional level

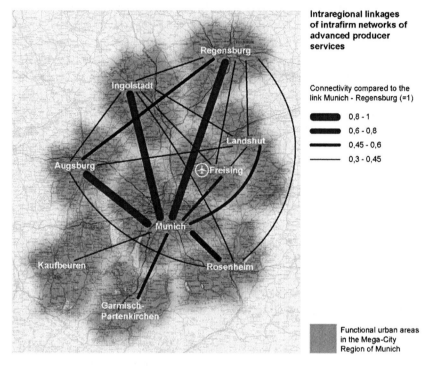

Source: authors' calculation.

The most important finding of Figure 2 is that the predominant part of intra-firm networks is located within the demarcation of what we have been labelling from the outset of our research as the emerging mega-city region of Munich. Since the FUAs within the study area are more closely linked with each other than with outlying FUAs, they begin to form a conglomerate of functionally linked FUAs that merits being labelled as 'emerging Mega-City Region of Munich'. The increasing complexity of network economies leads to a kind of paradox associated with this emergence. The inter-urban functional linkages are found to be extending and intensifying, while at the same time global functions are clustering and centralizing. While specialized global functions are concentrated in Munich itself, proximate FUAs are gaining complementary service functions. Interlocking networks of APS firms link these different agglomerations together, thus defining the emerging mega-city region of Munich as physically separated but functionally networked socio-economic space.

The greater Munich area as a hierarchical urban system

We shall now deal with the question of to what extent the greater Munich area can be understood as a hierarchical urban system. Figures 3 and 4 show the spatial dimension of the intra-firm connectivity for APS and high-tech firms on the national and international scale. For each FUA, the six most closely connected locations are listed. The thickness of the lines reflects the total international connectivity value of the FUAs created by intra-firm interlocking networks.

Figure 3: Intensity and ranking of connectivity values created by intra-firm networks of APS companies

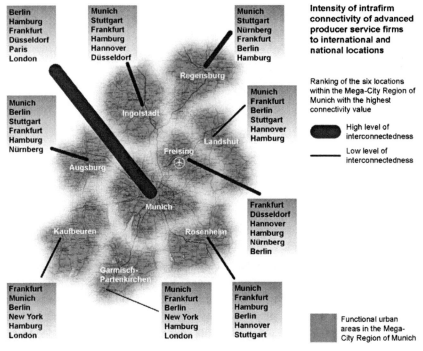

Source: authors' calculation.

Regarding the APS sector in Figure 3, Munich is most strongly linked with four large national cities (Berlin, Hamburg, Frankfurt and Düsseldorf) followed by Paris and London as the first European destinations. This is a surprising finding because it could be assumed that – in an increasingly globalized world – international linkages would be more important for the APS sector in Munich. Another interesting feature concerns the connectivities in the

Figure 4: Intensity and ranking of connectivity values created by intra-firm networks of high-tech companies

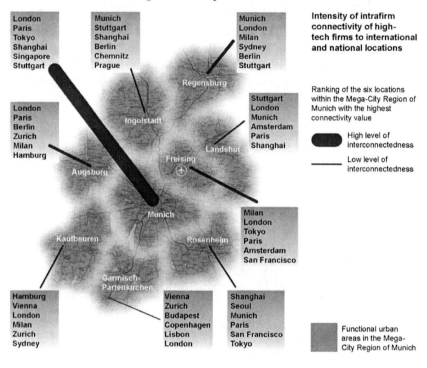

Source: authors' calculation.

secondary cities around Munich. Most of them are primarily connected to Munich, generally followed by further German locations. This means that APS firms in these locations mainly have offices in Munich or other national urban centres, whereas offices in European or even international locations are quite rare. Hence, in the case of APS interlocking networks, medium-sized and small urban centres in the greater Munich area are not directly integrated into international networks of knowledge-intensive economic activities. Instead, they are well integrated into large-scale regional networks of knowledge exchange. The city of Munich, however, is a central node and international gateway for smaller centres in the emerging mega-city region and acts as an important international knowledge-hub.

The globalization of intra-firm networks becomes particularly clear in the case of high-tech companies (Figure 4). Both, Munich and the surrounding secondary FUAs are dominated by international and national connectivities.

The reason for this lies in the physical fragmentation of production whereby the various stages are optimally located across different sites as firms find it advantageous to source more of their inputs globally. This finding is supported by an OECD (2008) study, showing that high-tech and medium-high tech industries are on average more internationalized than less technology-intensive industries or service sectors. However, as we shall see in the next section, the globalization of intra-firm networks does not mean that geographical proximity is unimportant. De Backer and Basri (2008) for example show that location decisions for research and development facilities are not only based on the host country's technological infrastructure, but also on the presence of other firms and institutions that may create spillover benefits that investing firms can absorb. In a similar way, Simmie (2003) argues that knowledge intensive firms combine a strong local knowledge capital base with high levels of connectivity to similar regions in the international economy. By doing so they are able to combine and decode both codified and tacit knowledge originating from multiple regional, national and international sources.

Another way to show the hierarchical polycentric pattern within the greater Munich area is to plot the connectivity values in a graph. Figure 5 shows the functional urban hierarchy for both the global and the regional scale and for the APS and high-tech sector. On the X-axis, there are the nine FUA, which have been under investigation. On the Y-axis, the connectivity values relative to the FUA of Munich are displayed. A strongly concave curve progression indicates a steep functional urban hierarchy, whereas a strongly convex progression shows a flat functional urban hierarchy indicating a rather pronounced functional polycentricity within the mega-city region.

The results show considerable differences between the two geographical scales. On the global level, the gap between Munich and the other FUAs of the mega-city region is remarkably wide. That means that small FUAs are less integrated in global intra-firm networks of APS and high-tech firms. On the regional level, however, the secondary cities reach a considerable portion of the connectivity value of Munich. On this geographical scale, the functional urban hierarchy is clearly less pronounced. Generally speaking, the larger the geographical scale of intra-firm networks is, the higher the significance of the FUA of Munich gets in comparison with its surrounding secondary cities.

In the framework of the POLYNET study, similar results are found for the APS sector in Germany's Rhine-Main region, which encompasses the cities of Frankfurt am Main, Wiesbaden and Mainz, but extending widely outwards as far as Hanau and Aschaffenburg in the east and Darmstadt in the south. The analysis of network connectivities confirms Frankfurt's dominant position as

Figure 5: Global and regional connectivity of the FUAs in the mega-city region of Munich – APS and high-tech firms

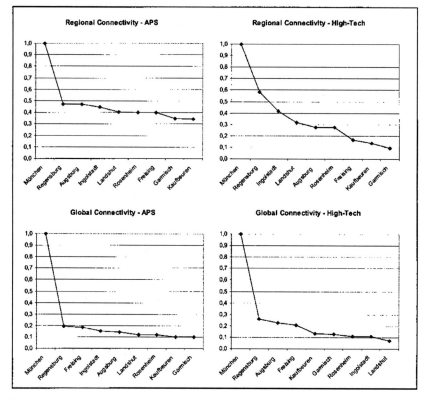

Source: authors' calculation.

the major hub of knowledge-intensive business services on both national and international scale. On the national scale, Frankfurt is part of the 'urban circuit' of those German cities (Frankfurt, Hamburg, Munich, Düsseldorf, Berlin, Stuttgart and Cologne) that have long constituted the apex of a polycentric national configuration of cities and metropolitan regions, characterized by complementary functional and sectoral specialization (Blotevogel 2000). On the international scale, Frankfurt clearly acts as 'first city' for internationally orientated APS firms and therefore constitutes a key gateway to the other major cities and towns in Germany and the world (Hoyler et al. 2008a).

In contrast to Munich and Rhine-Main, the RhineRuhr region – one of the world's largest polycentric Mega-City Regions, embracing 30 to 40 towns and cities with a total population of ten million people – has no obvious 'core city'. As the POLYNET study shows, the metropolitan cores of RhineRuhr – Dortmund, Essen, Duisburg, Düsseldorf, Cologne and Bonn – are characterized by quite balanced regional and national connectivity patterns. This means that these regional centres are interconnected almost to the same extent by regional and nationally-oriented APS firms. For international connectivities, however, the relative importance of Düsseldorf increases drastically, which underlines its important function as an international knowledge gateway connecting the mega-city region to a wider space of flows. The reason for this lies in Düsseldorf's increasing tertiary sector, which emerged during the second half of the twentieth century. Today it is one of the leading centres of the German advertising and fashion industry (Knapp and Schmitt 2008).

The greater Munich area as a localized system of value chains

The analyses so far outline the structural organization and spatial impact of intra-firm networks. In this section we present the results of the extra-firm analysis, which has been conceptualized by a value chain approach and realized by means of a web survey.

Figure 6 highlights the spatial patterns of extra-firm connectivities of APS firms on a regional, national, European and global scale. It is important to note that Figure 6 is a diagram based on the number of interactions as stated by the responding firms in the internet-based survey. The different shades of the grey colour in the legend illustrate the amount of firm-external interrelations. The darker the grey colour, the greater the number of interactions reported by the responding APS firms.

For APS firms, the strongest relations are located within the own mega-city region. The most frequent interactions are with other APS firms, in particular insurance, law, advertising and media companies. Extra-firm relations to the high-tech sector, on the other hand, are less pronounced, but still strongly concentrated within the greater Munich area. Hence, the figure shows quite clearly that geographical proximity to other enterprises appears to be a driving force towards generating extra-firm networks and interactions.

For high-tech firms, the spatial pattern of extra-firm networks is slightly different. Figure 7 shows the findings for high-tech enterprises. As in the case of APS firms, the predominant part of extra-firm networks is located within the demarcation of the emerging mega-city region of Munich. Hence, geographical proximity to other enterprises appears to be of importance for high-tech enterprises too.

Figure 6: Extra-firm relations of APS firms of the emerging mega-city region of Munich

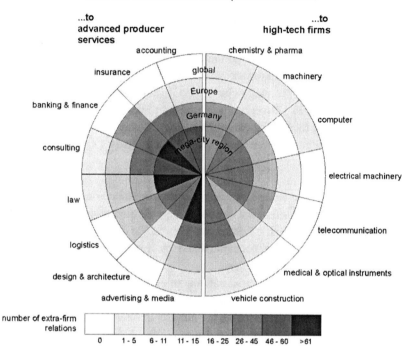

Extra-firm relations of advanced producer services...

Source: authors' calculation.

However, in contrast to the APS networks, high-tech firms within the greater Munich area display a remarkable level of global relations. This can be seen by the many dark sectors in the outer ring of Figure 7. To compete successfully in the global economy, high-tech firms have to rely on resources and expertise provided by firms in other economic areas. In this sense, the greater Munich area is not a self-sustaining system, but interconnected in a wide space of flows composed of flows of information, capital, goods and people travelling along infrastructure such as roads, railways, aviation routes and, increasingly, telecommunications.

Furthermore, Figure 7 indicates that third and fourth party logistic services play a central role in high-tech enterprises, even on the global scale. This highly sophisticated set of logistics service providers has emerged as a result of time and quality-based global competition with some developing out of traditional transportation companies (rail, road, shipping, airlines), some from wholesalers and trading companies, while others are entirely new forms of logistics organizations (Coe et al. 2008b). These firms appear to be important integrators that assemble the resources, capabilities and technology of their own and other organizations to design, build and run comprehensive global supply-chain solutions.

Figure 7: Extra-firm relations of high-tech firms in the mega-city region of Munich

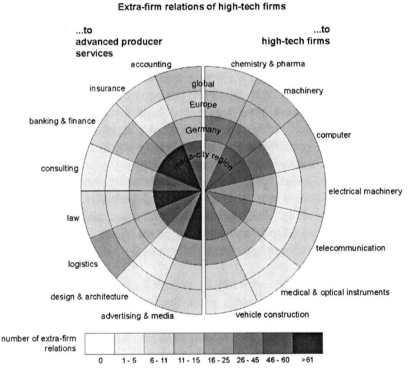

Source: authors' calculation.

However, as in the case of APS firms, the high-tech firms' strongest relations, namely to the accounting, insurance, law as well as the advertising and media sectors, are located on the mega-city-region scale. This means that these sectors provide important services for the knowledge economy of the mega-city region as a whole and for high-tech firms in particular. These branches assume an important role as an entrepreneurial support network within the emerging mega-city region of Munich.

In sum, all of these findings provide clear evidence for the initially proposed hypothesis that extra-firm linkages of knowledge-intensive enterprises concentrate in the emerging mega-city region of Munich, which, as a consequence, is evolving into a high-grade localized system of value chains. However, it must be stressed that such localized systems of value chains are not self-contained urban systems; instead, they are integrated into wide economic networks on different geographical scales.

Conclusion

Mega-city regions cannot be studied in isolation. Each city is connected to other places in the world in many different ways and through many different actors who form networks on different spatial scales. More than the pure locational perspective, this relational perspective makes it possible to highlight how different parts within and beyond mega-city regions are interacting with each other. The debate in the social sciences about the importance of geographical proximity has recently begun to acknowledge that local and global ties contribute positively to knowledge generation (Boschma 2005; Torre and Rallet 2005). Geographical clustering promotes a depth of knowledge production and is driven by the globalization of markets and services facilitated by developments in information and communication technologies. Knowledge-intensive businesses are agents that build spatially concentrated knowledge gateways between the regional and global economies.

The greater Munich area can be regarded simultaneously as a hier-archically organized polycentric mega-city region and as a high-grade localized system of value chains. Hence, the three initially suggested hypotheses can be verified. This process involving the emergence of a newly networked urban hierarchy is driven above all by knowledge-intensive enterprises. The examination of their value creation processes clearly reveals that they follow a functional and networked logic of both independent and interdependent institutions throughout the value chain. Here, we found evidence that Munich plays an important role for all other FUAs in the mega-city region, particularly in relation to its international gateway-function for knowledge-intensive businesses. However, the FUA of Munich, which has around 2.2 million inhabitants, is too small to concentrate all of the major functions of the mega-city region in its own location. The complementary combination of Munich and the supplemental centres elevates the emerging mega-city region of Munich to a competitive level in the context of the global economy.

The real impact of changing value chains on spatial development is difficult to grasp. On the one hand, there is an accelerated concentration of highly advanced and knowledge-intensive functions in just a few centres, while on the other hand a diffusion of associated functions and urban sprawl can be found (Lüthi et al. 2007). These contradictory processes pose an enormous challenge for the forthcoming research agenda, as both polycentric and monocentric tendencies are outcomes of the same process towards a more knowledge-intensive economy. Thus, further research activities must deal with the following specific aspects.

First, to understand spatial development processes more thoroughly, we need a conceptualization that integrates both economic and non-economic actors in a comprehensive research design. Each of the non-economic actors – such as nation-states, civil society organizations, labour and consumers – has very different spatialities from those of firms (Coe et al. 2008b). Second, to obtain a picture of the spatial patterns of Global Production Networks, future research must place a special focus on international gateway infrastructures, such as airports, seaports and high-speed train nodes. These sites are locations of highly specialized logistics services. It is safe to assume that these third and fourth party logistics providers will play an important role in the increasingly globalizing knowledge economy. Third, intra-firm and extra-firm linkages between APS and high-tech firms must be analysed on a more detailed regional scale. The smallest analytical entities should be at least functional urban areas. This makes it possible to identify and contextualize large-scale urban structures and hierarchies and the role of small and medium sized cities and towns within the globalizing knowledge economy. Fourth, to understand better the interplay between location strategies of knowledge-intensive enterprises, geographical proximity and polycentric mega-city regions, additional qualitative investigations need to be carried out, for example by means of qualitative network analyses. Finally, new methods of analysing and visualizing polycentric development need to be established to show and understand the potential contradictions of polycentricity between different geographical levels. Obtaining a picture of mega-city regions is crucial for comprehension, identification, motivation and commitment (Thierstein and Förster 2008). Raising awareness of this nascent spatial scale is a prerequisite to the establishment of large-scale metropolitan governance.

References

Blotevogel, H. H. (2000) 'Gibt es in Deutschland Metropolen?', in D. Matejovski (ed.) *Metropolen: Laboratorien der Moderne*, Frankfurt am Main: Campus, 179–208.

Boschma, R. (2005) 'Proximity and innovation: a critical assessment', *Regional Studies* 39 (1), 61–74.

Brown, E., B. Derudder, C. Parnreiter, W. Pelupessy, P. J. Taylor and F. Witlox (2010) 'World City Networks and Global Commodity Chains: towards a world systems integration, *Global Networks*, 10 (1), 12–34.

Castells, M. (1996) *The rise of the network society*, Malden: Blackwell Publishers.

Coe, N. M., M. Hess, H. W-c. Yeung, P. Dicken and J. Henderson (2004) 'Globalizing regional development: a Global Production Networks perspective', *Transactions of the Institute of British Geographers*, 29 (4), 468–84.

Coe, N. M., P. Dicken and M. Hess (2008a) 'Introduction: Global Production Networks – debates and challenges', *Journal of Economic Geography*, 8, 267–69.

Coe, N. M., P. Dicken and M. Hess (2008b) 'Global Production Networks: realizing the potential', *Journal of Economic Geography*, 8, 271–95.

De Backer, K. and E. Basri (2008) 'The internationalisation of R&D', in OECD (ed.) *Staying competitive in the global economy*, Paris: OECD, 219–48.

Derudder, B. (2006) 'On conceptual confusion in empirical analyses of a transnational urban network', *Urban Studies*, 43 (11), 2027–46.

Derudder, B. and P. Taylor (2005) 'The cliquishness of world cities', *Global Networks*, 5 (1), 71–91.

ESPON (2004) *ESPON Project 1.1.1. Potentials for polycentric development in Europe. Final Report*, Luxembourg: European Spatial Planning Observation Network. http://www.espon.eu/mmp/online/website/content/projects/259/648/file_1174/fr-1.1.1_revised-full.pdf, accessed 18 April 2009.

Friedmann, J. (1986) 'The world city hypothesis', *Development and Change*, 17, 69–83.

GEMACA (1996) *North-west European metropolitan regions*, Paris: Group for European Metropolitan Area Comparative Analysis.

Gereffi, G., J. Humphrey and T. Sturgeon (2005) 'The governance of Global Value Chains', *Review of International Political Economy*, 12 (1), 78–104.

Gottmann, J. (1961) *Megalopolis: the urbanized northeastern seaboard of the United States*, New York: Twentieth Century Fund.

Hall, P. (1966) *The world cities*, London: Weidenfeld & Nicolson.

Hall, P. (1999) 'Planning for the mega-city: a new Eastern Asian urban form?', in J. F. Brotchie, P. Hall, P. Newton and J. Dickey (eds) *East West perspectives on 21st century urban development: sustainable Eastern and Western cities in the new millennium*, Aldershot: Ashgate, 3–36.

Hall, P. (2007) 'Delineating urban territories. Is this a relevant issue?', in N. Cattan (ed.) *Cities and networks in Europe: a critical approach of polycentrism*, Paris: John Libbey Eurotext, 3–14.

Hall, P. and K. Pain (2006) *The polycentric metropolis: learning from mega-city regions in Europe*, London: Earthscan.

Hassler, M. (2003) 'The global clothing production system: commodity chains and business networks', *Global Networks*, 3 (4), 513–31.

Henderson, J., P. Dicken, M. Hess, N. M. Coe and H. W-c. Yeung (2002) 'Global Production Networks and the analysis of economic development', *Review of International Political Economy*, 9 (3), 436–64.

Hoyler, M., T. Freytag and C. Mager (2006) 'Advantageous fragmentation? Reimagining metropolitan governance and spatial planning in Rhine-Main', *Built Environment*, 32 (2), 124–36.

Hoyler, M., T. Freytag and C. Mager (2008a) 'Connecting Rhine-Main: the production of multi-scalar polycentricities through knowledge-intensive business services', *Regional Studies*, 42 (8), 1095–111.

Hoyler, M., R. C. Kloosterman and M. Sokol (2008b) 'Polycentric puzzles: emerging mega-city regions seen through the lens of advanced producer services', *Regional Studies*, 42 (8), 1055–64.

Jacobs, W. (2008) 'Global Value Chains, port clusters and advanced producer services: a framework for analysis', paper presented at the Annual Meeting of the Association of American Geographers, 15–19 April, Boston, MA.

Jacobs, W. C. Ducruet and P. de Langen (2010) 'Integrating world cities into production networks: the case of port cities', *Global Networks*, 10 (1), 92–113.

Kloosterman, R. and S. Musterd (2001) 'The polycentric urban region: towards a research agenda', *Urban Studies*, 38, 623–33.

Knapp, W. and P. Schmitt (2008) 'Discourse on "metropolitan driving forces" and "uneven development": Germany and the RhineRuhr conurbation', *Regional Studies*, 42 (8), 187–204.

Kogut, B. (1985) 'Designing global strategies: comparative and competitive value-added chains', *Sloan Management Review*, 26 (4), 15–28.

Krätke, S. (2007) 'Metropolisation of the European economic territory as a consequence of increasing specialisation of urban agglomerations in the knowledge economy', *European Planning Studies*, 15 (1), 1–27.

Krätke, S. and A. Brandt (2009) 'Knowledge networks as a regional development resource: a network analysis of the interlinks between scientific institutions and regional firms in the metropolitan region of Hanover, Germany', *European Planning Studies*, 17 (1), 43–63.

Kujath, H. J. (ed.) (2005) *Knoten im Netz*, Münster: Lit Verlag.

Kujath, H. J. and S. Schmidt (2007) 'Wissensökonomie und die Entwicklung von Städtesystemen', http://www.irs-net.de/download/wp_staedtesysteme.pdf, accessed 20 April 2009.

Lüthi, S., A. Thierstein and V. Goebel (2007) 'Spatial development on the quiet in the mega-city region of Munich', paper presented at the European Regional Science Association (ERSA) September 2007.

Lüthi, S., A. Thierstein and V. Goebel (2008) 'Intra-firm and extra-firm linkages of the knowledge economy: the case of the mega-city region of Munich', paper presented at the annual meeting of the Association of American Geographers (AAG), Boston, 26 March.

OECD (2005) *Oslo manual: guidelines for collecting and interpreting innovation data*, Paris: OECD.

OECD (2008) *Staying competitive in the global economy*, Paris: OECD.

Palpacuer, F. and A. Parisotto (2003) 'Global production and local jobs: can global enterprise networks be used as levers for local development?', *Global Networks*, 3 (2), 97–120.

Pike, A. (2007) 'Editorial: whither regional studies?', *Regional Studies*, 41 (9), 1143–48.

Pilat, D., A. Cimper, K. Olsen and C. Webb (2008) 'The changing nature of manufacturing in OECD economies', in OECD (ed.) *Staying competitive in the global economy: compendium of studies on Global Value Chains*, Paris: OECD, 103–40.

Rothenberg-Aalami, J. (2004) '"Coming full circle"? Forging missing links along Nike's integrated production networks', *Global Networks*, 4 (4), 335–54.

Sassen, S. (2001) *The global city: New York, London, Tokyo*, second edition, Princeton, NJ: Princeton University Press.

Schmitt, P. and W. Knapp (2006) 'RheinRuhr als polyzentrischer "Raum der Orte" im "Raum der Ströme"', *Zeitschrift für Wirtschaftsgeographie*, 50, 217–31.

Schürmann, C. (2004) *Morphological analysis of urban areas based on 45-minute isochrones: annex report D to ESPON project 111 potentials for polycentric development in Europe*, Luxembourg: ESPON Monitoring Committee.

Scott, A. J. (2001) *Global city-regions: trends, theory, policy*, Oxford: Oxford University Press.

Simmie, J. (2003) 'Innovation and urban regions as national and international nodes for the transfer and sharing of knowledge', *Regional Studies*, 37 (6), 607–20.

Taylor, P. J. (2004) *World City Network: a global urban analysis*, London: Routledge.

Taylor, P. J., D. M. Evans and K. Pain (2008) 'Application of the interlocking network model to mega-city-regions: measuring polycentricity within and beyond city-regions', *Regional Studies*, 42 (8), 1079–93.

Thierstein, A. and A. Förster (eds) (2008) *The image and the region: making mega-city regions visible!*, Baden: Lars Müller Publishers.

Thierstein, A., C. Kruse, L. Glanzmann, S. Gabi and N. Grillon (2006) *Raumentwicklung im Verborgenen: Untersuchungen und Handlungsfelder für die Entwicklung der Metropolregion Nordschweiz*, Zürich: NZZ Buchverlag.

Thierstein, A., S. Lüthi, C. Kruse, S. Gabi and L. Glanzmann (2008) 'Changing value chain of the knowledge economy: spatial impact of intra-firm and inter-firm networks within the emerging mega-city region of northern Switzerland', *Regional Studies*, 42 (8), 1113–31.

Tokatli, N., N. Wrigley and Ö. Kizilgün (2008) 'Shifting global supply networks and fast fashion: made in Turkey for Mark & Spencer', *Global Networks*, 8 (3), 261–80.

Torre, A. and A. Rallet (2005) 'Proximity and localization', *Regional Studies*, 39 (1), 47–59.

Wildemann, H. (2003) *Supply chain management: Effizienzsteigerung in der unter-nehmensübergreifenden Wertschöpfungskette*, Münster: TCW Transfer-Centrum.

8

Making connections: Global Production Networks and World City Networks

NEIL M. COE, PETER DICKEN, MARTIN HESS AND HENRY WAI-CHEUNG YEUNG

Among the myriad networks that make up the complex fabric of the global economy two, in particular, stand out. One is constituted by the circuitous processes of production, distribution and consumption. How these are articulated and coordinated derives from complex, asymmetrical interactions between a number of actors and institutions. Such actors and institutions are, themselves, deeply embedded in broad social structures and firmly grounded in specific places and geographies. These geographies constitute the second major network. The global economy, therefore, can be conceptualized as the complex inter-digitation of *organizational* networks, in the form of production circuits and networks, and *geographical* networks, in the form of localized clusters and webs of economic activities (Dicken 2007; Dicken et al. 2001). In fact, of course, the two networks are totally interconnected. They constitute two sides of the same coin. We cannot understand how the global economy works without appreciating its complete embeddedness in, and shaping by, specific geographies. Equally, we cannot understand such geographies without appreciating how they are shaped by the complex interconnections within and between production networks organized at different spatial scales (often regional and global). So far, however, there is relatively little work on the connections between these two kinds of network. Within geography, for example, political/economic geographers concern themselves with production networks while political/urban geographers concern themselves with cities and networks of cities. The twain rarely, if ever, meets.

In that respect, the theme of this book is especially apposite. It is concerned with the conceptual relationship between two particular variants of these two kinds of network: World City Networks (WCNs) and Global Commodity Chains (GCCs). In the individual chapters, the authors address, to a greater or lesser degree, and to a more theoretical or empirical extent, how these two approaches can be productively integrated and recombined into 'a key analytical lens through which the geographies of contemporary globalization are being studied' (Brown et al. this book). As economic geographers with vested interests in heated debates in both strands of the literature in geography, urban studies, development studies and international political economy, we welcome this analytical effort towards integration and synthesis. We believe that such cross-fertilization of different analytical frameworks in the study of global networks is not only crucial in engendering the future viability of their subject matter for research, but also reflective of the growing maturity and acceptance of these frameworks in the wider social sciences.

In this brief commentary, however, we do not attempt a critique of the chapters themselves, each of which makes a useful contribution to aspects of the debate. Rather, we reflect on some of the broader issues involved, deriving our position from our joint conceptual and empirical work on Global Productions Networks (GPNs) over the past decade (Coe and Hess 2005; Coe et al. 2004, 2008; Dicken 2007; Dicken and Malmberg 2001; Dicken et al. 2001; Henderson et al. 2002; Hess and Coe 2006; Hess and Yeung 2006; Yeung 2005a, 2005b, 2009). Pitched mostly at the conceptual level, the chapter looks at three issues – the world-system framework as a suitable basis for conceptual integration; the question of essentialism; and the issue of relationality. In addressing these issues, we hope to make a constructive contribution to what is undoubtedly a key debate within the social sciences.

Core concerns, peripheral visions

The intellectual origins of both WCN and GCC analysis are rooted in world systems theory as put forward by Terence Hopkins and Immanuel Wallerstein (Hopkins and Wallerstein 1977. See also Friedmann 1986; Gereffi and Korzeniewicz 1994; Wallerstein 1974). However, while still concerned with the same fundamental issues of the highly uneven nature of capitalist development, WCN and GCC literatures – especially in their more recent incarnations – have attempted new ways of investigating and explaining this phenomenon by refocusing on the firms and inter-firm networks that constitute the production networks and urban hierarchies in the world economy (Bair 2009; Brown et al. this book). Since their initial formulations, both approaches have developed further into new epistemological terrain. From our point of view, this makes it increasingly difficult if not impossible to reunify WCN and GCC analysis under the umbrella of world systems theory. We want to highlight two related areas of conceptual disjuncture and incompatibility here to illustrate our argument: the core–periphery framework and hierarchical ordering of the global economy, and the role of space and place in this ordering.

There can be no doubt that capitalist development is based on power asymmetries and therefore is highly uneven in terms of the distribution of value among different actors and places in the global economic system. In world systems theory, this has been represented through the language of core, semi-periphery and periphery, indicating the loci of power and capital accumulation. Such a (structuralist) reading of the geographies of power, however, implies a Braudelian world of nested scalar hierarchies, which, arguably, no longer exists. Indeed, this neat classification of the world system depicts a highly problematic conception of places and regions as relatively stable and enduring territorialized ensembles, without sufficient allowance for the possibilities of a multitude of flows and connections that cut across and reconfigure these different territories. Cognizant of such ontological weakness, contemporary concepts of Global Production Networks and world city formation recognize a world that consists of multiple webs and networks 'made from a complex addition, crossing and entanglement of transversal business chains and social and intellectual communities' (Hess 2009: 21; see also Veltz 2004).

Given the multiplicity of actors, and the connections and power relations they establish, a clear distinction between core and periphery as a core concern for both WCN and GCC approaches is hard to maintain in a meaningful way. It is not surprising, therefore, that more recent work on global cities and Global Production Networks pays attention not only to increasingly networked forms of governance via the possession of economic power by different actors, but also to governmentality via the practice of different technologies of control (see Vind and Fold this book, referring to Sassen's work). As Prince and Dufty (2009: 1752) observe: 'A governmentality perspective can incorporate the variety of actors who impact on a production network/value chain such as state agencies, NGOs, trade unions, health organisations and so on ..., not just as external pressures on the system but as constitutively involved in making the kinds of linked, productive subjects and spaces that make up the system' (see also Gibbon and Ponte 2008; Hess 2008). This leads us to the second area of conceptual disjuncture, namely the role and nature of space and place.

The core–periphery dichotomy of world systems theory not only presents us with a conceptual cul-de-sac when it comes to understanding power relations and multiple hierarchies in the global economy, but also represents a rather problematic theoretical basis for investigating the geographies and scales of uneven capitalist development. This is because there is a strong conceptual tendency to correlate core and periphery with absolute forms of territoriality, which in the literature more often than not is the nation-state. Pries (2005) calls this the trap of 'methodological nationalism' in the social sciences, and even a more sensitive approach to scale that recognizes other levels of territory (for example the city, the region) still tends to conflate power and hierarchy with particular geographies of bounded space, hence producing what we could call 'methodological territorialism'. In other words, world systems theory creates a geographical imagery of 'quasi-natural levels of subsidiarity' that does not allow for consideration of the complex ways in which space and place co-constitute each other (for a critical and more detailed discussion of the space–place distinction, see Wainwright and Barnes 2009). This is in stark contrast to the multiple hierarchies and socio-economic relations that are found not only between, but also within, places.

The dynamic flows and relations among actors and institutions have indeed reconstituted what it means to be territories such as core or periphery. A world made up of discrete cores and peripheries can no longer hold much analytical purchase in today's globalizing era. For instance, global cities may assume a powerful position in some networks, but not in others. Their socioeconomic fabric is made up by powerful and powerless actors alike. GCC/GPNs encompass multiple sites of governance and control across space. Massey (2005: 9) makes an important point by proposing a reading of space as 'the sphere ... of coexisting heterogeneity. Without space, no multiplicity; without multiplicity, no space. If space is indeed the product of interrelations, then it must be predicated upon the existence of plurality. Multiplicity and space as co-constitutive.' The language of core, semi-periphery and periphery is clearly not suited to acknowledge this and therefore we need a different conceptual grounding.

The argument we have developed so far is not intended to dismiss plainly important insights generated by work in the tradition of world systems theory. Indeed, the epistemological shift in WCN and GCC/GPN literature – while producing new foci of analysis – may inadvertently have confined some important aspects to our peripheral vision. Much empirical work is concentrating on *how the world economy is organized* through multiple networks of material and immaterial flows controlled and coordinated by actors in various places like global cities (or the islands in the global archipelago economy) and at various scales. This is crucial if we want to better understand the contemporary world economy. However, pressing issues of social injustice and inequality – the question of who is included and excluded, *who wins and who loses* – must not be sidelined if WCN and GCC analysis are to be politically and societally relevant strands of research. In this more normative sense, world systems theory provides a powerful reminder of the fundamental capitalist imperatives at work, impacting on the ways in which production and World City Networks develop and are transformed, leading to highly uneven developmental outcomes. But this does not mean world systems theory is well placed to build the unifying conceptual core for WCN and GCC analysis, for the reasons outlined above. In the following sections, we discuss in more detail the dangers of essentialism with regard to place/territory and elaborate on a relational perspective which in our view might be better positioned to provide a conceptual bridge between the WCN and GCC/GPN frameworks.

Limiting essentialisms

One key issue we take with the WCN literature in particular and also the GCC literature to a certain extent concerns the excessive attention paid to certain places and/or sectors at the expense of others that are omitted as being less glamorous and too 'ordinary'. Indeed, this tendency towards essentializing *the* global city has been critiqued for over a decade now (see Amin and Graham 1997; Robinson 2002, 2006). Still, we sense the continual reproduction of the dominant global city discourses through accounts that frame and essentialize cities such as New York and London as 'instants in a global space of flows' (Thrift 1997: 139). This 'one city tells all' approach in WCN analysis reflects the dominance of representational theories of urban change and the subtle effects of Eurocentrism and structurally influenced globalist perspectives in urban studies (see further critique in Olds and Yeung 2004: 497). For example, the dominant focus on intra-firm networks in the global cities of North America and Western Europe has led to the circulation of a relatively *coherent* global city discourse (*the* global city). This is a discourse that generates resource allocation bias towards essentializing commonalities between global cities, or possible global city status in terms of function, role, linkages, structure, problems, form and process. As Amin and Graham (1997: 417; our emphasis) noted over a decade ago:

> The problem with paradigmatic examples is that analysis inevitably tends to generalise from very specific cities, both in identifying the changing nature of urban assets and highlighting normative suggestions for policy innovation elsewhere. What should be a debate on *variety and specificity* quickly reduces to the assumption that some degree of interurban homogeneity can be assumed, either in the nature of the

sectors leading urban transformation or in the processes of urban change. The exception, by a process of reduction or totalizing, becomes the norm.

To us, the academic field of urban studies and WCN analysis needs to become more open about the limited purchase of all of our situated knowledges and local epistemologies. We believe that *the* global city model as an essentialized end-state is in serious doubt because of its tendency to shut down alternative development scenarios that have the potential to be more appropriate and achievable given the continued diversity of conditions across space and time. Global cities, be they Alpha, Beta, Gamma, hyper, or emerging global cities or even global city-states, should not be viewed as an idealized end-state phenomenon. Instead, all these cities are the intended and unintended outcome of a wide range of relational networks constituted and governed by diverse actors and institutions. Given the diversity of actor roles and capacities around the world, we should therefore expect equally diverse forms of world city formation and transformation processes mediated by actors spearheading Global Commodity Chains and Global Production Networks.

In this regard, we are gratified to see in this book empirical chapters that focus on Mexico City, Santiago de Chile, Ho Chi Minh City and Munich. Because of the kind of analytical essentialism in the earlier phase of WCN analysis, these 'ordinary' cities have quite often fallen out of the analytical map of what constitutes global cities and how they relate to and co-constitute with other organizational networks. Parnreiter's chapter, for example, offers telling evidence about the linkages between business services firms located in Mexico City and the globalization of the 'Mexican' economy and demonstrates the need of global service firms for access to 'localized' knowledge and the desire to maintain close contacts with clients. The work of Lüthi et al., on the other hand, provides an actual mapping of the functional and spatial linkages between production and its servicing in a particular 'global' city – Munich. The authors illustrate empirically how multi-location firms from the so-called 'knowledge economy' develop their intra-firm networks internationally, after which they establish the spatial location of the partners with whom these firms have working relationships along individual Global Commodity Chains. In both cases, there seems to be a particular analytical choice made in relation to the empirical focus on firms offering knowledge intensive business services (KIBS).

This calls for another careful (re)consideration: the almost 'mythical' nature afforded to KIBS or advanced producer services (APS) in WCN analysis. While GCC and GPN analyses undoubtedly tend to pay insufficient attention to these APS, WCN research has swung the pendulum so far as to take APS for granted as its foundational sector. Understandably, KIBS and APS do exhibit an organizational tendency towards locating in mega cities in connection with the unfolding of the dynamics of agglomeration economies or, more broadly, urbanization economies. They are thus a relevant lens through which to examine the organizational interrelationships between different urban centres and regions in the global economy. However, it is quite another matter if we *equate* world cities with only the location and domination of APS. This essentializing approach is often visible in WCN analysis and can be dangerous for at least two reasons. First, it privileges only a very select number of world cities that come to dominate in the global provision and control of APS, for example London and New York. In turn, other cities are always measured against a biased benchmark established on the basis of essentializing APS as the necessary (and sometimes sufficient) condition for a city's globality.

Second, an excessive concentration on APS or, for that matter, any other sector produces a caricatured view of complex organizational ecologies and sector dynamics that not only produce the underlying dynamics of contemporary cities, but also enable these cities to be interconnected and thus constitute global networks. One important element of such organizational dynamics is the *vertical specialization* through which global lead firms in different production networks and sectors are moving towards a business model of increasing specialization in value chain activities. This trend has been much further accelerated since the late 1990s, particularly in the electronics, automobile, clothing, retailing, finance and logistics sectors (Dicken 2007; Gereffi et al. 2005; Yeung 2007, 2009). What this value chain specialization entails is a more strategically focused role played by global lead firms in the upstream (R&D) and downstream (marketing, distribution and post-sale services) segments of the value chain, leaving much of the manufacturing portion of the value chain to its international strategic partners and dedicated supply chain managers. This vertical specialization thus refers to the multiple specializations of a lead firm in different stages of the same value chain. It is vertical because both upstream and downstream specializations can be possible within the same lead firm. It is also different from vertical disintegration, a process not necessarily associated with multiple specializations. The implication of vertical specialization for world cities and regional development is highly contingent on the strategies of lead firms and their changing organization of Global Production Networks.

To compete more effectively in today's global economy, lead firms begin to opt for what can be broadly termed an *organizational fix*. Lead firms now realize that competitive advantage can be obtained through a more flexible and efficient form of organizing production on a global scale, sometimes bypassing archetypical global cities altogether. This idea of an organizational fix must be distinguished from the earlier Marxian notion of a spatial fix (cf. World Systems Theory). The reorganization of production networks does not necessarily entail the spatial relocation of production, particularly one's own production facilities. Instead, an organizational fix results primarily from a firm-specific choice of different business strategies; it is about strategizing the organizational principle that affords the most competitive advantage. The strategy of outsourcing, for example, represents an organizational fix through which global lead firms are able to increase their production flexibility without incurring substantial liability in owning manufacturing facilities (for example contract manufacturing and electronic manufacturing services) or service provision (for example financial, auditing, human resources and logistics).

Through these different organizational arrangements, production networks become more globally oriented and integrated, leading to the emergence of sophisticated Global Production Networks orchestrated by transnational lead firms. Organizational fixes therefore produce highly differentiated geographies of production and service provision that in turn impact on different con-figurations of cities and regional fortunes. Competing in today's global economy is no longer just about finding a niche in the paradigmatic global cities; it is as important for lead firms and their GPNs to search for new sites beyond these cities for production and service activities. We argue that these kind of organizational dynamics are central in driving the global economy through new connections made by the relentless search by lead firms and their partners in establishing and reproducing Global Production Networks.

Unpacking relationality: actors, governance and methods

Our position is that the project to bring together GPN and WCN perspectives would benefit from a widening of the urban and sectoral lenses being used. To paraphrase Brown et al. (this book), all Global Production Networks run through cities, and all cities are integrated into Global Production Networks. What is more, all sectors are characterized by Global Production Networks, not just primary commodity and manufacturing industries. From this broader perspective, much of the supposed analytical distance between WCNs and GPNs disappears: GPNs, across the full range of industries, are what bind cities together.[1] What is more interesting to us are the *kinds* of relationships connecting cities, as reflected in the constantly changing and evolving structures of GPNs.

First, identification of the full range of network actors, their inter-relationships and power configurations, and the structural outcomes of these relationships is central to understanding the operation of global economic networks. As Lüthi et al. (this book) argue, 'we need a conceptualization that integrates both economic and non-economic actors. ... Each of the non-economic actors – such as nation states, civil society organizations, labour and consumers – has very different spatialities from those of firms.' In some WCN analyses, the city appears to be simply a point in Cartesian space. Such a broadening of scope necessitates thinking seriously about the city as a territorial entity, one that extends beyond the central business district where APS firms congregate to incorporate the broader hinterland of the city-region (Vind and Fold this book; see also Scott 2001). Brown et al. (this book) are attuned to this relative downplaying of urban theories in WCN analysis, and in some of the key theoretical contributions to the approach (for example Beaverstock et al. 2002; Taylor 2004), city formation processes are explained as occurring through the complex relationships between 'territorial' communities (the city and the state) and 'functional-economic' communities (firms and sectors). Service firms, city governments, service sector institutions and nation-states are argued to be the key 'agents' shaping WCNs.

As the empirical analysis unfolds, however, the territorial dimension, and the huge range of political and economic actors that affect economic development within city-regions, become subsumed in favour of the corporate strategies of APS firms (see earlier critique). This is a deliberate move, as Taylor (2004: 59) explains: 'first ... it is the firms as economic agents that produce the wealth upon which the network has been built and sustained. Second, it is the firms through their office networks that have created the overall structure of the network.' However, to our minds at least, this is a dangerously narrow interpretation of the range of non-firm actors and multi-scalar regulatory/institutional contexts involved in shaping the intersections between global networks and uneven development processes (Coe et al. 2004; Yeung 2005a). Even within the corporate sector, there are complex and differentiated power relations among actors within the same business groups, let alone different firms and corporate groups in the global economy. In short, it might be fair enough for WCN analysis to take APS firms as a proxy for measuring the relational globality of world cities. But it is quite a different matter to assume some kind of autonomous power in the hands of these APS firms as *the* actors in the creation of wealth and the network structure through which value is appropriated. We should not forget that some of the most important actors in the global economy do not necessarily operate out of the paradigmatic 'global' cities.

Second, power and governance must be brought onto centre stage, as manifested not only in intra-firm networks, but also through inter-firm and extra-firm networks, which are arguably grasped far less effectively by WCN analysis. GCC/GPN approaches have very effectively demonstrated the wide range of *inter-firm* governance regimes that exist within and across different sectors (for example Gereffi et al. 2005; Vind and Fold this book; Yang and Coe 2009) and, in turn, their implications for territorial development in the places they connect. In dynamic terms, upgrading processes of various kinds can start to redress the power configurations of GPNs. However, as Parnreiter (this book) notes, understanding the 'practice of exercising management and command functions' remains an ongoing concern for research. These inter-firm relations of power and interdependency are also heavily shaped by *extra-firm* networks of many stripes, incorporating, as noted above, a wide range of regulatory, institutional and civil society actors. Many inter-city networks, therefore, go well beyond what is typically captured in WCN analyses. The intra-firm hierarchies of leading producer service companies are an important part of this complex mesh, but they are only one set of connections among many – the centrality of APS networks to WCNs needs to be empirically established, not assumed *a priori*. Moving forward, the challenge is to identify the actual flows and connectivities between cities, or in Vind and Fold's (this book) terms, to add 'flesh' to WCNs through industry-specific analyses that reveal the connections and material links between cities.

Third, we need to address questions of methodology. For us, the chapters in this book clearly reiterate the necessity of combining both quantitative and qualitative approaches in studying global networks (cf. Hess and Yeung 2006; Yeung 2003). On one level, it is easy to criticize WCN analysis – based as it is on somewhat crude estimations of intra-corporate hierarchies and their connectivities – for its limitations in explaining the actual flows, practices and strategies of firms within wider GPNs.[2] As Vind and Fold (this book) argue, and we would agree, 'it is impossible to do this without intensive fieldwork, including corporate interviews; databases or surveys cannot provide the data needed'. And yet, as a plethora of publications in recent years have demonstrated, WCN analysis does provide a systemic global overview, and one that can be mapped over time and extended to a wider network of cities and sectors. GCC/GPN research, however, has tended to use qualitative and/or case study evidence to demonstrate *how* networks function, and to what effect, shedding considerable light on the issues of asymmetric power and divergent governance discussed above.

That said, the over-dependence on qualitative methods is something of a weakness, and the evidence cannot always be pieced together to provide a synthetic, macro-perspective. The potential for a methodological rapprochement between the two approaches is one of the key lessons we take from this set of chapters. For example, the kinds of 'outside-in' approaches characteristic of WCN research need to be combined with 'inside-out' studies that look in depth at how particular places 'plug in' to wider networks, as evidenced by the studies of Ho Chi Minh City (Vind and Fold this book), Mexico City (Parnreiter this book) and Munich (Lüthi et al. this book) offered here. Meeting the challenge of what Lüthi et al. term 'analysing and visualizing polycentric development' can only be achieved through multiple field studies and secondary analyses working in tandem.

Conclusion

The chapters in this book open a welcome dialogue between proponents of World City Network and Global Commodity Chain approaches to global economic transformation. While we are broadly supportive of such a project, as our commentary suggests we are concerned that the frames of reference for such an analytical engagement should not be too restrictive. Overly dwelling upon the common world systems heritage of both approaches is one risk, while constraining the sectoral and urban lenses we use to analyse the global system is another. Circumscribing the range of actors and spaces taken to define the urban arena is also unnecessarily limiting. Drawing upon a Global Production Network (GPN) perspective, we have argued for a conceptualization that is open to all aspects of the sectoral and geographical complexity that characterizes the contemporary global economy. Moving forward, it is also important to recognize that World City and Global Production Networks are not 'neutral' forms of socio-economic and spatial organization, but deeply political, contested projects (cf. Levy 2008). Ultimately, perhaps, revealing the highly variegated socio-economic *impacts* of the global networks that we identify and describe is what should centrally concern us.

Notes

1. An argument can be made that they are complemented by global *reproduction* networks that bind migrants, households and communities together and also

influence territorial processes of economic development (see Kelly 2009, for more). Such connections are another notable silence in the recent WCN literature although international migration processes were central to the earlier analyses of Friedmann (1986), Sassen (2001) and others.

2. It is important to note that it is only one strand of WCN research, albeit a formative one, that uses this particular methodology of mapping 'interlocking' APS firms. A quick scan through the now over 300 Research Bulletins on the GaWC website (http://www.lboro.ac.uk/gawc/) reveals that WCN research more generally utilizes a broad range of methodologies.

References

Amin, A. and S. Graham (1997) 'The ordinary city', *Transactions of the Institute of British Geographers*, 22, 411–29.

Bair, J. (2009) 'Global Commodity Chains: genealogy and review', in J. Bair (ed.) *Frontiers of commodity chain research*, Stanford: Stanford University Press, 1–34.

Beaverstock, J. V., M. A. Doel, P. J. Hubbard and P. J. Taylor (2002) 'Attending to the world: competition, cooperation and connectivity in the World City Network', *Global Networks*, 2, 111–32.

Brown, E., B. Derudder, C. Parnreiter, W. Pelupessy, P. J. Taylor and F. Witlox (2010) 'World City Networks and Global Commodity Chains: towards a world systems integration, *Global Networks*, 10 (1), 12–34.

Coe, N. M. and M. Hess (2005) 'The internationalization of retailing: implications for supply network restructuring in East Asia and Eastern Europe', *Journal of Economic Geography*, 5, 449–73.

Coe, N. M., M. Hess, H. W-c. Yeung, P. Dicken and J. Henderson (2004) '"Globalizing" regional development: a Global Production Networks perspective', *Transactions of the Institute of British Geographers*, 29, 468–84.

Coe, N. M., P. Dicken and M. Hess (2008) 'Global Production Networks: realizing the potential', *Journal of Economic Geography*, 8, 271–95.

Dicken, P. (2007) *Global shift: mapping the changing contours of the world economy*, London: Sage, New York: Guilford, fifth edition.

Dicken, P. and A. Malmberg (2001) 'Firms in territories: a relational perspective', *Economic Geography*, 77, 345–63.

Dicken, P., P. F. Kelly, K. Olds and H. W-c. Yeung (2001) 'Chains and networks, territories and scales: towards a relational framework for analysing the global economy', *Global Networks*, 1, 89–112.

Friedmann, J. (1986) 'The world city hypothesis', *Development and Change*, 17, 69–83.

Gereffi, G. and M. Korzeniewicz (eds) (1994) *Commodity chains and global capitalism*, Westport, CT: Praeger.

Gereffi, G., J. Humphrey and T. Sturgeon (2005) 'The governance of Global Value Chains', *Review of International Political Economy*, 12, 78–104.

Gibbon, P. and S. Ponte (2008) 'Global Value Chains: from governance to govern-mentality?', *Economy and Society*, 37, 365–92.

Henderson, J., P. Dicken, M. Hess, N. M. Coe and H. W-c. Yeung (2002) 'Global Production Networks and the analysis of economic development', *Review of International Political Economy*, 9, 436–64.

Hess, M. (2008) 'Governance, value chains and networks: an afterword', *Economy and Society*, 37, 452–9.

Hess, M. (2009) 'Investigating the archipelago economy: chains, networks and the study of uneven development', *Journal für Entwicklungspolitik*, 2, 20–37.

Hess, M. and N. M. Coe (2006) 'Making connections: Global Production Networks, standards and embeddedness in the mobile telecommunications industry', *Environment and Planning A*, 38, 1205–27.

Hess, M. and H. W-c. Yeung (2006) 'Whither Global Production Networks in economic geography? Past, present and future', *Environment and Planning A*, 38, 1193–204.

Hopkins, T. and I. Wallerstein (1977) 'Patterns of development of the modern world system', *Review*, 1 (2), 111–45.

Kelly, P. F. (2009) 'From Global Production Networks to Global Reproduction Networks: households, migration, and regional development in Cavite, the Philippines', *Regional Studies*, 43, 449–61.

Levy, D. L. (2008) 'Political contestation in Global Production Networks', *Academy of Management Review*, 33, 943–63.

Lüthi, S., A. Thierstein, and V. Goebel (2010) 'Intra-firm and extra-firm linkages in the knowledge economy: the case of the emerging mega-city region of Munich', *Global Networks*, 10 (1), 114–37.

Massey, D. (2005) *For space*, London: Sage.

Olds, K. and H. W-c. Yeung (2004) 'Pathways to global city formation: a view from the developmental city-state of Singapore', *Review of International Political Economy*, 11, 489–521.

Parnreiter, C. (2010) 'Global cities in Global Commodity Chains: exploring the role of Mexico City in the geography of governance of the world economy', *Global Networks*, 10 (1), 35–53.

Pries, L. (2005) 'Configurations of geographic and societal spaces: a sociological proposal between "methodological nationalism" and the "spaces of flows"', *Global Networks*, 5, 167–90.

Prince, R. and R. Dufty (2009) 'Assembling the space economy: governmentality and economic geography', *Geography Compass*, 3, 1744–56.

Robinson, J. (2002) 'Global and world cities: a view from off the map', *International Journal of Urban and Regional Research*, 26, 531–54.

Robinson, J. (2006) *Ordinary cities: between modernity and development*, London: Routledge.

Sassen, S. (2001) *The global city: New York, London, Tokyo*, 2nd edition, Princeton: Princeton University Press.

Scott, A. J. (ed.) (2001) *Global city-regions: trends, theory, policy*, Oxford: Oxford University Press.

Taylor, P. J. (2004) *World City Network: a global urban analysis*, London: Routledge.

Thrift, N. (1997) 'Cities without modernity, cities with magic', *Scottish Geographical Magazine*, 113, 138–49.

Veltz, P. (2004) 'The rationale for a resurgence in the major cities of advanced economies', paper presented at the Leverhulme International Symposium, London School of Economics, 19–21 April.

Vind, I. and N. Fold (2010) 'City networks and commodity chains: identifying global flows and local connections in Ho Chi Minh City', *Global Networks*, 10 (1), 54–74.

Wainwright, J. and T. Barnes (forthcoming) 'Nature, economy and the space–place distinction', *Environment and Planning D: Society and Space*, advance online publication, doi: 10.1068/d7707.

Wallerstein, I. (1974) *The modern world system 1: capitalist agriculture and the origins of the European world economy in the sixteenth century*, New York: Academic Press.

Yang, Y.-R. and N. M. Coe (2009) 'The governance of Global Production Networks and regional development: a case study of Taiwanese PC production networks', *Growth and Change*, 40, 30–53.

Yeung, H. W-c. (2003) 'Practicing new economic geographies: a methodological examination', *Annals of the Association of American Geographers*, 93, 442–62.

Yeung, H. W-c. (2005a) 'Rethinking relational economic geography', *Transactions of the Institute of British Geographers*, 30, 37–51.

Yeung, H. W-c. (2005b) 'The firm as social network', *Growth and Change*, 36, 307–28.

Yeung, H. W-c. (2007) 'From followers to market leaders: Asian electronics firms in the global economy', *Asia Pacific Viewpoint*, 48, 1–25.

Yeung, H. W-c. (2009) 'Regional development and the competitive dynamics of Global Production Networks', *Regional Studies*, 43, 325–51.

9

Global inter-city networks and commodity chains: any intersections?

SASKIA SASSEN

The editors have asked me to address the conceptual relationship between two particular variants of these two kinds of networks: World City Networks (WCNs) and Global Commodity Chains (GCCs).[1] This is a timely project; indeed it is surprising that after a few early research suggestions (Smith and Timberlake 1995) not much has happened. It is an exciting project and one on the agenda not only of geographers, who have been key researchers in both fields, but also of a much wider social science spectrum. But, it will require some work and, I would argue, some analytical developments and experimentation if we are to go beyond attempts at finding the lowest common denominators. We need to find an analytical triangulation that goes beyond each, inter-city networks and commodity chains.

I promptly confront a dilemma in addressing the editors' request to think about the linking of these two fields. WCN is one, albeit critical, component of a much larger analytical frame: I cannot properly address potential intersections by confining myself to the WCN analysis. Peter Taylor has insisted that 'the focus of the GaWC research network on APS firms was launched as "a simple empirical hook in an interesting theoretical area"' (Taylor 2000: 29).[2] And it has served us well, producing a continuously growing and diversifying data set, unique in the world and used by many around the world. Neither Taylor's (2000) work, mine (Sassen 1991), nor Friedmann's (1986) can be reduced to this specific empirical component. Addressing the agenda put forward by the editors requires working off the complexity of that earlier scholarship, returning to some of the many themes that were central to it and that have been developed richly in diverse scholarships, from anthropology to political theory. These themes are not present in the WCN work because that was not the purpose of this empirical research – indeed, the actual WCN research group is clear in specifying that this is an empirical component of a much larger conceptual frame.

I shall address the matter of substance asked from me by the editors, and in

179

this process discuss the various contributions that the chapters in this book can make to that larger analytical effort that we need if we are to go beyond mere aggregation and move on to developing a key analytical lens through which the geographies of contemporary globalization are being studied (Brown et al. this book).

Five propositions towards an analytic lens

I should perhaps start by explicating a core methodological principle that organizes my scholarship: explaining the x requires a focus also on the non-x. Confining an analysis to description of the x that is the object of explanation provides a description, potentially enormously rich and revealing, but falls short of explaining. It also, thereby, falls short of theorizing – and theorizing is a way of seeing what the empirical details do not allow you to see.

Let me use a familiar example to illustrate what I mean: Adam Smith's 'invisible hand' is precisely such a non-x that explains how a market economy works; the mere functioning of a market brings about a governing dynamic, but they are not analytically the same. Post-Marshallian neoclassical economics evicted this analytic distance between the actual market and some larger concept positing that the market is more than a price mechanism. Thereby, the model lost explanatory power, setting the stage for the rise of institutional economics and, most recently, behavioural economics, all of which can be seen as aiming to reintroduce analytical distance between the market as price-mechanism and equivalents to the invisible hand. To take an example from my own work, in this case in political theory, when I write about immigrants or citizens, I need to find a non-x that allows me to explain who these subjects are. I cannot simply say the citizen is the citizen, and the immigrant is the immigrant – no matter how much empirical detail I have to describe each – and presume that I am explaining. Thus, I use the concept of the rights-bearing subject: both citizens and immigrants are such (and it allows one for instance to recognize that the immigrant is also the carrier of the rights that she has as a citizen of another country). Could it be that when we reduce global city analysis to WCN analysis we have arrived at some juncture similar to the post-Marshallian moment in economics? From this perspective, the project of connecting to a very different yet cognate field such as commodity chains is a very interesting one. But, it will mean regaining a larger analytical terrain and taking Taylor's warning that WCN analysis is simply an 'empirical hook', one to which neither Taylor's nor my work can be reduced.

I can think of at least five propositions I developed in my global city analysis (Sassen 1991; Sassen 2007) that provide the non-x. This non-x gives us a third analytic stance to that of the WCN and GCC, and thereby might help in articulating these two fields in ways that go beyond mere aggregation or overlap. Inevitably, this is a perspective from the city side rather than the GCC side, as that is what I know, and knowledge and precision are important for this type of effort. Again, these five propositions come straight out of my global city analysis, not to be confused with the much narrower empirical component that is WCN analysis.

Incomplete knowledge

The first concerns the problematic of incomplete knowledge in market economies and its especially acute consequences in a global economy. This is present in both, commodity chains and APS inter-city networks. Firms have always confronted incomplete knowledge in market economies. When such firms go global, this problem becomes acute. From the start of my work on the subject I saw the producer services as an organizational commodity that becomes more and more important the more a firm (or an economic sector) operates in globalized space. This holds for global firms and markets, no matter what the sector – mining, agribusiness, finance, insurance and so on. One question is whether this also holds for Global Commodity Chains, no matter what the sector. In brief, one potential non-x variable articulating these scholarships is that their market actors are subject to incomplete knowledge. The proposition I developed to organize the many different conditions and needs is that the more digitized and the more globalized the operations of a firm, the more acute is its incomplete knowledge problem, and hence the more dependent on APS.[3]

The city's specificity *vis-à-vis* the incomplete knowledge problem, especially for global actors, is that its diverse networks, information loops, professionals coming from diverse parts of the world, produce a particular type of knowledge capital. I refer to it as urban knowledge capital – which is more than the sum of the knowledges of the professionals and the firms in a city. Analytically, I posit that this is a key element in the economic production function of the global city (Sassen 1991: ch. 6); there is also a political production function (developed in Sassen 1991: part 3; 2008: ch. 6).

This then also explains why global capitalism produced a systemic demand for a growing number of global cities across the world as globalization expanded in the 1990s and onwards. Each of these is a site for the production of urban knowledge capital, in good part specific to each city. Indeed, since the beginning I have argued that this phase of globalization needs and stimulates the specialized differences of cities. Thus, already in the 1980s, I found a division of functions among what were at the time the three strategic global cities for articulating an emergent new phase of global capitalism.[4] I argued that the intensifying problem of incomplete knowledge as globalization expands is partly addressed through a systemic demand for more strategic sites (global cities) and multiplying divisions of functions among such sites.

One question I have is whether this might also hold for GCCs, which seem to have diversified and each chain now aggregates more and more specialized steps. The recurrent observation in these chapters that GCC and WCN analyses generate different types of knowledge begins to go in this direction, though the WCN frame is too narrow to encompass some of the issues I raise here –it would require focusing on global cities. I do like some of the methodological issues posited by these authors, in that they can generate knowledge that could eventually move on to what I am here referring to as the systemic demand for particular forms of knowledge on the part of global actors – the non-x.

Thus, Vind and Fold (2010: 58) note:

> We believe the GCC approach can inform the WCN approach in two respects. The first is the application of commodity-specific lenses. By moving beyond selecting TNCs based on size criteria, industry-specific analyses will give more 'flesh' to the global city network by providing insights into the real-life connections and material links between specific cities. The second is the provision of qualitative information on the practices and strategies of firms, including on the role and significance of APS firms for TNCs in other industries.

We need to take the analysis one step further. Let me elaborate. The effort in these chapters is to see how the different types of knowledge produced by each approach can potentially inform each other. Researchers gain additional knowledge by using each other's research findings. The perspective is that of the researcher's understanding of the process. Indeed, even when mention is made of them, for instance in descriptions of the GPN framework (for example, Henderson et al. 2002: 444), they are not active, working concepts analytically speaking. Whether GCC analysis can benefit from incorporating producer services is yet to be seen, but it does seem a promising possibility for articulating with WCN analysis, and more foundationally, with global city analysis (Brown et al. 2010; Parnreiter 2010).[5]

The further step we need is to understand what these findings about different types of knowledge tell us about the incomplete knowledge problem that actors in respectively WCNs and GCCs confront and seek to solve. Incomplete knowledge is a variable – its specifics will vary for diverse actors in respectively GCCs and WCNs. The comparative data that can be gathered should be put to work to address a larger analytical/theoretical problematic that cuts across CGCs and WCNs so that we can recover where the locations on that variable that they share and those where they diverge.

Producing organizational commodities

The second proposition concerns the production of the organizational commodities I referred to above and how to capture analytically the systemic demand that leads to their production (Sassen 1991: chapters 4 and 5). By systemic demand I seek to refer to a type of demand that is not merely a market-promoted demand – such as a fashion, or a supply-induced demand as might be the case with some forms of consulting, and such entities as credit-rating agencies which have become partly a sort of rubber-stamp. I refer to a demand that comes out of actual organizational needs, in this case linked to new organizational formats, such as cross-border operations. The articulation of this proposition with the global city is that these cities are production places for such organizational commodities. This is a second key element of the economic production function of the global city.

The input–output models of national economies indicate clearly that firms in all sectors, from mining and agriculture to health and transport, to advanced services, are buying more of these organizational commodities – accounting, legal, insurance, finance and all sorts of new technology-linked specialized services for firms. This holds for firms in local, regional, national and global markets. Thus, the production of these organizational commodities is a variable: at one end they cater to local firms and at the other to global firms. The particularity of the global city is that it is a production place for the most complex version of these organizational commodities. But the larger underlying process is present also at the national level.[6] This explains why a growing number of small and medium-sized cities marked by more routinized economies also evince some of the patterns we see in global cities: for instance, the growth of a high-income managerial and professional class and the consequent gentrification of central urban space (see Sassen 1991: chapter 9, 'Economic Restructuring as Class and Spatial Polarization').

The natural experiment case

A third proposition has to do with the heuristics of the choice of empirical data – in other words, preferring a case that can tell a far larger story than that of its own specifics (that is rather than merely the x). When the social sciences deal with emergent complex real-world processes, a case that can function as a natural experiment is enormously useful. Thus, the choice of APS is meant to function as indicating a far larger tale than the characteristics of that sector *per se*. One can choose a case that approximates an intuitive understanding of that emergent process, or take the counterfactual – the case that is counter-intuitive.

For instance, I used the case of finance as a natural experiment case that is counterintuitive. It is the extreme case of hypermobility and digitization and hence the case most likely not to need a territorial insertion, such as a global city. Such a need somehow seemed far less counterintuitive for the case of transnational corporations selling consumer products and services. Yet, these could also have served as a natural experiment: as I argued extensively, even a TNC selling an elementary consumer product or service needs organizational complexity to handle operations in many different countries; hence, it will also have an embedded demand for organizational commodities. This would have been far easier to demonstrate than the case of finance; it is also the case that the needs of such TNCs are easier to standardize than those of finance. Finance is caught in multiplying inter-connected markets, continuous innovation in products and all of it at increasing velocities. From my perspective, then, focusing on finance was heuristically more productive because it pushed matters to the limit.

It is not clear to me what the equivalent methodological move might be in the case of GCC analysis, but it would have to be one that is heuristic and shows a larger set of characteristics about the current phase of global capitalism. It must get at non-x elements. In so doing there could be a rich research agenda using both approaches to specify some of the strategic mobilities of this era.

The spatial correlates of centrality

The fourth proposition points to a potentially fruitful articulation of global city analysis, and especially of WCN analysis, with GCC analysis: the specification of the variable locations of the most complex managerial/organizational functions of commodity chains. That is to say, thinking of the locations of these most complex managerial/organizational functions of GCC as a variable: at one extreme the locations are global cities, at the other they are not – they could be suburban office parks. I would posit that at the other extreme from global cities is a format that consists of distributed inputs across the whole chain. That is, the embedded demand for organizational commodities (the producer services of the WCN) is distributed across the chain, providing a sharp contrast to the global city analysis and at the same time situating both extremes in a shared analytic frame – a non-x.

Thus, I read the contribution of the two pieces in this volume (Hesse this book; Jacobs et al. this book) focused on material commodity chains from a WCN perspective as potentially contributing to specify this locational variable. The authors do not quite see this. They see their contribution as the focus on material commodity chains in contrast to the non-material contents of APS. Perhaps they have more developed versions of their work but, as presented, there is no non-x in their analysis. Thus, they confine their own understanding of their contribution to what is ultimately a modest empirical addition – though a very nice one![7] This confinement then also means that they leave unaddressed what is potentially fruitful analytically: the fact that many commodity chains do not need global cities. In my reading this work would gain analytical strength by understanding how their data specify one of the positions on that locational variable (to repeat, the locational variable of the most complex organizational/managerial functions in commodity chains ... not just any functions).

Thus, Jacobs et al. suggest their finding of a 'weak relation between commodity flow patterns in ports and APS firm localization in port cities' is problematic. But, it is not! Seen against a larger analytic space, it is yet another point on the locational variable I propose above, one that adds rather than detracts. Their findings for Hamburg, Rotterdam and Houston specify yet another type of location for complex functions. In my reading what they are finding is that global cities that actually arise from the need to handle the complex functions of ports are different from a city like London, which arises not only from its past port functions, but also from finance and commerce. I am not an expert on ports but have a keen interest in them, and have by now gathered quite a bit of information, thus allow me this observation: Rotterdam as a centre for producer services (which it also is) is an extended port space; and, in fact, it exports services that have to do with the management of ports. Singapore is probably the major exporter of a knowledge economy about port management – which takes the form of managing ports around the world. In my reading, the authors should be specifying the particularity of the global city function as instantiated in the cases of these three port cities – Rotterdam, Hamburg and Houston. In the larger analytical frame these are a specific location on a variable that goes from one extreme, the global city, to another extreme, distributed embedded complex functions. Somewhere in the middle are complex ports.

I would make a similar comment on the piece about 'the emerging mega-city region of Munich' by Lüthi, Thierstein and Goebel. They document how Munich based high-tech firms have their management operations distributed over a broad 'mega-region'. They see their contribution in terms of the details of the 'x'. They could situate this contribution against a broader analytic frame, which would allow them to specify yet another position on the locational variable for complex functions I propose above.[8]

By limiting themselves to describing the details of their very interesting x, they miss a chance to make their findings work more analytically, both in the sense of an extended space of centrality and in the sense of marking one point on that larger locational variable discussed earlier.

I should add that in my analysis (Sassen 1991: 122 ff), which the authors seem to have misunderstood or not read, there is a new type of formation that is the extension of a space of centrality into older social geographies, such as the suburb or the metro area. Indeed, I identify at least four territorial correlates for the space of centrality, of which the downtown traditional business centre is but one. I include, for instance, a space of centrality for global finance that has diverse nodes in the suburbs, notably the hedge funds in Connecticut; to see this simply as the hedge funds that moved to the suburbs is imprecise. Just because there was an older social geography does not mean that it cannot accommodate other spaces over time. My proposition is that a given territory can be occupied by several distinct types of spaces.[9]

Parnreiter's extensive research documents the ways in which global cities are critical nodes in Global Commodity Chains. Access to local knowledge and close contact to clients are both key factors. His analysis is far more comprehensive in terms of the complexities of WCNs in its documenting of how Mexico City is such a critical node in GCCs. With such detailed knowledge, and years of research, Parnreiter could also specify some of the locations for complex corporate functions in each, the GCC and the WCN, where these diverge from each other and where they intersect. The negative – in this case, the absence of similar locations for headquarter functions – can be a plus analytically in that it shows us the extent of variability between GCCs and WCNs, from active intersections to absent intersections.[10]

Command functions: the shift from imperial centres to distributed operations

The fifth proposition develops the question of a larger shared analytic frame by specifying the meaning of 'command' functions in global city analysis; I would think that the narrower focus of WCN analysis can be seen as providing one of the empirical platforms for this understanding of 'command' functions. Parnreiter and Vind and Fold's research makes a contribution to the specifying of this larger analytic field through a focus on a third analytic point for interpretation that is neither a WCN nor a GCC. They do this by bringing into the analysis respectively, command functions, and labour migration.

Vind and Fold (2010: 61) find that it is important to understand 'the structure and dynamics of GCCs that constitute the crucial linkages (in terms of material flows) from globalizing cities to world markets'. This requires intensive fieldwork on the linkages, which in turn requires 'the need to include labour migration patterns and processes from the rural hinterland of globalizing cities'.[11] Such detailed analysis also makes visible a spatial dimension that marks a globality that is specific to a region. They posit, convincingly, that a detailed examination along these lines shows 'how traditional GCC analyses could be realigned and integrated with the WCN approach'. I find this an extension of the analytic field that introduces more urban variables than a mere WCN analysis.[12] What also makes this interesting is that their project was not initially about these types of issues, but they wound up showing that 'detailed and qualitative accounts of "how HCMC is going global" may supplement and integrate with quantitative indicators of "how global HCMC is"'.

An important specification is the existence of an 'East-Asian city network for globalizing HCMC'.[13] I find this very persuasive; it was already evident in the 1980s when Japan had considerable economic and financial influence in several Southeast Asian countries – through banks, construction companies and the foreign development aid office of the Japanese government. It also fits into my long-term argument that the current forms of globalization produce novel geographies of centrality that cut across the old north–south divide, even as many aspects of this old divide remain in place.

Parnreiter (2010) raises the level of complexity in his analysis by introducing the notion of governance when he discusses the position of Mexico City in the geography of governance of commodity chains. 'The analysis suggests that it is useful to break up global city functions into the management of the world economy and into its command and control.' Introducing the notion of governance is one way of finding a third analytic point to deal with both. I do think this is critical for making these GCC and global city analysis work together. But I am not clear about how he precisely conceives of 'command functions'. Thus he writes:

> However, as regards influences on value creation and distribution within the 'Mexican segments' of Global Commodity Chains, the – still tentative – results indicate that the scope of influence of both local affiliates of TNCs and of local offices of global producer service firms is rather limited, namely to issues such as taxes or labour laws and unions, where the need for in-depth knowledge of local conditions is required.

In my conception, he is describing how elements of governance get embedded in command functions – a disaggregated distributed, multi-sited networked system, with territorial insertions in each pertinent country, in the shape of both global cities and GCCs. I use command functions to refer to the series of activities that need to be done for global firms to execute their operations without losing sight of the corporation's aims. It is a kind of embedded governance – embedded in the lawyering, the accounting and the investment choices of the firm, often via the APS to which it outsources some of its management functions. From here then my observations about creative accounting and lawyering in the case of some of the more speculative financial services firms; but it is also evident in less speculative firms.

Parnreiter's chapter raises several foundational questions, and is a more complex analysis than is typical in some of this literature. Its conceptual architecture encompasses a far larger range of variables. In this regard it offers us more complex articulations with GCCs analysis.

In brief, these command functions are not like the command functions of older imperial bureaucracies headquartered in the empire's capital and some of its major colonial centres. Each global city, no matter how minor, contributes a component because each articulates the wealth of a national economy with global circuits, either through 'national' firms or through foreign firms. So, yes, Mexico fulfils 'command' functions. I do think the term command lends itself to this confusion. I use it, true, but always insist that the global city is a space for the production of organizational commodities needed by firms and markets to operate globally and to shift national wealth to global circuits, and that this entails command functions that are distributed across those operations. Here I see an interesting and potentially fruitful point of analytical collaboration with GCC analysis. It is that cross-border operations nowadays require a whole series of organizational capabilities, and they are distributed across the chain in a far more evident way than is the case with WCNs. Here, the category governance assumes substantive meaning and operational meaning, and it intersects with major power logics. Some of these power logics are shared by the actors, in each WCNs and GCCs, and others are not.

What does a focus on cities add?

It seems to me that one critical question is to ask what does a focus on each of the core categories –WCN and GCC – add to the analysis. I also think that to make this a fruitful, productive question, we need to find a broader analytic context – the non-x.

A first point might be to use the city as that broader context, where the non-x are the multiple urban conditions that keep interfering conceptually, we might say, with a narrow, controllable empirical component such as WCN. Having that broader analytic context then allows us to recognize the conceptual potential of all sorts of urban conditions and actors: for instance the by now familiar fact that APS contribute to gentrification and to a demand for low-wage migrant and minoritized citizen labour. What the equivalent would be for GCCs is not immediately clear to me, though the chapters by Parnreiter and by Vind and Fold provide us with some hints.

A second point is situating 'the city' analytically in the larger effort that is world city and global city analysis. This can be addressed by using three faulty assertions that recur in most of these chapters which point to a foundational misunderstanding as to the role of the city in global city analysis. I am not certain about the origin(s) of these assertions but they are sufficiently elementary that it does not really matter. One is that the WCN excludes most cities. The second is that it focuses on a Western process. The third is that it focuses only on the Global North.

The problem with the first two assertions is that the larger global city and world city analyses are not urban theories: their aim is, rather, to explain a new phase of global capitalism, its strategic spaces and its exclusions.[14] In brief, they seek to capture a system of power. The analysis is not about cities *per se*, it is about novel types of imperial geographies. The contribution they make is to discover and specify that this new imperial geography includes as strategic spaces a variety of cities and inter-city networks. Imperial geographies are rarely inclusive. And in our modern history they are indeed Western – though this is now shifting. Thus to complain that this analysis excludes too many cities and is too Western in focus is misunderstanding what this type of theorization is about. The issue here is not a theory of the city. It is a theory of how the new empire functions.[15]

The third assertion is factually incorrect. This holds even for the narrow focus of the WCN, which includes cities from all parts of the world; it includes these not because the researchers decided that it was time to be more inclusive, but because the actual practices and projects that constitute the expanding global corporate economy incorporate more and more cities – or rather particular sectors of those cities.[16] Global firms and markets do not want to operate only in a few cities of the Global North. They want to operate in multiple cities worldwide. This generates what I described earlier as a systemic demand for a growing number of global cities.

In my own work I found that the current global phase has engendered new types of geographies of centrality. These cut across the old North–South divide – even though many aspects of this divide persist. They disaggregate 'the city' and cut across the North–South divide via a range of networks. I have long argued that the powerful and rich elites and corporate sectors of a growing number of global south cities (whether in São Paulo or Jakarta, or so many others) are deeply linked with similar centres of the North. And, at the same time, cities that fall out of this new geography of centrality lose ground whether they are in the North or in the South. This is also why these new geographies of centrality cannot be easily grafted onto the core/semiperiphery/ periphery geometry even when the core dynamics underlying this geometry are in fact at work in these new geographies of centrality. Perhaps it would be helpful to return to the original concept developed by Karl Polanyi! Many GCCs, on the other hand, correspond more closely to the core/semiperiphery/ periphery division – though other formats are also emerging, as Parnreiter and Vind and Fold's chapters indicate.

A focus on cities brings to the fore some of the contradictions of this particular geography of power. The fact that cities are strategic in the new imperial geography allows us to capture in great detail the multiple and variable conditionalities of power. What is straightforward in the GCC analysis is more intermediated in cities. A focus on cities also allows us to capture a changing process. Thus Vind and Fold note that many 'so-called "third-world cities" that are growing on the basis of booming export-oriented industrializ-ation and migration from rural hinterlands and distant regions' constitute their global linkages in a ways that are different from the Western modes that have dominated the global corporate map. A city like Ho Chi Minh City has now gained a foothold in the new geography of centrality. Jakarta, Manila,

Bangalore did in the 1990s, each through its own particular economic sectors ... and so on. A very different process that can be captured in the city is the shift to new so-called flexible and deregulated modes of operating. In my research I found that the equivalent of deregulation at the top takes the form of informalization at the bottom of the economic system. There are many more aspects of the current structuration of advanced economies that become concrete and legible in cities pointing to the diverse contingencies and contradictions of this new geography of power.

In brief, a focus on cities rather than just WCNs brings in the messiness and the contradictions of a system of power marked by strong territorial insertions in cities. What would be the equivalent analytic operation for GCCs?

Notes

1. There are now three kindred yet different terms: GCCs, Global Value Chains (GVCs) and Global Production Networks (GPNs). All three are well developed and their differences are specified analytically and empirically (see Coe et al. 2008).
2. Elsewhere Taylor writes that APS firms may be an 'indicator species' of a larger entity (namely the global economy) (Taylor 2005; see also Derudder and Taylor 2005). It seems to me there might also be such a parallel between narrow empirical elements of GCCs and the greater complexity of the GCC work evident in works such as Gereffi and Korzeniewicz (1994) and Gereffi et al. (2005)
3. I should note that for me they have always included a range of engineering and technical services that need to be customized.
4. Basically, I found Tokyo to be an exporter of the raw commodity money to London and New York, and an exporter of massive infrastructure knowhow to Southeast Asia and Australia for rebuilding vast parts of those regions. London functioned as the most strategic entrepôt financial centre and a platform for firms from the entire world (including the USA) seeking to enter Europe. New York was the Silicon Valley for financial innovations, creative accounting and lawyering, plus the invention of all sorts of new APS.
5. Vind and Fold (2010) posit that 'The absence of producer services in GCC analyses is linked to their underdeveloped spatial dimension. Chain-based analyses of cluster upgrading dynamics and their linkages to global firms and markets ... have an obvious spatial dimension, as, more or less by definition, cluster-based firms share the same geographical location. Otherwise, there are typically no references to spatial connections other than company locations within different national territories; the role of (global) cities is not discussed.' See also Brown et al. (2010).
6. The chapter in *The global city* (chapter 5) that focuses on producer services owes a lot to an early geography scholarship that had gone completely unnoticed by the other social sciences. I recall first presenting some of my early research in the late 1970s to an audience of economists in New York City: they had never heard of this term; but soon they began to understand the usefulness of the distinction contained in the concept.

7. Hesse's (2010) statement that 'the ability of urban places to act as a spatial fix in an environment of increasing flows is becoming questioned' might indeed be the case, but (a) I still find David Harvey's analysis remains unmatched in this regard, and (b) I am afraid Hesse makes a literal – rather than a theoretical – reading of Harvey's notion of the spatial fix: it is not that flows are the opposite of spatial fix. We cannot interpret spatial fix as a literal description. It is a theoretical term.

8. Two further comments on this piece. 'Megaregion' is now used to describe a territory that includes multiple metro regions; thus, one would not say, for example, New York's mega-region but the NorthEast Corridor. Besides the designation issue, I was not aware that Munich's surrounding region actually incorporates several cities and their metro areas. If it does, it should not be called Munich's mega-region – even if Munich is the absolutely dominant city.

9. What would make this more significant as a contribution to the global cities analysis (which, again, covers far more than the WCN analysis) is to understand not simply the details of regional location – that is an old story – but whether those offices in the larger Munich area are actually constituting a space of centrality or whether they are the more routinized activities in the longer chain of activities they describe. Producer services are a variable, as I described earlier – extremely complex and innovative at one end, and fairly routinized at the other, with all kinds of intermediate mixes. Final point, all advanced economies show that the intermediate economy (which includes producer services) is growing and that firms in all economic sectors (though not all firms in those sectors) are buying more of these services. It is not completely clear to me where this Munich case fits on the 'made-in-house versus bought' spectrum (for a development of these issues see Sassen, 2007).

10. Throughout the scholarship on global cities and world cities there are instances of recognition that the analytic terrain needs to be expanded (for example Rozenblat and Pumain 2007; Samers 2002). And while this is a bit of a challenge, the beginning steps towards such an analytically expanded terrain need not be complicated. Thus Alderson and Beckfield (2006: 902) posit that 'while it could be the producer-services sector that leads the way in binding cities into a global network, it is likely that the industrial sector also constructs connections of control among cities.'

11. One of the findings is that the foreign-owned electronics companies rely more on female migrant workers than the domestic-owned companies. These migrants are perceived to be more amenable and harder working. This confirms findings of studies made over the last 40 years – let us recall that outsourcing was already happening in the 1960s, especially in garments, electronics and toys. The destinations were different, but some of the patterns, aiming at controlling the workforce were already evident, with foreign-owned firms far more dependent on control techniques and domestic firms more embedded in traditional cultures of male entrenchment. A separate issue is their mention that several interviewees in the electronics study believed the growing labour shortage was caused by former or prospective migrants finding jobs nearer to home. A similar trend is evident in China today; initially the 2007–8 crisis closed firms and forced migrants to return home but today the factories have shortages because the migrants are not coming

back as they are finding jobs in the factories that have been opening closer to the traditional migrant sourcing areas in China.

12. I read in this article a recognition that a third analytic frame is needed. 'We have argued that the World City Network and Global Commodity Chain literatures can inform each other, but that an integrative framework is needed to explore empirically the assumption of the WCN approach that APS firms are the critical agents in connecting (producers in) cities' (Vind and Fold 2010: 70). Further, 'an integrative approach also calls for a broader perspective than closer scrutiny of the links between APS and their corporate customers in Global Commodity Chains' (2010: 60).

13. We can extend this Southeast Asian regionality to labour migrations today as well, see for example the research by Gracia Farrer (2007) on migrations link between Tokyo and Shanghai that emerged over the last ten years, and include manual workers as well as professionals.

14. It is worth noting that all three of us came from non-urban fields. Friedmann came from development studies, Taylor from work on the state, and I from development and migration. We stumbled on the city, so to speak – the strategic role of some cities was a discovery. But this also explains why our approach to the question of the city is not perhaps typical of traditional urbanists, and why our effort is not to make taxonomies or even typologies of cities. It is a different type of intellectual and research project.

15. Using some of the propositions I developed in 2008, I would posit that the diverse types of mobilities of each WCNs and GCCs require a mix of conditions that aggregate in the form of assemblages. The distinction between physical and non-physical that runs through several of the articles might be better understood as functioning in diverse assemblages, rather than whether they are about the movement of materials or of financial instruments. Think of the international art circuit: it is now well established that the development of the producer services to handle global operations has greatly facilitated the movement of art pieces for museum shows and international art events.

16. It is important to recover the trajectory, not only across space as in a commodity chain, but also across time. Thus, in the early 1980s the new phase of globalization was emergent. As it proceeds through the 1990s and 2000s, the geography of power expands and includes more and more cities. It is conceptually spurious to say that the WCN literature is now more acceptable because it covers more cities. That is not the point. The point is that we are studying a process, and this process came to include more cities. It is not a question of including as many cities as possible: it is to include those that are part of the geography of power. The study of cities as such is a different project, and there are millions of them.

References

Alderson, A. S. and J. Beckfield (2006) 'Reply: whither the parallel paths? The future of scholarship on the world city system', *American Journal of Sociology*, 112, 895–904.

Brown, E., B. Derudder, C. Parnreiter, W. Pelupessy, P. J. Taylor and F. Witlox (2010) 'World City Networks and Global Commodity Chains: towards a world systems integration, *Global Networks*, 10 (1), 12–34.

Coe, N. M., P. Dicken and M. Hess (2008) 'Global Production Networks: realizing the potential', *Journal of Economic Geography*, 8, 271–95.

Derudder B. and P. J. Taylor (2005) 'The cliquishness of world cities', *Global Networks*, 5 (1), 71–91.

Farrer, G. L. (2007) 'From corporate employees to business owners: Chinese immigrant transnational entrepreneurship in Japan', in S. Sassen (ed.) *Deciphering the global: its spaces, scales and subjects*, London: Routledge.

Friedmann, J. (1986) 'The world city hypothesis', *Development and Change*, 17 (1), 69–84.

Gereffi, G. and M. Korzeniewicz (eds) (1994) *Commodity chains and global capitalism*, Westport: Praeger.

Gereffi, G., J. Humphrey and T. J. Sturgeon (2005) 'The governance of Global Value Chains', *Review of International Political Economy*, 12, 78–104.

Henderson, J., P. Dicken, M. Hess, N. Coe and H. W-c. Yeung (2002) 'Global Production Networks and the analysis of economic development', *Review of International Political Economy*, 9, 436–64.

Hesse, M. (2010) 'Cities, material flows and the geography of spatial interaction: urban places in the system of chains', *Global Networks*, 10 (1), 75–91.

Jacobs, W. C. Ducruet and P. de Langen (2010) 'Integrating world cities into production networks: the case of port cities', *Global Networks*, 10 (1), 92–113.

Parnreiter, C. (2010) 'Global cities in Global Commodity Chains: exploring the role of Mexico City in the geography of governance of the world economy', *Global Networks*, 10 (1), 35–53.

Rozenblat, C. and D. Pumain (2007) 'Firm linkages, innovation and the evolution of urban systems', in P. J. Taylor, B. Derudder, P. Saey and F. Witlox (eds) *Cities in globalization: practices, policies and theories*, London: Routledge, 130–56.

Samers, M. (2002) 'Immigration and the global city hypothesis: towards an alternative research agenda', *International Journal of Urban and Regional Research*, 26, 389–402.

Sassen, S. (1991) *The global city: New York, London, Tokyo*, Princeton: Princeton University Press, 2nd edition 2001.

Sassen, S. (2007) 'Whither global cities: the analysis and the debates', in J. R. Bryson and P. W. Daniels (eds) *The handbook of service industries*, Cheltenham: Edward Elgar, 186–208.

Sassen, S. (2008) *Territory, authority, rights: from medieval to global assemblages*, 2nd edition (updated), Princeton University Press, first published 2006.

Smith, D. A. and M. Timberlake (1995) 'Cities in global matrices: toward mapping the world-system's city system', in P. L. Knox and P. J. Taylor (eds) *World cities in a world-system*, Cambridge: Cambridge University Press, 79–97.

Taylor, P. J. (2000) 'World cities and territorial states under conditions of contemporary globalization', *Political Geography*, 19, 5–32.

Taylor, P. J. (2005) 'New political geographies: global civil society and global governance through World City Networks', *Political Geography*, 24, 703–30.

Vind, I. and N. Fold (2010) 'City networks and commodity chains: identifying global flows and local connections in Ho Chi Minh City', *Global Networks*, 10 (1), 54–74.

Index

197

LaVergne, TN USA
21 February 2011
217026LV00015B/2/P